# Stories, Stats and Stuff
# About Syracuse® Sports

## By Bob Snyder
## Forewords by Jim Boeheim
## & Paul Pasqualoni

Printed in the United States of America by
Mennonite Press, Inc.

ISBN 1-880652-83-8

**PHOTO CREDITS** All photographs were supplied
by the Syracuse University Sports Information
Office, the Syracuse Newspapers and Syracuse
University Archives.

# ACKNOWLEDGMENTS

We were at the bowling alley, downstairs in the Women's Building, that Saturday afternoon — all afternoon — in the winter of 1961.

There on a dare. From my fraternity brothers, who said — and 10 of them each put up a $5 bill against my 50 bucks — that this Syracuse University junior couldn't bowl 50 games in a row. Non-stop, 120 minimum per game.

When day had turned to night and this academic pursuit, a scientific study of how much strain an arm and hand could withstand, had taken 8½ hours, where did I head? To bed? No.

*For Marsha and our Lesley, the stars of our family, whose love and support brighten every day.*

*— R.L.S.*

To the Onondaga County War Memorial, where the Orangemen were about to tip off against St. John's. That may not seem so strange; but you had to be a hoop junkie to really want to be there. That 1960-61 SU team was 2-12 at the time ... and would finish with five straight losses.

The next season, Sports Information Director Val Pinchbeck Jr. and I (his student assistant) watched loss after loss after ... 22 in a row that winter, an NCAA-record 27 straight over two seasons.

And then along came Dave Bing.

I was more fortunate when it came to football; sophomore year, National Champions, perfect season. And lucky, too, to cover SU's first trip to the Final Four.

But to package plays and players I've covered, and all those precedent, it took the assistance and cooperation of countless others.

Many of the stories and information come from clippings from *The Syracuse Newspapers*, from files at the SU sports information office, media guides and photos. I'm indebted to players and coaches who provided comments and anecdotes. And to those writers, photographers and others who have followed the Orangemen over the years, particularly Arnie Burdick and "Red" Parton.

Special thanks to the sports information staff, including the dean of sports info directors, Larry Kimball, and assistant SID Bill Dyer, who provided the stats and records section.

Finally, thanks to Sandy Thomas, a computer whiz who made sure I wouldn't panic and cause the system to crash before we were in print.

Oh, yes, those first 47 games were a snap, so I tried to roll a 600 triple for closers. Had to settle for 590-something, pocketed the $50 ... and watched the Orangemen lose by 35.

*— R.L.S.*

# FOREWORDS

Tracing the history of Syracuse football can be as elusive as holding onto a slippery pigskin. But Bob Snyder has witnessed highs — certainly none greater than as a student, when Coach Schwartzwalder's team won the national championship — in three decades with the *Syracuse Herald-Journal*, as Orange fortunes have taken some peculiar bounces. His good grasp of well-known stories, served up with some new slants and little-known incidents, make for an easy, enjoyable read. Events and personalities he presents — from days of Archbold to the Carrier Dome — provide a handy reference for those interested in what our program was and is today.

— *Paul Pasqualoni*

If anyone is going to write a history of Syracuse basketball, why not Bob Snyder? He's been around forever, matriculating at SU … even claiming to have earned a degree. He was working for the *Syracuse Herald-Journal* when Dave Bing was transforming the program. As a beat writer for 20 years, from Fred Lewis to Roy Danforth to long after I took over, he's tasted the dust of Manley, gained the confidence of players, able to put his twist and those of others on games and rivalries going back to before even he was around. This is more than Final Fours and Big East Tournaments. It's All-Americans and walk-ons; it's their stories, told by him, told by them. If you bleed Orange, I hope you'll enjoy a new look at Syracuse basketball.

— *Jim Boeheim*

# TABLE OF CONTENTS

# *1889-1980*
# **Football**

*In 1890, Syracuse players took postgame baths by raising a trap door and dropping into icy water beneath the library basement.*

Mention Syracuse football, and what pops in your head? A number … 44.

Images of Brown and Davis, Little and now, Konrad. There have been those whose numerals — Csonka (39), Morris (47) — made them no less great land rovers.

And in more than a century of playing the game, from days of a makeshift field to Archbold's concrete oval that was a wonder of its time to the teflon bubble that is the Carrier Dome, the game on the Hill was more than merely a parade of great running backs.

The legendary strength of Horr and numerous positions played by Alexander were highlights of SU's

*A few memories from the first 100 years of Syracuse football, celebrated in 1989.*

earliest days.

Hanson, a man for all seasons.

Could a horseshoe tossed over the goalpost snap the Colgate jinx?

The shame of school officials not telling Maryland: "If Sidat-Singh doesn't play, we don't play!"

A first bowl trip drowned by the onrushing Tide.

SU's only national championship won on the field (and polls), a 1959 team that bowled over everyone, then Hook(ed) 'em Horns on New Year's Day.

Racial strife tore at a team and brought down a legend.

Green stayed home, energizing a defense and town.

Would we EVER beat Penn State?

Fans were fit to be tied by a deadlock off Bourbon Street.

From 0-4 and a step ahead of the SacMacPac to MacPherson for Mayor, but Coach Mac opted to play a Pat(s) hand.

Pasqualoni never loses bowl games.

From Custis to Hurley to McPherson to Graves, the line of great quarterbacks has been thin. McNabb might set the standard by which all SU signal-callers are judged.

But first, back to a time when SU's behemoths were clad in …

# ORANGE
## ·Q U I Z·

*1. Who is the only quarterback to throw for more than 425 yards against the Orange? (hint: he did it in the Carrier Dome)*

**STUNNING IN PINK?** Had students not come up $1.25 short of $5 needed to buy a football, Syracuse's first game would have been played a year earlier. A committee raised $75, John Blake Hillyer put together the players, and a coachless team rode the morning train to Rochester on Nov. 23, 1889. In a mudbath, U of R so manhandled the visitors, the *Rochester Democrat & Chronicle* said SU "showed a deplorable lack of teamwork …" Pink-clad football players? That was SU in 1889, pink and blue. The next year, orange became the official school color.

*The Big Orange played with a football that resembled a big watermelon when Syracuse's first edition posed in the snow.*

**THE FIRST COACH** Bobby Winston had come to SU from the Athletic Club of London, where he established a reputation as a pugilist. Hired for $35 per month plus expenses, he'd run his players three miles in the rain. SU's initial victory came in a rematch with U of R, 4-0, and his 1890 team went 8-3.

Syracuse's fortunes weren't so good throughout the first decade of play, though. The 1800s ended with SU's record at 50-46-8.

**1900-09: 'BIG BILL'** The 1900s brought a more enthusiastic view of football on the Hill. Ed Sweetland, a former Cornell oarsman/football star, coached SU three seasons (20-5-2).

# ARCHBOLD STADIUM

Once referred to as "the eighth wonder of the world," Consolidated Engineering and Construction Company billed Syracuse's new stadium as "the greatest athletic arena in America."

It was the country's first complete concrete oval but just the third concrete stadium built in the USA (California and Harvard were constructed four years earlier).

Named for John D. Archbold, who would give $4 million to SU during his lifetime, and modeled after Greek arenas, the $400,000 facility covered 6.3 acres, was 670 feet long and 475 feet wide, required excavation of 250,000 cubic yards of earth and used 20,000 cubic yards of concrete, 1 million feet of lumber and 500,000 tons of steel.

Ahead of schedule, Archbold opened on Sept. 25, 1907 (it was completed in 1908). Art Stein booted the opening kickoff at 3:05 p.m. Captain Ford Park scored the first touchdown 3½ minutes later. SU beat Hobart, 28-0.

*They were still putting the finishing touches on Archbold Stadium in 1907 when play began in the country's first complete concrete oval.*

And Frank "Buck" O'Neill, who had coached Colgate to an unbeaten season in 1902 and been attending Syracuse Law School, began the first of three stints as SU coach (eight-year mark: 52-19-6 in 1906-07, 1913-15, 1917-19).

Marquis "Big Bill" Horr was a giant of his era at 240 pounds, a tackle who ran 75 yards for a touchdown in the first game played at Archbold. In 1908, he became Syracuse's first All-American. So skillful an athlete was the native of nearby Central Square that Horr won national track and field championships in shot put, hammer and discus throws, and was an Olympian.

In the first decade of the 1900s, SU's record was 60-29-5.

*Marquis F. "Bill" Horr, SU's first football All-American (1908), was a 240-pound tackle who could run the 100-yard dash in 11 seconds, very fast for his era.*

## 1910-19: DEVELOPING SUCCESS
O'Neill returned in 1913. Regarded as the "Father of the off-tackle play," he devised a peculiar exercise called the "fanny play":

Rather than snap the ball between his legs to the quarterback, the center keeps it, putting it in his crotch. Running backs scamper, faking runs left and right until a designated player grabs the ball from the center and takes off on the run.

A rules change required the ball to leave the snapper back's (center's) hands. The "fanny play" had been given the boot.

Prior to the era of platoon football, the 1915 team ranks as one of SU's greatest.

*The "Big Four" — T.R. Johnson, "Babe" White, Chris Schlachter and "Ty" Cobb — were a powerful, virtually immovable defensive force in 1915.*

# A RINGER OF A TRADITION

Prior to beating Colgate in 1915 for the first time in 10 years, a spectator threw an orange-colored horseshoe with orange ribbon onto the field. A sportswriter picked it up and tossed it over a goalpost. In the wake of SU's 38-0 thrashing of Colgate —which writer Arthur Evans described as "a flaming masterpiece of football" — an SU tradition was born. A gold-plated horseshoe (stolen 10 times) was used at every Colgate pregame pep rally until the series ended in 1961.

## ORANGE ·QUIZ·

*2. Name the lone opposing ball-carrier to rush for more than 200 yards twice?*

*An All-American at two positions, lineman Joe Alexander played 60 minutes of every game but one (SU had a big lead) from 1917 through 1920, despite finding out later he had torn adhesive in his shoulder joint, internal bleeding and a cracked collarbone.*

The tackle-to-tackle quartet of T.R. Johnson, Harold "Babe" White, Chris Schlachter and Alfred "Ty" Cobb was huge, averaging 222 pounds. Schlachter and White were first team All-American guards, tackle Cobb All-American in 1917.

A 24-day Western trip depleted the travel budget in '15, causing SU officials to decline a Rose Bowl invitation to face Washington. SU (9-1-2), with its power sweep directed by quarterback Chick Meehan and an immovable defense, outscored foes, 331-16, had seven shutouts (including the first five games) and allowed 16 first downs in 12 games.

Syracuse finished the decade with a 60-29-8 mark.

O'Neill, paid approximately $2,000 a year at SU, left to coach Columbia in 1920 for a salary said to be "the highest received by any coach in the country."

**ALEXANDER THE GREAT** The most publicized lineman of his day, guard Joe Alexander was exceptional because he often scored on pass interceptions, fumble recoveries and blocked kicks.

One series of downs in 1920 summarized his career. Dartmouth was on SU's 3-yard line. After helping stop three successive plays, Alexander intercepted a fourth-down pass, returning it beyond midfield. The loss was Dartmouth's first at home in 16 years.

Alexander, a medical school student, became SU's first repeat All-American, in 1918 and '19.

**1920-29: CHICK(ANERY)** Former player Chich Meehan was both showman and disciplinarian when it came to physical conditioning. But he was also a master psychologist, although a mere 25 years old after returning from Navy duty in WWI to succeed O'Neill.

No SU coach lasting five seasons or more has had such a winning percentage (35-8-4 in 1920-24). His teams were stingy: allowing 4.2 points per game, tossing

26 shutouts.

Meehan, who'd later coach NYU and Manhattan, was not above coaching chicanery, such as the time the Maryland punter had his worst day. Why? Meehan deflated every available football.

Meehan coached plenty of star athletes at Syracuse, including speedster Ray Barbuti, a back who was a gold medalist in the 1928 Olympics (400 meters, a leg on the 1,600-meter relay). Another Olympic gold medalist Chet Bowman (gold in the 1,600-meter relay, silver in the 100-meter dash in the 1924 Games) could outrun defenses. Meehan widened the field for the 1923 Colgate game to make use of Bowman's speed, but the plan backfired when Eddie Tryon intercepted along the sideline (which would have been out of bounds), and set up the score that handed SU its only loss.

The decade ledger: 65-21-9.

**HALL(S) OF FAMER** As player, Vic Hanson was an All-American end in 1926, captain of football, basketball and baseball (he played one season in the New York Yankees' farm system), and later, the only inductee in the College Football and Basketball Halls of Fame. Yale and Harvard wanted him; Michigan was interested, too.

The "Black Menace" — as the kid from Syracuse's Central High was called, for his dark complexion and hair — would be persuaded by Meehan to come to Piety Hill.

At 5-foot-10, 174 pounds, he was both soft-handed receiver and sure-handed tackler.

Until Jim Brown, Hanson was unquestionably the greatest all-around athlete in Syracuse history.

**1930-39: COLGATE GAME WAS THE YARDSTICK** Named coach in 1930 at age 27, Hanson's teams in '31, '34 and '35 went into the next-to-last game with perfect records. Each time, the Orangemen lost to Colgate.

A Hanson-coached Syracuse team never beat Colgate, his seven-year tenure (33-21-5) just part of a 13-year drought at the hands of the Red Raiders.

The Orangemen finished the decade with a record of 46-29-8.

## 'THE VOICE' REGRETS HIS SILENCE

Marty Glickman would be known as the first of a breed called jock broadcasters. He'd scored both touchdowns in the 1937 win over Cornell. Glickman relates what happened the following week:

"We're in the locker room at Maryland, our T-shirts, jocks and socks on. Wil (Wilmeth Sidat-Singh) is sitting alongside me; we're starting halfbacks in the single-wing. Ossie Solem and Lew Andreas (SU coach and athletic director, respectively) come in and tell us Maryland knows Wil's not a Hindu (as he'd been billed); they know he's a black man."

The game was off unless Sidat-Singh did not play. Shamefully, SU officials agreed to Maryland's demand.

"The Cornell game was the best day I ever had. I was the star of the team," Glickman said, by way of explaining his status in that dressing room.

"I say to myself, 'Marty, get up and say if Wil doesn't play, I don't play.' Then, I tell myself, 'Whoa! Just a year ago (at the '36 Berlin Olympics), you were the Jewish kid who caused all the furor in Germany.' "

He'd not been allowed to run on the USA's 400-meter relay team, because American Olympic officials didn't want to embarrass Hitler on German soil. Jesse Owens stood up, saying Glickman earned the right to run. But his plea went unanswered. "I didn't say anything (in support of Sidat-Singh). I'm ashamed of it. ... That," said Glickman, "stays with me still, the one thing I'll always regret."

*Marty Glickman scored both touchdowns in a stunning, 14-6 upset of powerhouse Cornell in 1937.*

## WHERE THERE'S A WIL, THERE'S A WAY

Years ago, Roy Simmons declared:

"If he (Sidat-Singh) had played under a T system, he would have been the greatest T-quarterback this town ever saw."

As it was, Sidat-Singh was, according to teammate/SU assistant/Michigan State head coach Duffy Daugherty, "one of the great stories of the 1930s."

A nationally-acclaimed scholastic basketball player, he'd been discovered as a gridiron gem the fall of his sophomore year by Simmons, who caught a glimpse of him playing touch football.

A sweltering crowd of 25,000 at Archbold caught more than a glimpse on an October day in '38. After Sidat-Singh's 35-yard touchdown pass to Harold "Babe"

Ruth was answered by Kenny Brown's 94-yard touchdown kickoff return, SU trailed Cornell by 11.

Sidat-Singh ran the kickoff deep into Big Red territory, two passes to Ruth resulted in a score and it was 17-12 with three minutes to go.

Cornell wanted to ice it by running out the clock. Vinnie Eichler ran a buck up the middle. As he was being tackled, SU left end Phil Allen yelled, "Over here Vinnie." Eichler lateraled … to Allen. Orange ball on Cornell's 25-yard line.

Next play: Sidat-Singh hit Allen in the end zone to win the game.

SU fans would refer to that game as "The Game."

Grantland Rice, who was there, called it the greatest college game he'd ever seen.

*Even more dramatic than the 1937 win over the Big Red was the incredible rally engineered by Wilmeth Sidat-Singh, who passed for three scores in the final nine minutes of the 1938 game.*

**WHAT 'HOODOO?'** Later in the 1938 season, the 40th edition of what had become the "annual loss to Colgate" was played at Archbold. Colgate was looking to extend its dominance over SU to 14 years.

It was scoreless in the third quarter, when Dick Banger returned a punt to the Colgate 14-yard line. Two plays later, Allen went the final 14 yards on a rarely-used end-around play, SU's first touchdown against Colgate since 1931. The 7-0 lead held up.

SU repeated its 7-0 victory over Colgate in '39.

**1940-49: PARDON MY POSTERIOR** Ossie Solem was among the nation's most innovative coaches. While his Y formation was first thought of as wacky, the system featured an element totally foreign to the game, a Reverse Center.

Ken Beehner was described by one writer as "the only

*Walter "Slivers" Slovenski, who dashed 65 yards to score on the old Statue of Liberty play to upset Colgate in 1947, had 13 interceptions in a 27-game career in the 1940s.*

*Syracuse ran up a five-year win streak over Penn State. In the 1935 game (SU, 7-3), fullback Vannie "Iron Man" Albanese carried the ball on 19 consecutive plays, gained 282 yards rushing and receiving, and scored in the closing minutes on a 17-yard pass play.*

center in the nation who faces North when his team is going South."

Jokingly, Beehner was called "the most impolite player in football."

And why not! Literally, he stuck his behind in his opponents' faces.

But he could snap the ball easily to any of his backs, then become a backfield man himself, able to lead interference, pass, run, block or kick.

"Emily Post has not given a ruling on it yet," wrote one scribe.

Officials were perplexed by the Reverse Center. In the 1941 Cornell game, referee Red Freisell whistled a successful SU play — a buck-lateral series in which the ball is returned to Beehner.

Solem's Reverse Center would die shortly after the devastation at Pearl Harbor. Amos Alonzo Stagg was the prime mover behind the decision to kill the formation, saying, "During these times of war, it's a poor example to turn your back on your enemy."

As WWII escalated, SU football declined. Syracuse suspended play in '43.

Solem exited after 1945. His staffs in the 1930s included Charles "Bud" Wilkinson, who'd coach some of college football's greatest teams at Oklahoma, and Clarence "Biggie" Munn (Michigan State).

The '40s produced SU's only losing decade (29-43-3).

# BEN SCHWARTZWALDER

*Years coached at SU: 1949-1973*
*SU record: 153-91-3; 22 straight non-losing seasons; Seven bowl games; 1959 National Championship*

The first three seasons under Floyd Burdette "Ben" Schwartzwalder began a building process with .500 results (14-14). Custis threw for a school-record 1,121 yards in '49, when George Davis ran for more than 800 yards and 11 touchdowns, and Ben's boys beat Colgate before a record crowd of 36,500.

"That was the one ultimatum they served on me," Schwartzwalder would say years later. "I had to beat Colgate."

In 1950, when Custis was injured, Schwartzwalder inserted Avatus Stone — one of SU's premier punters — into the quarterback spot.

Curious that 20 years later Schwartzwalder would be called a racist; his first two quarterbacks were black, a rarity in those days.

The 5-4 record in '51 marked SU's first winning season since 1942.

Ben sought help from the administration. Chancellor

*Chancellor William Pearson Tolley helped elevate the status of football on the Hill under Schwartzwalder.*

Bill Tolley agreed to increase scholarships from 12 to 16 a year. But the recruiting budget was so low the coaching staff couldn't get mileage.

Before increased scholarships could pay a dividend, the 1952 team directed by quarterback Pat Stark and snapped into action by center Jim Ringo, a future Pro Hall of Famer, went 7-2, beat Penn State, claimed the Lambert Trophy (symbolic of Eastern supremacy) and received the first bowl invite in school history.

The team was captained by Dick Beyer, whose pro wrestling career took him globetrotting, and Joe Szombathy, who led SU in receptions three consecutive seasons. Joe 'Z' would later coach receivers under Schwartzwalder and then become the longtime director of the Orange Pack.

**1953 ORANGE BOWL** "I don't think anybody could have told us, 'Don't go play Alabama, you're not good enough,' because we wouldn't have listened to them," reflected guard/tackle Bob Fleck who, in a 1953 season of 5-3-1 modest post-bowl success, would become SU's first All-American in 19 years. It was a 7-6 game after the first quarter and still in reach at halftime, 21-6. But Bama, whose backup quarterback was Bart Starr, scored 20 points in each of the final two quarters, setting 12 bowl records.

Eastern football was scorned. Even fans berated SU, surely no match for the Tide.

"They all came back sun-tanned, and we came back with our asses kicked (61-6)," Fleck said.

*Coach Ben Schwartzwalder and Jim Brown go over the X's and O's of the game.*

*Lineman Bob Fleck (above) and quarterback Pat Stark were second-round NFL draft picks in 1954, highest in SU history until Jim Brown.*

# NUMBER 44

Equipment manager Al Zak, an ol' curmudgeon, stood opposite a 16-year-kid who identified himself as Jimmy Brown.

Zak took an orange jersey that day in 1954 and handed it to the kid. The number — 44 — was without meaning, yet not without irony.

Brown would make history on the Hill, though coming to SU without a scholarship, preferring his high school number (33) and being fifth-string on the depth chart as a sophomore left halfback.

Brown was an Orangeman because Ken Molloy, his champion, had gotten 44 Manhasset, Long Island, businessman to ante up $100 apiece to pay Big Jim's way his freshman year.

The legend of '44' was launched, though nobody knew it.

It has taken a circuitous route, this fabled number worn by Brown — a College/Pro Football Hall of Famer whose 43 points scored vs. Colgate remains an NCAA record.

Others to wear '44':

■ Ernie Davis, the first black to win the Heisman Trophy, whose life was snuffed out by leukemia at age 23.

■ Floyd Little, who was a three-time first-team All-American.

Each rushed for more than 2,000 yards, surpassing his predecessor's records along the way.

No. 44 was worn well by Tom Stephens, who led the 1958 team to the Orange Bowl; Bill Schoonover, who gained 5-plus yards a carry; and Michael Owens, whose two-point conversion run vs. West Virginia completed a perfect regular season in 1987, and is the most famous play of the post-Schwartzwalder era.

But Rich Panczyszyn, a running quarterback in the mid-'60s struggled, and local schoolboy phenom Mandel Robinson, so weighted by the pressure, transferred to Wyoming before he found collegiate success.

The ghosts of Brown, Davis and Little are stepping aside to provide running room for greatness. In 1995, freshman Rob Konrad ate up yardage at 6.9 a clip.

Brown, who liked what he saw of Konrad in '95, told *The Syracuse Newspapers* the legacy of 44 "isn't infallible and it doesn't always predict itself correctly, but it's a good thing to have."

*Floyd Little*

**BIG JIM** The 1954 team was .500. In '55 the team finished 5-3, the loss at Penn State a 21-20 thriller featuring a memorable ground duel between Brown (159 yards, three touchdowns, two PATs) and the Nittany Lions' Lenny Moore (146 yards, one touchdown).

A foundation had been built for 1956, when Brown finished fifth in Heisman balloting to "Golden Boy" Paul Hornung (though Notre Dame had a 2-8 record).

SU rebounded from a one-touchdown loss at Pitt, winning its last six to post a 7-1 mark.

Brown rushed for 154 yards in the opener vs. Maryland, 165 vs. West Virginia.

"Brown developed so fast that we couldn't keep up with him … he was too fast for us," Schwartzwalder admitted. "We were not ready for Jim Brown."

But Brown was ready for Army. The game was regionally-televised, a big deal in those days. The gate swelled to the largest in upstate New York college football history. The Eastern title figured to be on the line.

Brown carried 22 times for 125 yards. This was not a game for the faint-hearted; there was only one real drive all day — SU marching 80 yards in 11 plays in the second quarter to win, 7-0. Brown's 37-yard run off right tackle had put the ball at the 4-yard line.

Jim Ridlon, so often a blocker for Big Jim and later a fine NFL defensive back, punched in the lone score, with Brown adding the PAT.

Late in the game, Army had a first down at SU's 7-yard line. Three times, Brown was in on the tackle — at the 4-yard line, twice at the 1-yard line. On fourth down, Ridlon and Ed Bailey preserved the shutout.

*Jim Brown wanted No. 33, but made No. 44 special when he had seven 100-yard games in the nine-game 1956 schedule.*

*Brown backfield mate Jim Ridlon led Orange receivers in 1956 with 19.1 yards per reception and in interceptions in '55 and '56.*

Later, SU edged Penn State, 13-9, and, in the finale, Brown scored an NCAA-record 43 points — touchdown runs of 1, 15, 50, 8, 19 and 1, and seven PAT kicks — in a rout of Colgate.

When Navy turned down a Cotton Bowl bid, SU was Dallas-bound.

*Jim Brown in 1989.*

**1957 COTTON BOWL** Syracuse trailed Texas Christian University by two touchdowns with 11 minutes to go. Brown returned TCU's kickoff 46 yards, then scored for the third time to make it 28-20. But TCU end Chico Mendoza's kamikaze dive blocked Brown's PAT.

Chuck Zimmerman tossed a 28-yard scoring pass to a leaping Ridlon, with 1:16 to go and Brown's PAT (there was no two-point conversion) left it a 28-27 heartbreaker.

Brown (26 carries, 132 yards) outplayed TCU All-American Jim Swink, but SU still had not won a bowl game.

**POINT FROM UNBEATEN** Without Big Jim, SU went 5-3-1 in 1957.

But '58 was different. Following a one-point loss to Holy Cross for the second year in a row, the Orange reeled off seven wins, including SU's first at Penn State's Beaver Stadium since 1934. An 8-1 regular-season ledger was tops on the Hill in 27 years.

After a 15-12 win at West Virginia, SU accepted a bid to play Bud Wilkinson's Oklahoma Sooners in the Orange Bowl, where the Orangemen lost, 21-6.

The Orange had an All-American in tackle Ron Luciano, who made fun of his own lack of football skills, became an outstanding American League umpire/best-selling author yet, sadly, took his own life.

**ORANGE**
**·QUIZ·**

*3. What made guard Joe Alexander and tackle Lou Usher unique for nearly 70 years?*

# 1959: CHAMPIONSHIP SEASON

In 1959, players climbed 20-foot ropes at Hendricks Field and ran half-miles as never before in practice.

This was a tough bunch; talented and deep, too. Big up front for its day — the "Sizeable Seven" averaged 6-foot-3, 215 pounds.

"If you're not a hitter, you're not a hard-nose. And if you're not a hard-nose," an SU player once said, "you don't play football for Benny."

The essence of what might have been the decade's best team was up front:

Fred Mautino, Maury Youmans, Bob Yates, Bruce Tarbox, Al Bemiller, Roger Davis, Gerry Skonieczski.

Unbalanced line, offensively; Schwartzwalder, a single-wing coach, felt two to one side of center, four to

Coach Ben Schwartzwalder is surrounded by the Sizeable Seven (from left): end Fred "Chief" Mautino, tackle Maury "Yo-Yo" Youmans, tackle Bob "Toe" Yates, guard Bruce "Cinderella" Tarbox, center Al "Tombstone" Bemiller, guard Roger "Hound Dog" Davis (kneeling, in front of Bemiller) and end Gerry "Hands" Skonieczki.

the other gave him an advantage. Foes weren't used to such an alignment. He'd try a million-and-one ways to run at you off-tackle.

A 6-2, 212-pound sophomore wearing No. 44 would carry the Orange to glory.

**GAME 1: SARETTE'S THE ONE** Captain Ger Schwedes, a halfback, began the season opener at quarterback. John Hadl was the quarterback for Kansas. But sophomore Dave Sarette's performance that day was such he won the job for the rest of the season, allowing Schwedes and Ernie Davis to form a formidable halfback duo, flanking Art Baker. Sarette was 9 of 13 passing for 177 of SU's 491 total yards, SU rallied from a 15-12 deficit late in the third period to win, 35-21.

Quarterback Dave Sarette, shown picking up a first down against Pitt, threw with 59 percent accuracy in 1959 and became a great field leader of the national championship team his sophomore year.

**ORANGE**
**·QUIZ·**

*4. Who coached the team that ended SU's nation-leading 16-game winning streak in 1960?*

**GAME 2: FIRST OF MANY SHUTOUTS** Maryland suffered its worst offensive day in history (eight yards rushing, 21 total offense). The Terps never crossed Archbold's mid-stripe. Davis' 26-yard touchdown jaunt was a hint of what No. 44 would do over three seasons. SU rolled, 29-0.

**GAME 3: OYSTER STEW** For the first time, blacks played in the Oyster Bowl in Norfolk, Va. Baker, who's black, was voted the outstanding player. A fullback/linebacker, Baker was also quick as a cat on the wrestling mat. He stopped a Navy drive that might have tied the game, returning an interception 97 yards for a touchdown. SU had five interceptions, returning a pair for scores in a 32-6 romp.

**GAME 4: THOU SHALT NOT RUN** Schwartzwalder bemoaned a lackluster performance, even though Holy Cross had minus-28 yards rushing in a 42-6 mismatch. Sarette and No. 2 quarterback Dick Easterly each tossed two touchdown passes.

*Fullback Art Baker (39) was a devastating linebacker whose record 97-yard interception return against Navy in 1959 was broken three games later by Dan Rackiewicz's 100-yarder against Pitt.*

**GAME 5: CUT UP BY 'THE SCISSORS'** SU's running game thrived on a misdirection play called "The Scissors." An inside reverse, it was sheer (or is that shear?) madness for opposing defenses. Rocky Pirro's linemen blocked it with precision, Bill Bell's backs finding daylight. Against WVU, Davis had nine carries for 141 yards on the ground. Syracuse — No. 1 in the East, sixth in the nation — amassed 589 total yards in a 44-0 slaughter.

**GAME 6: DAN(DY) RETURN** Third-stringer Dan Rackiewicz set an existing SU record, putting an exclamation point

on a 35-0 pillage of Pittsburgh by running 100 yards with an intercepted pass. Pitt's running game produced minus-6 yards.

## GAME 7: PASS THE TEST

There was one, but only one, game that saw the Orange pressured to the end. Penn State, too, was unbeaten. There were bowl/Lambert Trophy implications. Taking a 20-6 lead into the last quarter, SU seemed secure until Roger Kochman returned a kickoff 100 yards and a blocked punt to set up another Nittany Lion score. But the second of State's two-point conversion tries failed. Marching more than half the field in a clock-killing mode, SU sensed its 20-18 win was a ticket to the national championship.

## GAME 8: 'ATTILA THE BEN'

For the first time since 1945, an Eastern team was ranked No. 1 — in both national wire service polls. Criticized in defeat, Ben was berated for a 71-0 stomping of Colgate in which the Orange gained 607 yards, even though one player who saw action wasn't even on the roster. Called "Attila Schwartzwalder" by one columnist, the writer described SU's treatment of neighboring Colgate as "compassion for none and concussion for all."

## GAME 9: BRING ON THE DOGS

Boston University's Terriers were no match either. SU's defensive front suffocated BU (minus-88 yards rushing), the offense gained 510 yards. A 46-0 laugher was SU's fifth shutout.

## GAME 10: CALIFORNIA, HERE WE COME

Bruce Tarbox would later say, "There was a real rap against Syracuse, against Eastern football before that game (UCLA in Los Angeles). Texas was No. 2, and we were the No. 1-rated team, but I don't think people really believed we were No. 1 until we waxed UCLA in our last game real bad (36-8)." Schwedes scored twice, his 16 touchdowns setting an SU season record surpassed only by Floyd Little. Schwartzwalder termed the nationally-televised performance at UCLA "the greatest game any of our teams played." After 71 years, SU had gone unbeaten.

## NUMERO UNO IN SIX STATS

At the end of the regular season, Syracuse (10-0) led the nation in six major categories:

Total offense (451.4 yards a game); rushing offense (313.6 yards a game); total defense (96.2 yards a game); rushing defense (19.3 yards a game); scoring (39 points a game); touchdown passes (21). And they said Ol' Ben never threw the ball!

*7. Whose touchdown with 10 seconds remaining in the 1987 regular-season finale with West Virginia gave SU the chance to go undefeated?*

**LOOSENS THE REINS** Players favored the Orange Bowl atmosphere, but voted to go Cotton.

Al "Tombstone" Bemiller, SU's center, explained:

"We felt, let's let it all hang out. If we're going to be No. 1, we have to play Texas."

Bemiller saw a change in the approach to bowl game preparation by Schwartzwalder, the former 152-pound center at West Virginia, who wrestled college heavyweight foes, and was a decorated World War II company commander in Normandy.

In Ken Rappoport's *The Syracuse Football Story*, Bemiller related: "The year before, he took us down to the Orange Bowl and killed us. ... The team was not ready at all because he had worked us for two weeks, and I mean, really, really hard! ... He ran us into the ground, and that's why we lost to Oklahoma. ... When we went down to Texas — of course, it was a different breed of fellows — he knew how to handle us. We went down there, and we had a good time. It wasn't work. We wanted to play. That was nothing but fun, that Texas game."

**SPIT 'N POLISH** There was a distasteful part to the 24th Cotton Bowl Classic. It could be seen on faces of the Orangemen as they headed from playing field to dressing room.

"I have never in my life spent a more frustrating afternoon," said Schwartzwalder. "This was tougher on me than that long afternoon in Miami seven years ago (Orange Bowl, Jan. 1, '53)"

Officiating — particularly umpire Julius Truelson of

*The 1959 national champions outscored 10 regular-season opponents by an average of 33.1 points.*

Texas Christian — was questioned.

"We teach our kids to use a forearm lift on their defensive blocks, and that official (Truelson) told us we couldn't do it," Schwartzwalder told the *Herald-Journal*.

The well-polished SU offense, featuring the "Four Furies" backfield, would lack a coherent flow.

Whistles and flags didn't hurt some of the Orangemen as much as language they claimed they heard.

"They (the Longhorns) hit harder in the open field than they did along the line of scrimmage," said Bemiller. "We respected Oklahoma the way they hit us last year, but frankly, we don't have much respect for these guys the way they played.

"Some of the names they called John, Art and Ernie (Brown, Baker and Davis, SU's three black players) were just awful."

John Brown and Texas tackle Larry Stephens mixed it up just before halftime, and a melee ensued. SU tackle Al Gerlick said Brown had been called "a dirty nigger, and everybody got all heated up." Baker said a Texas player "spit in my face as I carried the ball through the line."

**1960 COTTON BOWL** The Orangemen were double-digit favorites despite the fact that leading rusher Davis' status was in doubt; he'd been treated 10 days for a pulled muscle in his left leg suffered during workouts.

While visibly favoring his injured limb, Davis was on the receiving end of a Cotton Bowl-record 87-yard scoring pass on the game's third play. Ger Schwedes took a pitch from Sarette, and protected by Baker's block, hurled a strike to Davis, who took it away from Texas

*8. Who holds the single-game receiving yardage record?*

*Winning the national championship gave Syracuse students and fans reason for a downtown celebration.*

# ORANGE ·QUIZ·

9. Can you name the
only Orange QB who
attempted at least
100 passes and had
a higher season
passing efficiency
rating than Donovan
McNabb's 162.3 in
1995?

Alpha Tau Omega
fraternity brothers
fired a cannon after
every SU touchdown
at Archbold, until an
accident on Oct. 15,
1960. Cannon fire
after SU's first TD
against Penn State
touched off a nearby
box of gunpowder,
injuring seven in the
second blast, none
fatally. The cannon
was "retired."

defender Bobby Lackey at SU's 48-yard line.

The "Elmira Express" raced, then limped his way the final few strides into the end zone.

SU never looked back. Davis (eight carries for 57 yards on the ground) also scored on a 4-yard run and pair of two-point conversion passes from Sarette. The Orange led at halftime, 15-0, and 23-6 after three periods, with Schwedes' 3-yard run providing SU's final touchdown.

The Longhorns' big strike was a 69-yard touchdown pass from Lackey to Jackie Collins. Lackey's late-game plunge ended the scoring.

In the annals of SU football, The Score of scores remains: Syracuse 23, Texas 14.

It spelled a perfect season — 11-0 — and a national championship.

**1960-69: ALL GOOD THINGS COME TO AN END** The 1950s produced a record of 62-29-2. Despite the loss of unanimous All-American guard Roger Davis, Yates and Youmans from the "Sizeable Seven," and captain Schwedes from the "Four Furies," SU won its first five games in 1960.

The Orangemen's 16-game winning streak was the nation's longest and best ever in school history. SU won 22 consecutive regular-season games prior to Pitt's Archbold invasion. Mike Ditka and the Panthers whitewashed the Orange, 10-0.

A 7-2 season, otherwise successful, was disappointing on the heels of 1959.

Bowls were interested in SU and No. 44. But Chancellor Tolley and Athletic Director Andreas said the season was history, protests of fans and bowl folks notwithstanding.

**IF AT FIRST YOU DON'T SUCCEED ...** Second only to Ernie Davis writing Heisman history, the 1961 season would never be forgotten because of "The Extra Play" at South Bend.

The Orange Bowl representative was at Notre Dame to tender the Orange a bid, which seemed secure after the visitors rallied from a 14-0 deficit and led, 15-14, with :03 left on the clock and Joe Perkowski set to try a desperation 56-yard field goal.

Wouldn't you know there'd be an Irish Leprechaun on the field. "Gus" Skibbie was his name, and when end Walt Sweeney (later all-pro with the San Diego Chargers before falling on hard times) crashed into holder George Sefcik, after Perkowski's failed attempt was shanked far short and farther right and his leg was on the way down, Skibbie dropped his handkerchief.

A 15-yard walkoff gave Perkowski another chance — a 41-yarder. He nailed it: Notre Dame 17, Syracuse 15.

"Rock" Pirro could hardly be restrained. The Orange had been jobbed by a call that didn't exist in the rule book … until 1962.

The game, according to '61 rules, should have been declared over with the failed field goal. But SU blew the game, too.

Lefty Bob Lelli, subbing late in the game for injured quarterback Dave Sarette, ran out of bounds, stopping the clock. Notre Dame took over on downs at its 30-yard line with 17 seconds remaining. Quarterback Frank Budka scrambled for 21 yards (:08 left), then passed for 11 to Sefcik, who stepped out of bounds (:03).

What ensued was a week-long critique in the national press: Should Notre Dame forfeit the win? Didn't Syracuse commit the foul and has no complaint?

There was no redress, though the error was acknowledged and the rule changed so as not to allow a game (or half) to end on a defensive penalty.

SU would spend a bone-chilling bowl-game afternoon in frozen Philadelphia.

**1961 LIBERTY BOWL** Bud Dudley wanted to match Syracuse and Notre Dame in a grudge (re)match in his Liberty Bowl. The Irish said no; it had a policy at the time against bowl games.

There were more than 85,000 unfilled seats in

*Ben Schwartzwalder congratulates his senior trio of (from left) quarterback Dave Sarette, MVP halfback Dick Easterly and Most Outstanding Back Ernie Davis after they accounted for all but one point in SU's 15-14 win over Miami in the 1961 Liberty Bowl. The Orange would go 18 years before winning another bowl.*

# TOO SOON, HE'S GONE

To know him at all was to like him a lot. As student assistant in the sports information office of Val Pinchbeck Jr. (who's had a distinguished career in the NFL office), I never heard a harsh word spoken of Ernie Davis.

A portion of what *Herald-Journal* Executive Sports Editor Arnie Burdick wrote just after Davis died of leukemia at age 23:

"We still see him as a runner with the power of a freight train as he powered over Miami in the last half of the Liberty Bowl game in his collegiate farewell ... as the flawless pass receiver in the Oyster Bowl game of '59 as Syracuse walloped Navy, 32-6 ... as a sprinter with a gait of a greyhound when he picked off a desperate Boston College pass and sped 55 yards for a touchdown to sew up the victory ... as a self-sacrificing blocker — a sure tackler, a fearless competitor and a complete team player.

"But the greatest memory ... is the sight of him winning the game no one ever thought he'd play ... the Cotton Bowl after the 1959 season ... Ernie always told me that he got more pleasure out of that game than any other."

With an engaging smile, great talent, desire not to seek center stage even for a two-time All-American, first of his race and only Orangeman to win the Heisman Trophy, Davis turned No. 44 into a legacy by the splendid way he wore it and courageous manner he fought his final battle.

To many of us in the Class of '62, the Carrier Dome's Ernie Davis Room, named for a special person, remains a special place.

*A smiling Ernie Davis appears bewildered, snowed under by a sea of footballs he and other members of the 1961 Walter Camp All-America team, selected by the American Football Coaches Association, autographed in New York.*

Philadelphia Stadium for what no one could suspect would be — other than a two-point conversion in the East-West Shrine Game — the last points Ernie Davis would score on a football field.

Quarterback George Mira had Miami in front at halftime, 14-0. Then, SU's No. 44 wrote a closing chapter to his brilliant football life. He scored on a 1-yard plunge late in the third period, caught a two-point conversion pass from Dave Sarette and set up the final touchdown (7-yard pass from Sarette to Dick Easterly, followed by Ken Ericson's PAT).

Ernie sustained a first-period back injury. But when the frost-bitten afternoon was over, he'd carried 30 times for 140 yards.

Still, Schwartzwalder would say, "It was pretty hard not to think about Notre Dame when the score got to 15-14."

Perhaps SU's defense did, after two Mira passes put the ball on the Hurricanes 42-yard line. Mira threw four incompletions, the last deflected away by Davis at SU's 20-yard line. The Orange ran out the clock on an 8-3 season highlighted by a second straight bowl victory, Schwartzwalder's last.

**PROMISES, PROMISES**  When Davis was a senior, Schwartzwalder's top recruiting priority was finding an heir to Ernie's numeral.

As Ben's staff fanned out in pursuit of a top-notch halfback, an inducement was No. 44. Ted Dailey offered it to Jim Nance, Bill Bell to Nat Duckett, Joe Szombathy to Billy Hunter. Each said they'd come to SU, expecting to wear No. 44.

They played well on the freshman team in 1961, wearing numbers other than 44.

After a varsity-frosh scrimmage during the season, Schwartzwalder worried about what to do with 44 in 1962.

"If we give it to one, the other two will probably leave," he told the staff.

Each assistant argued for his recruit. The discussion became heated.

Roy Simmons chimed in, " 'Pap' (that's what he called Ben privately), there's no problem. We'll just make 'em 44A … 44B … 44C!"

The staff broke into laughter. Simmie, renowned as a horrible horse player, had come up with a winning trifecta to break the tension.

As it turned out, each contributed to the SU program; none wore 44.

**BETWEEN BOWLS**  Flanker John Mackey and sophomore fullback Jim Nance were bright spots in an otherwise mediocre 1962 season (5-5), Schwartzwalder's first non-

10. What former Hobart coach holds the longest-standing offensive mark in SU's record book?

*Center Pat Killorin helped open up the middle for Floyd Little (above) in 1964-65, and gained All-American recognition both years.*

## ORANGE
### ·QUIZ·

11. Whose touchdown pass to Mike Siano upset No. 1 Nebraska in 1984?

*Charley Brown (left) was the first SU defensive back named to an All-America team in 1965.*

*Herb Stecker (middle) was an unheralded, undersized, but very dependable end in the mid-1960s.*

*Gary Bugenhagen (right) moved from guard to tackle, wore No. 78 and gained All-America honors in 1966.*

winner since '54.

Arguably the greatest tight end of all time, Mackey finally entered the Pro Football Hall of Fame in 1992.

The '63 campaign (8-2) saw SU avenge the '61 loss to Notre Dame in what was the 400th victory in Orange history. The defense stood tall nearly all fall.

Collegian Jim Nance never quite met expectations some held for him as the "next Jim Brown."

Inconsistent and always fighting weight problems, "Bo" Nance displayed as a senior in '64 the form that would make him the leading rusher in the American Football League.

Nance saved his best for last (951 yards, 13 touchdowns). Teaming with a squatty, bowlegged sophomore tailback named Floyd Little, SU's tandem conjured up comparisons with the original 'Mr. Inside and Mr. Outside' — Doc Blanchard and Glenn Davis of Army in the '40s.

Together, they ran for 1,779 yards in '64, a major share of the 251 yards SU averaged to rank No. 1 in the nation in rushing. The run game had another threat in the loping strides of quarterback Walley Mahle, whose 457 rushing yards (5.9 a carry) had led SU the year before.

Up front, center Pat Killorin was All-American along with Little.

**A LITTLE GOES A LONG WAY** SU opened 1964 losing at Boston College.

In the locker room before the home opener with Kansas, featuring the great Gale Sayers, Little learned he was starting at tailback.

What a response! Floyd was fabulous in his first start: 16 carries for 159 yards, two receptions, 254 all-purpose yards and all five SU touchdowns in a 38-6 rout. "... greatest performance by a back that I have ever seen," said Kansas coach Jack Mitchell.

Other opposing coaches would see even more.

The Orange (7-3) received a bid to the Sugar Bowl, where the Orangemen lost to Louisiana State. But at least the first integrated Sugar Bowl since 1956 went without incident.

"They didn't show any prejudice at all. ... I hope someday I can play against them again," said Little, the lone sophomore named to *Look Magazine's* All-America team.

A 7-3 season in 1965, in which Little and Killorin repeated as All-Americans, and defensive back Charley Brown also gained All-American recognition, earned no bowl trip.

**BUMPY START ON ROUTE '66** If the '66 season began in embarrassing fashion — a 35-12 debacle at Baylor on ABC television and 31-12 home loss to UCLA — it surely turned around dramatically, only to end in disbelief.

Schwartzwalder made some lineup changes. Southpaw Jim DelGaizo tied Pat Stark's 14-year-old record by pitching for four touchdowns against Maryland. But in the Boston College game, Rick Cassata took over as quarterback.

The Orangemen ran the regular-season table to an 8-2 mark. The hallmark victory — and only close game all fall — was at Happy Valley. SU held the ball nearly eight minutes, protecting a 12-10 lead over Penn State in the final period.

Larry Csonka and Little combined for 242 yards. That win was the fourth straight over the Nittany Lions.

Little fought his way through a season hobbled by an

*Floyd Little carried No. 44 to record heights, but lost his shirt and the Orange lost the game in the 1966 opener at Baylor.*

*Despite gaining 26 yards during SU's opening drive, Floyd Little ran for a mere 46 yards against LSU in the 1965 Sugar Bowl played in New Orleans.*

*Little scored three touchdowns, the most electrifying of which was a 91-yard punt return, in a 28-21 Archbold win over Penn State in 1965 and became the first Orangeman to rush for more than 1,000 yards in a season. His 19 touchdowns and 114 points remain SU single-season standards.*

*Larry Csonka, ever the battering ram, lowered his shoulder and prepared to pile drive his way through Tennessee in the 1966 Gator Bowl, an 18-12 loss.*

ankle sprain. No. 44 was team captain, a fiery orator in the dressing room, leader by example, yet criticized for stats that had fallen. Little never said a word about his injury.

Instead, he spoke loudly at Ol' Archbold. In his final game there, he turned the hat trick — three 24-yard touchdown runs against Florida State — and carried 25 times for 193 yards, passing Ernie Davis on the all-time rushing list.

Closing with a convincing win at West Virginia, SU accepted a Gator Bowl invitation, where the Orange lost, 18-12, despite 330 rushing yards combined from Csonka and Little (a record 216 by No. 44, who'd carry 29 times).

## 'ZONK' A ONE-MAN SHOW

As a senior in 1967, Larry Csonka came at linemen and linebackers with the power of a 238-pound Ohio farmboy.

He possessed none of the moves Floyd Little or Ernie Davis had, nor their speed. Jim Brown was that rare mixture of speed and power.

"Just run over them," Csonka said, when asked how he'd attack Penn State in '67.

Running behind a not-so-good line on a team that lacked a speed back, Csonka literally carried the 1967 offense on his broad shoulders.

He'd run for a record 216 yards against West Virginia as a sophomore, for more than 1,000 his junior year, and was a primary lead blocker for Little in 1965-66. But the first two games of '65, Csonka was a linebacker. In his first start on offense, however, "Zonk" gained an inconspicuous 26 yards against Maryland. The next week, the figure was 162 against UCLA.

When he rumbled for 216 against West Virginia, breaking Brown's mark (197), offensive backfield coach Bill Bell proclaimed: "Larry Csonka is the best back I've ever coached."

As the Orange carved out an 8-2 mark in '67, Csonka rushed for a school-record 1,127 yards, gaining much of that on his own. He dragged defenders keyed to

# LITTLE BIG MAN

All-American Floyd Little means more to Syracuse football than a stack of records.

His 46 touchdowns, 35 rushing, remain marks on the Hill. A great punt returner, his career average of 164.9 all-purpose yards may tell the true story of Little the player. His 39.9-yard average returning kickoffs adds to the statistical lore.

Little's greatest statistical season was 1965. He led the nation in all-purpose yards (199.0 per game), broke six single-season records, eight of his school-record 19 touchdowns were from 45 yards away or more and he led the team in receptions a second year in a row.

Even more important than his football skills, perhaps, is what he's meant in the ensuing 30 years to his alma mater. Overlooked by the Pro Football Hall of Fame despite an outstanding career toiling for the Denver Broncos, when he carried the offense on his bowed legs, he remains appreciated in his collegiate "hometown."

Little became an attorney and successful businessman. He'd made himself into a good student, from one whose scholastic days had not included academics.

But Little's true mark is an unflinching loyalty to his coach and alma mater. With Ol' Ben's

coaching glory gone and in his darkest hour — embattled by charges of racism during the black boycott of 1970 which gained support from Jim Brown — there was Little. On campus, by Ben's side, saying black players, not the coach, were wrongdoers.

Little was unjustly branded a Schwartzwalder mouthpiece.

A leader on and off the field, there has been no finer alum produced by the Syracuse football program than Floyd D. Little.

*At the 100 Years of SU Football dinner in 1989, three-time All-American Floyd Little posed in front of a photo mural of Ol' Archbold.*

stop No. 39.

"If I had a team of Mr. Csonkas," Schwartzwalder said, "I'd sit up in the stands and watch the fun."

Ben's last great back needed no mirror images that year, particularly when he lugged the ball 43 times in a 7-3 win at Maryland or rushed for 204 yards against California.

And to think, Larry Csonka almost went to Clemson.

*Linebacker Jim Cheyunski was a 12th round draft pick in 1968, who went on to play nine seasons in the NFL with the Patriots, Bills and Colts.*

*Marty "Jan the Man" Januszkiewicz finds a gaping hole on the right side and a sea of mud to navigate before gaining first down yardage against Army in 1972.*

**AND NOW, THE END IS NEAR** Syracuse football's fall from grace wasn't instantaneous, but gradual.

As the 1968 campaign began, one could look back to the 1967 closer and hope for more of the same. SU had gone to Los Angeles and with a defense led by middle guard Dennis Fitzgibbons, turned eventual Heisman-winning Gary Beban (3 of 11 passes for 17 yards, minus-9 rushing) into little more than a crumbling statue.

This was a time when campus revolts were part of the landscape, on the Hill, coast to coast. Ben's cupboard was no longer well-stocked. Csonka, a one-man wrecking crew, was gone.

There were those who tried to carry on. Marty Januszkiewicz ran for 769 yards in 1970, more than 2,000 in his career; Roger Praetorius plodded for 705

*Guard/tackle Dennis Fitzgibbons drove Heisman-winning Gary Beban of UCLA crazy in the 1967 finale in Los Angeles. SU won, 32-14, capping an 8-2 season that wouldn't be matched until 1987.*

and 11 touchdowns in '71, nearly 1,800 overall.

But before the program would return to glory, there would be a great deal of angst, a new stadium and a couple of coaching changes.

**1968-73: THE FINAL YEARS**  The numbers game tells the story of Schwartzwalder's last six seasons: 6-4, 5-5, 6-4 (closing the 1960s at 69-33), 5-5-1, 5-6, 2-9. A collective 29-33-1 ride to nowhere.

There were outstanding individual performances. Januszkiewicz carried 36 times against Penn State in '70 … Praetorius rushed for three scores in the '71 West Virginia game. … Tony Gabriel caught a record four touchdown passes in '70 against Miami. … Greg Allen returned four punts for a record 172 yards in the '69 Penn State game. … 1971 All-American safety Tommy Myers tied a Hill mark with three of his 18 career interceptions in the 1970 Penn State game.

But the only other All-America selections those last half-dozen seasons were Tony Kyasky (1968) and defensive tackle Joe Ehrmann (1970).

*Tackle Stan Walters had the largest helmet size among 1970-71 Orangemen. One day, you couldn't miss it. "Stan wore size 8," said teammate Roger Praetorius. "We painted it pink, with fairytale decals all over it, for the spring game. (Equipment manager) Jon Phillips was in on it. "Pro scouts were there … and Stan had to wear that pink helmet, because nothing else fit him."*

*Tackle Art Thoms (1966-68) went on to have an outstanding pro career with the Oakland Raiders (AFL).*

*Only Art Monk (14 with the Redskins) and Gary Anderson (13 with the Steelers) played more years with one NFL team than 1971 All-American defensive back Tommy Myers, who played his 12-year NFL career with the Saints.*

Following a 6-2 start in '68, no Schwartzwalder team would rise above two games over .500. And the final year was a desperate search for a win. After losing the first eight games (nine including the 1972 closer), a 5-3 baseball score in an awful game at Holy Cross seemed an embarrassing way to end the free fall.

**THE DARKEST HOUR** Schwartzwalder could withstand allegations made by a former player of improper recruiting practices and payoffs. Dave Meggyesy, an outstanding student and stellar lineman in 1960-62, bludgeoned Ol' Ben in his book, *Out Of Their League.*

The administration foolishly demurred from commenting, though some of Meggyesy's teammates denied the charges.

Syracuse prepared to play Kansas on Sept. 26, 1970. The game meant little in light of racial turmoil on the Hill. Police security was beefed up from 40 to nearly 200.

Dialogue between blacks and whites was bitter, if at all. What began with a boycott by eight members of the team — claiming betrayal by Schwartzwalder who, they said, promised them a black assistant coach would be hired — was now ominous.

New York State Human Rights Commission and the university had Schwartzwalder discussing allegations of racism with his team.

"It was a big mistake," Schwartzwalder later conceded. "Before the talk, the team was a unit. After that, it was two groups — one black, one white. If I had known what was going to happen, I would have refused to hold that stupid meeting."

Floyd Little came to the 1970 spring practice, which only irritated black players.

Starting fullback Al Newton, the team's leading rusher in 1968 and '69, and eight others boycotted spring practice.

John Corbally was chancellor, and only now did he enter the dispute.

Eventually, seven of the nine black players were no longer team members. An eighth joined boycotters; ergo, the label "The Syracuse 8" — acknowledged leader Newton, Greg Allen, Richard Bullis, John Godbolt, Dana

# ORANGE
# ·QUIZ·

*12. Name the starting QB in the opener of the 1959 championship season?*

*Two-time team rushing leader Al Newton was the acknowledged leader of the 1970 black boycott rather than the starting fullback his senior year.*

*Guard Dave Meggyesy (1960-62), a seven-year linebacker with the St. Louis Cardinals, was very critical of SU when he authored the book,* Out of Their League.

Harrell, John Lobon, Bucky McGill and Duane Walker. Blacks Robin Griffin and Ron Page, who was injured, remained with the team.

SU's first black coach, Carlmon Jones, joined the staff.

"The Syracuse 8" levied four charges (later eight) against Schwartzwalder and the university. Among them, they claimed white athletes gained preferential treatment.

"They claimed we got preferential medical treatment," Roger Praetorius said recently, still in disbelief. "Who got good treatment from Doc (Bill) Pelow?"

Corbally said any player not at the opening of formal fall practice "has removed himself from participation as a member of the squad for the 1970 season."

None of the boycotting blacks showed up. Jim Brown came to town; battle lines stiffened.

The season began with a 42-15 defeat at Houston.

To lessen fears of any organized disruption of the Syracuse-Kansas game, terms of a reconciliation were drawn. A statement said Schwartzwalder "recommended" reinstatement of the black players to the chancellor.

The embattled coach quoted the team as saying, "We'll take the suspended players back in order to play the game."

# BEN'S LEGACY

You can crunch numbers and they add up to Hall of Fame:
- 153-91-3 in 25 years
- 22 consecutive non-losing seasons
- 15 first-team All-Americans (two two-time All-Americans, one three-time selection)
- seven bowl games (five on New Year's Day)
- four Lambert Trophies
- one national championship.

Still, the man had his detractors. Only the 1959 kings of college football and '61 squad won bowl games; he ran the ball too much, they'd say.

If you had Brown, Davis, Nance, Little and Csonka (four of 'em College Hall of Famers), wouldn't you run the ball? And yet, not until 1987 did an Orange squad toss more touchdown passes than the 21 thrown in 1959.

Ben Schwartzwalder's teams from 1958-67 won 75 of 98 regular-season games, during which time Syracuse was 7-3 vs. Penn State and the Benny-Rip Engle personal tug o' war became legendary among Eastern football folks.

He could be different (i.e., unbalanced line, "Scissors" play).

He could be stubborn (not exiting until nudged by time — mandatory retirement age of 65 — and an administration that turned its back on him in the face of the boycott).

But his career on the Hill was — and is — the golden moment of Syracuse football.

White players Tommy Myers and Gary Bletsch told the press: "We never voted to take the blacks back. … We were forced to take them back."

"We've been sold out by the university," said Bill Coghill, another white player.

Ticket refunds were sought. A six-foot chain link fence was erected around the field. Syracuse lost, 31-14.

**ONE LAST GRAND STAND** The next weekend, SU lost at Illinois, 27-0. But in a surrealistic twist, the given-up-for-dead Orange (0-3) won its next five games, six of the last seven. Schwartzwalder was UPI's Eastern Coach of the Year.

Most amazing was a 24-7 victory over Penn State, in which Myers' three interceptions tied a school record and Marty "Jan the Man" Januszkiewicz carried the ball all afternoon, scoring twice.

Schwartzwalder would say, in light of the situation, "I think this is probably the greatest upset in my 22 years here."

It would be 17 years before SU would enjoy another win over Penn State.

In 1972, Schwartzwalder suffered his first losing campaign since '49.

**THE MALONEY YEARS** "I feel like I'm walking into the shoes of a giant," new head coach Frank Maloney said of his predecessor. "I feel like it's 1939 and I'm replacing

## ORANGE ·QUIZ·

*13. Only one player captained the Orange three seasons. Who was he?*

*Frank Maloney endured some tumultuous moments trying to rebuild the Orange program. But he was a happy guy as he hugged Joe Morris during the 1980 Dome unveiling.*

Lou Gehrig."

Ironically, Ben Schwartzwalder's successor would find his job security not in football, but baseball. Since his seven-year struggle on the Hill ended with the first season of Syracuse's Carrier Dome, Maloney has directed the Chicago Cubs' ticket office and is a vice-president of the ballclub.

It's a good fit; even as football coach, he loved talking baseball.

Maloney had coached Chicago's scholastic powerhouse (Moeller High) and been an assistant to Michigan's Bo Schembechler. But he never endeared himself to SU alums.

He alienated the old guard by not cultivating a friendship with Schwartzwalder, and totally sweeping the old staff out of the house despite efforts by influential backers to retain receivers coach Joe Szombathy, a former star player.

Maloney felt he needed to make a statement by selecting his own staff.

The new coach inherited little talent, and Ol' Archbold's concrete was cracking.

Maloney gave the team a new uniform and canned the unbalanced line, running out of the I-formation. He switched sidelines, from north to south; if the sun ever shined on a football Saturday in Syracuse, it ought to glare in opponents' eyes.

The administration was more favorable toward returning football to its glory days; scholarships and

*Linebacker Ray Preston toiled for bad teams, but was an All-American in 1975.*

*No Orangeman has played longer for a professional football team than classy possession receiver Art Monk, who spent 14 seasons with the Redskins.*

funding increased.

Maloney sought improved facilities. Local industrialist J. Stanley Coyne donated $600,000 for an artificial turf practice field. In 1975, Coyne Field (now Coyne Stadium) was dedicated.

**WON ONLY IN ODD YEARS** Homegrown Ken Kinsey didn't wish to carry the weight of No. 44. But he carried the ball for 169 yards in the 1974 opening-game win over Oregon State.

Four games into Maloney's first season, the Orange had accumulated a total of 120 passing yards. SU (2-9) scored 121 points all fall, the most anemic output in 36 years.

The next season (6-5), Kinsey quit.

Syracuse's trend continued, with a 3-8 season in 1976, a 6-5 record in '77 and another losing campaign in 1978 (SU's 0-4 start was the second worst since 1892).

**I AIN'T GOT A HOME** A new stadium wouldn't be ready until 1980, so 1979 was a road show. Two "home" games were played in the Meadowlands, two at Buffalo's Rich Stadium, one at Cornell's Schoellkopf Field.

The stellar performances were by Joe Morris at Kansas

*Tackle Ken Clarke (1975-77) played 15 NFL seasons, though not drafted and signing as a free agent with the Eagles.*

*South African native Gary Anderson had the most accurate season kicking field goals in SU history (18 of 19 in 1981) and didn't miss any of 72 points-after in his three years as the Orange placekicker.*

and linebacker Jim Collins in a Meadowlands loss to Penn State.

The Ayer Express set a single-game rushing record of 252 yards (11.0 yards per carry, three touchdowns vs. KU). Collins set existing records for tackles (42), solos (22), assists (20), and that season set a mark for total stops (229); only Tony Romano (198 in 1982) has come close to 200.

At 4-1 and the talk of the East, SU's lead evaporated at Temple in a 49-17 whipping, and after the Nittany Lions clawed Syracuse, 1959 captain Ger Schwedes and teammate Dick Easterly, both Syracuse residents, called a press conference and demanded a "more dynamic" coach than Maloney, who responded in a seven-page

## UNDER THE TEFLON BUBBLE

Constructed between April of 1979 and September of 1980, the Carrier Dome was built at a cost of $28 million.

A $15 million grant from New York State paved the way, the other $13 million coming from private donations, of which Carrier Corporation kicked in $2.75 million.

The 49,900 seats (33,000 capacity for basketball in the DemiDome) include 24,000 on the upper level, 6,000 mezzanine and 19,000 lower level. Additionally, there are 38 private boxes providing 900 seats.

Requiring 30,000 cubic yards of concrete and 880 tons of steel to

*The $28 million Carrier Dome was a hot box for the opening of indoor football on Sept. 20, 1980, and some of the record 50,564 on hand passed out in the stands.*

press release.

Then, when Gary Anderson's four field goals beat Miami at empty Rich Stadium, Maloney was given the game ball. Bill Hurley asked, "Where's the '59 boys now?"

**1979 INDEPENDENCE BOWL** When the 4-year-old Independence Bowl invited SU to play in Shreveport, La., players voted to go.

Skeptics wondered what was to be gained playing tiny McNeese State, 11-0 yet a four-point underdog.

"A lot of people were saying it was the 'toilet bowl,' " Morris would say later.

Money? Peanuts! SU hadn't gone bowling since the 1966 Gator, that's why.

# ORANGE
## ·Q U I Z·

*15. Whose touchdown broke the Colgate jinx?*

build, the Dome spans 7.7 acres, is 570 feet long and 497 feet wide and has 527,320 square feet of floor space 160 feet below the top of the Dome. The roof weighs 200 tons, is constructed of 287,000 square feet of Teflon-coated fiberglass and steel bridge cables.

Air pressure, provided by 16 five-foot diameter fans located in walls, keeps the roof inflated. Zippers hold together 28 rolls of Astro Turf (each 13½ feet wide) installed by a machine called a grasshopper.

Utilitarian in design, it's the fifth-largest domed stadium in the country.

*A look inside the Teflon Bubble, which is covered by a 200-ton roof constructed of Teflon-coated fiberglass and steel bridge cables.*

SU had only Anderson's 40-yard field goal to show for a half. Ken Mandeville's 1-yard touchdown run in the third period was matched by McNeese's lone score, and it was 10-7 going into the final period.

Hurley hit Art Monk on a 9-yard touchdown pass and ran one in from a yard out, before Tom Matichak closed out the scoring with a 6-yard run.

Morris (33 for 155 yards) was selected the outstanding offensive player. SU's 31-7 victory marked the school's first bowl win in 18 years. The sorry '70s ended 45-64-1, the only losing decade in SU history.

## MONK AND HURLEY

The new 50,000-seat stadium on Irving Avenue was going up as Monk and Hurley were leaving.

The offense faced rebuilding; tackle Craig Wolfley was gone, too.

Monk had been an exquisite receiver in a ground-oriented system, catching 41 balls in 1977 and 40 (for 790 yards) in '79, when he was an All-American.

Hurley, walking wounded during a career that included a medical redshirt year, was a fearless leader who ran for 12 touchdowns in '79.

Only Marvin Graves and Don McPherson have passed for more yards or accounted for more total offense than Hurley, whose 2,551 rushing yards is a quarterback standard that appears untouchable and is No. 5 on SU's all-time list, ahead of 44s Davis and Brown.

## RECORDS FOR MORRIS

The Dome would allow Syracuse to go to the air more, but sans Hurley, SU was grounded.

That wasn't so bad, because Morris was certain to pass Csonka and become SU's all-time rusher.

The 1980 season began in front of 87,000 fans at Ohio State; Morris carried 25 times for 150 yards in a 10-point loss.

On Sept. 20, the indoor football era began on the Hill. On a sweltering evening under the billowy bubble, the largest crowd to ever see a football game in Syracuse (50,564) saw some of its own pass out in the stands.

"We were hyperventilating on the sidelines," said Morris, who scored four touchdowns (one a 94-yard kickoff return) and rushed for 170 yards in a 36-24 win over Miami of Ohio.

Morris rushed for 492 yards and five touchdowns in three games, seemingly a lock for a third successive 1,000-yard campaign.

But he went out with a shoulder injury in the loss to Kansas. After missing the loss at Penn State, Morris' 157 yards in a win over Rutgers put him No. 1 on the all-time rushing list.

*Bill Hurley ran for more than twice as much positive yardage (2,551, fifth on the all-time rushing list) as any SU quarterback, and is the only quarterback to rank in the top five in rushing and passing.*

*Thousands of No. 44 jerseys were handed out as the Ernie Davis Room was dedicated in the east end of the Dome in 1980. Ernie's mother, along with Jim Brown and Floyd Little, were on hand. Ernie's Heisman Trophy and countless memorabilia were placed in the room.*

Morris wasn't the only weapon for the Orangemen, though. Glenn Moore, wearing No. 44, carried 37 times for 192 yards in a win at WVU that ended another losing season.

**THE PLAYERS' COACH RESIGNS** Two days later, Maloney announced his resignation. He cited family reasons and a desire to return to Chicago. But he was also shoved, taking with him a settlement of what remained on his contract.

Joe Morris was in tears; he thought about transferring. "I'm emotionally attached to him. He took a chance with me, because no one wanted a 5-7 running back in Division I. He wasn't popular because he cared only about his players. ... He put it (the program) in modern times."

Maloney, whose seven-year record was 32-46, resisted rancor, saying, "The biggest plus for me was that the program was in the basement in 1973 and we made it better ... built it back to respectability. The minus is that we never won enough to satisfy the general public."

*It was fitting that Joe Morris, who had set game and season records on the ground and would become the all-time rushing leader, scored SU's first touchdown in the Dome.*

# 1981-Present
# Football

## DICK MacPHERSON

16. What receiver is
SU's all-time leader
in yards-per-catch?
Shelby Hill, Marvin
Harrison, Tommy
Kane or Rob Moore?

*Years coached at SU: 1981-1990*
*SU record: 66-46-4; Only unbeaten 11-game winner; three straight*
*bowl wins.*

Modern-day football at Syracuse is measured by the
Schwartzwalder Era. Its resurrection took place under
Dick MacPherson.

That rise would take awhile. Along the way, there'd
be more losses than wins, and the SacMacPac that
wanted him out of town when a bowl game was followed
by a 0-4 start.

But no other coach in SU history won 11 regular-
season games in one season. The culmination of that
1987 season — a march down the Dome carpet to beat
West Virginia on a two-point conversion, and the TieDye
Sugar Bowl that smudged perfection — are games among
the most memorable in Orange history.

*Think Dick*
*MacPherson enjoyed*
*what transpired on*
*Sept. 29, 1984?*
*Coach Mac hoisted*
*quarterback Todd*
*Norley, who had*
*delivered the bomb*
*that blew up No. 1*
*Nebraska.*

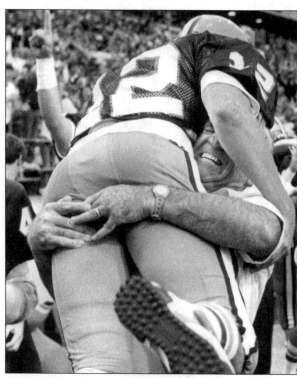

The craggy-faced man from Maine had come from the NFL, an assistant in Denver and Cleveland, sandwiched around a successful stint as head coach at University of Massachusetts. He'd leave SU after 10 years to be head coach of the New England Patriots.

MacPherson became the most popular person in town. He might have been elected to political office (some urged him to run for mayor).

His mark will always be the 11-0-1 record of 1987, three bowl wins his last three seasons and a Stengelese manner in which MacSpeak took on special meaning for Central New Yorkers, even as he destroyed the King's English.

### ONCE, TWICE, THREE TIMES A LOSER
Initially dubbed "The Mac Pack," MacPherson's first edition began the 1981 season dropping three in a row.

Morris ripped off a 95-yard kickoff return and got his 100 yards rushing, but Jamie Kimmel and Ike Bogosian went down with knee injuries, and Rutgers won the lid-lifter in the Dome, 29-27. There were 12,000 unfilled seats.

Temple passed SU silly in Philly, 31-19. And folks in Champaign toasted Illinois' 17-14 win.

Finally, Mac got a 'W' — 21-7 over Indiana — as Morris ran for 164 yards.

### NO MO' JOE
Morris rebounded from 1980 shoulder injuries to put together an '81 campaign that preceded a great NFL career with the New York Giants.

As a senior, he carried a record 261 times for 1,194 yards and scored 10 touchdowns. But he was also an electrifying kickoff returner and competent pass receiver.

Morris' career marks of 813 carries for 4,299 yards, and 21 100-yard rushing performances won't soon — if ever — be surpassed.

Lil' Joe never opted for comparisons with great backs who had run before him on the Hill.

"I'm my own man; not the greatest, just the latest," he said.

### 500 AND COUNTING
Not since Schwartzwalder's finale and Maloney's debut had Syracuse sunk so low as 1982. SU (2-9) lost six in a row, was twice shut out and averaged an anemic 8.8 points in its nine losses.

The '83 road to victory No. 500 was filled with potholes. After a turnover-plagued, season-opening loss at Temple, SU needed a record five field goals by Don McAulay at home to beat pitiful Kent State, 22-10. The defense sacked lowly Northwestern, 35-0. No. 500 was a 17-13 squeaker over Rutgers.

*17. What was the most famous play in the 1959 national champions' arsenal?*

*18. Can you name the only alum in the Pro Football Hall of Fame not to letter in football for the Orange?*

Then, reality — in Lincoln, Neb. The Cornhuskers emasculated the Orange, 63-7.

Well, Nebraska needed fourth-down situations for seven of those scores, Mac pointed out.

Three losses followed, but solid defensive efforts paid season-ending dividends.

At Navy, Tim Green scored the game-winner on a fumble recovery. BC had thoughts of a Fiesta Bowl bid, but an SU defensive front of tackles Green and Blaise Winter, outside linebacker Jamie Kimmel and nose guard Bill Pendock — they called themselves "Four-Wheel Drive" — ran down quarterback Doug Flutie (four sacks, three interceptions). And the West Virginia finale was more of the same.

With a record of 6-5, the 1983 team turned in Syracuse's first winning season of the '80s.

**UPSET OF UPSETS** Defense was the name of Syracuse's game. In nine of 11 games in 1983, SU limited foes to 17 points or less. The 'D' in 1984 would be the stingiest in 15 years.

*ORANGE*
*·QUIZ·*

*19. An Orangeman said in 1987: "I was told during warmups to be alert, because they might throw some kind of trick play, and they wanted me to be in there for it." Who was he?*

*The catch? There have been a few; perhaps none more memorable than when Mike Siano (14) elevated between a pair of Nebraska defenders in the west end zone of the Dome to snare Todd Norley's 47-yard pass that upset the No. 1 Cornhuskers and shocked the nation in 1984.*

Following two road wins, the Orange was No. 20 in the land. Perhaps Dome lights blinded them into a false sense of security. Or was SU looking ahead? Regardless, the crowd booed as SU coughed up the ball seven times in a 19-0 gift-wrapping to Rutgers.

Next, No. 1 Nebraska, favored by 24 points, on Sept. 29, 1984.

Tim Green was at his All-American best (12 tackles, two sacks). When quarterback Todd Norley let go the most memorable pass of his career, the Orange trailed, 7-3, late in the third period. When Mike Siano leaped between red-clad defenders in the west end zone and grabbed it, the noise was deafening and SU held a lead it would not surrender.

The Cornhuskers shot themselves in the foot with a 12th man on the field for a punt, allowing SU to retain possession, killing any chance of a late UN score.

Syracuse 17, Nebraska 9. The nation thought it must be a misprint in Sunday's papers.

"The euphoria of Nebraska was something," MacPherson said. "Ben was happy again!"

**CAN'T SCORE, CAN'T WIN** As quickly as the Orangemen and their fans tasted euphoria, they were faced with road kill. Easy as 1-2-3, they fell at Florida, West Virginia and Penn State, scoring one touchdown in 12 quarters.

MacPherson conceded his team had nothing left after the Gators' super-quick defense stuffed SU, 16-0.

The Orange did rebound for home wins over Army

**ORANGE**
**·Q U I Z·**

*20. Which school has faced SU the most and holds the most wins over the Orange?*

*Jaime Covington was a workman-like back who never gained 800 yards in a season, but led the 1982-84 teams in rushing and is No. 7 all-time (2,188).*

(Jaime Covington went over the 2,000-yard mark), Pitt and Navy.

But any bowl talk fell on deaf ears when SU went to Sullivan Stadium and Cotton Bowl-bound Boston College, directed by Flutie, beat the Orange, 24-16.

Another 6-5 season, but with a memorable victory.

**WE'VE GOT HIGH HOPES**  With Liverpool's own Tim Green touted for Outland and Lombardi trophies, and a Rhodes Scholar candidate to boot, expectations were lofty when the 1985 season kicked off in Starkville, Miss.

But the Mississippi State Bulldogs knocked Green cold and the Orange silly, 30-3. If safety Pete Ewald had to make 15 solos, where was the up-front defense?

SU did fashion home shutouts over Kent State and Howard Schnellenberger's Louisville squad (Don McPherson getting the latter start at quarterback) around a road loss to Virginia Tech.

Penn State's yearly victory figured next, even in the Dome. Yet, the ball was in SU's hand near midfield. Time (4:43 to play) and score (20-17) in favor of the Orangemen suggested another shocker.

Then, the ball was coughed up by fullback Roland Grimes. Penn Staters covered the carpet, and the ball. A packed house was resigned to what would ensue. The Lions drove for the winning score … 24-20 was close, but when would this bitterest of Eastern rivalries, now so one-sided, turn SU's way if not today?

**LONGEST WIN STREAK SINCE 1970**  For the first time since the Schwartzwalder Era, the Orange ran off five wins in succession: Temple, at Pitt and Navy, Boston College, at Rutgers, where Siano scored three touchdowns and eclipsed Monk's season reception yardage mark. Not since 1967 had SU won seven regular-season games.

The second-year Cherry Bowl invited SU.

For the regular-season closer against West Virginia, much of the crowd was clad in green on Tim Green Day. It was the last game in the Dome for a National Football Foundation Hall of Fame Scholar-Athlete and unanimous first-team All-American who would be a first-round NFL pick.

A late 44-yard pass set up West Virginia's go-ahead touchdown, SU's five-game streak halted in disappointing fashion, 13-10.

**GREEN WITH ENVY**  MacPherson saw Green as a pivotal player in the program's turnaround.

"He was the star of the local area. The key was getting Tim Green to come here.

"We said, 'He's the kind of kid who won't let those

guys be an ordinary team' … and he led 'em to the
Cherry Bowl."

**1985 CHERRY BOWL**  No money-maker, this Cherry Bowl
in Pontiac, Mich. Muddy Waters, the old Michigan State
coach, was the front-man for a bowl whose financial
status was, indeed, murky.

SU led Maryland, 10-6, and was still in it at 14-10 late
in the first half. Then, quicker than you could say
turnover, turnover, turnover, the Terrapins scored twice.
They'd score again in the third period — a total of 29
unanswered points — and go on to a 35-18 win.

Don McPherson threw and ran for 315 yards, Robert
Drummond was 10 for 93 on the ground, Siano and
Scott Schwedes combined for nine catches and 129
yards. SU had 28 first downs and lost by 17 points.

The program was no longer in an abyss, nor was it all
the way back.

Still, Mac could reflect recently, knowing it had been

*Another local
schoolboy product
and son of a former
Orange captain who
wore the same
uniform number,
Scott Schwedes (16)
clutches this Cherry
Bowl toss in the
Silverdome.*

a step in the right direction.

"It was the only time Jake (Crouthamel, SU's athletic director) ever got the short end financially," he said. "But it was the best investment we ever made."

**'THE PEOPLE ARE GETTING RESTLESS'**  The Cherry Bowl didn't help SU's coffers, but enhanced recruiting.

The Dome opener was a 24-17 nocturnal loss to Mississippi State, which capitalized on two fumbles for scores. It would get much worse before getting better.

At Army, nose guard Ted Gregory was lost for the season with a broken leg.

Asked 10 years later what was the lowest point in his tenure at SU, MacPherson replied, "Some coaches have a great gift of forgetting those things. But I can't forget coming back from West Point (a 33-28 loser). Not one kid of theirs could start for us, and they kicked our ass."

Back home, SU lost to Virginia Tech by nine and Rutgers by six.

The SacMacPac was alive and feeling its oats.

A 5-6 ledger in 1986 provided no sign of what was a year away.

# 1987: NEAR-PERFECT SEASON

**GAME 1: TRICKING THE TERPS**  On SU's first play of the season, the Orangemen gave a hint of what was to become a fall to remember.

Drummond took a pitch from McPherson at his 26-yard line, began to sweep right, pulled up and fired a 55-yard strike to Tommy Kane. SU settled for Tim Vesling's 32-yard field goal, first of his four, and the Orange marched to a 22-0 halftime cushion over ex-SU lineman/assistant coach Joe Krivak's Maryland Terrapins.

Kane caught four passes for 125 yards. Gregory, after missing all but five quarters of the 1986 season, was one of a trio of Orangemen with double-figure stops as SU's run defense allowed 48 yards in 36 attempts in a 25-11 win.

**GAME 2: FULLBACK UP THE MIDDLE**  Criticized at home for a too predictable fullback-up-the-middle-on-first-down-offense, Coach Mac ran this so often with success at Rutgers, SU enjoyed a better than 2-to-1 possession advantage, rushing 59 times for 292 yards.

The heralded Michael Owens, who sat out in 1986 (Proposition 48), scored his first SU touchdown. The Scarlet Knights, 20-3 losers, gained just 161 total yards.

**GAME 3: KANE AND ABLE**  Miami of Ohio couldn't run (44 yards in 27 tries).

*Tommy Kane, beating a Maryland defender in the end zone, is SU's yards-per-catch leader for a season (22.0 in 1987) and career (20.7).*

SU scored on its first possession, McPherson hitting fullback Daryl Johnston on a 38-yard pass. Kane caught six passes for 113 yards.

Not since '75 had an SU team started 3-0; that year, the Orange collapsed. Would this team, following its 24-10 win, be able to avoid a similar fall?

**GAME 4: OVERCOMING SOME HOKIE POKIE** Two touchdown passes (one set up by a bad punt snap) and blocked punt in the end zone found SU trailing Virginia Tech, 21-7, in Blacksburg.

"We took a gut check at the half," Coach Mac said at the time.

25. *What backup QB holds SU's record for passing percentage in a bowl game?*

SU marched 80 yards in eight plays on its first possession of the third quarter, Chris Barnes going the last four. And Donnie Mc's 17-yard pass to Kane capped a 71-yard march to tie it. In the final period, Drummond dashed 51 yards for the game-winner, and McPherson to Kane for 11 was insurance in a 35-21 win

SU limited Tech to minus-1 yard rushing. Gregory (12 stops) was a thorn in Tech's side. And second-half double coverage left the Hokies no where to go.

### GAME 5: A SANDLOT PLAY
No style points awarded in Columbia, Mo., where the teams fumbled 13 times and SU squandered a 10-0 first-quarter lead.

Trailing Missouri in the third period, 13-10, and faced with a third-and-14 on his 29-yard line, Donnie Mc had freshman Rob Moore streaking down the left sideline. Moore was supposed to be a decoy, opening up the middle for what was called a "nine route."

Mizzou was in a three-deep, but Moore slipped past corner Pat Ray. McPherson fired, Moore caught it at the 25-yard line and sprinted for the score.

"You run as far as you can, I throw as far as I can, and if we match up, we match up," Donnie Mc said of the play that broke Mizzou's back.

Backer Dan Bucey had 15 stops in a 24-13 win, SU moving into the AP Top 20 (No. 17) for the first time in 16 years.

### GAME 6: BEN RIDES MAC'S HORSES
It only took the first play from scrimmage to turn 50,011 people into a

*26. Which school is the only one to face the Orange in more than one bowl game?*

*All-American center John Flannery hoists Rob Moore after one of his career-record 22 touchdown grabs.*

frenzied Dome crowd that partied the whole day long. And when it was over, Ben Schwartzwalder rode off on the shoulders of Coach Mac's troops.

Penn State had won the last 16 meetings by an average of 21.4 points.

It was 17 years, to the day, that Schwartzwalder's 1970 team beat the Nittany Lions.

But when SU snapped the ball at its 20-yard line, and Donnie Mc faked an option right, stopped, stepped back and let go a bomb, the game of Oct. 19, 1987, was about to become one SU fans won't soon forget.

Moore was streaking toward the middle of the field, and Nittany Lion defensive back Brian Chizmar was slipping to the carpet. Moore grabbed the ball and dashed to the end zone. The noise would have registered on the Richter Scale.

The beating Penn State took was such that MacPherson pulled regulars in the third quarter. The score was 41-0; it ended, 48-21, the worst licking State's ever been dealt by SU.

Moore was told during warmups of a possible trick play. "I only knew they were going to throw the play 30 seconds before it happened," he said after the game.

SU had lined up with only 10 men, Moore sprinting on the field at the last instant.

SU cut up Penn State every which way. Heisman candidate Blair Thomas was shut down all day by Gregory & Co., leaving the Lions with little offense.

Donnie Mc threw for 336 yards, 163 of those to Kane, who caught two for touchdowns — one a spectacular change of direction in mid-leap to grab an underthrown ball.

When Vesling booted the final point, it broke

*The last great ride Ben Schwartzwalder took on Orange shoulders came, as Dick MacPherson beams approval, moments after SU ended the Penn State series losing streak at 16.*

## ORANGE ·QUIZ·

27. Can you name the last player to lead SU in tackles three years in a row?

Alabama's NCAA record of 199 consecutive PAT kicks.

SU was 6-0 for the first time since 1959. Coach Mac, his team about to crash the Top 10 (No. 9), took the game ball and ran a victory lap around the Dome.

Every 17 years, why not!

28. What passing leader threw the fewest interceptions-per-attempt in a season? Dave Sarette, Chuck Zimmerman, Bob Woodruff or Donovan McNabb?

**GAME 7: UGLY END TO A RIVALRY LONG PAST** Syracuse-Colgate was a rivalry in name only. SU's Division I-AA neighbors hadn't beaten the Orange since 1950.

The schools decided enough was enough. And if the 52-6 rout wasn't sufficient proof, the dirty tactics of which each team accused the other surely was.

The verdict was rendered early, McPherson to Kane tacking three scores on the board from 18, 44 and 42 yards out. It was 42-0 at intermission. McPherson tied a school record with four touchdown passes (and he caught one from Drummond for a score), Kane did likewise with four touchdown grabs, Vesling equaled Jim Brown's single-game PAT mark with seven, and SU gained 560 total yards.

SU paid a heavy price in victory. Greg Robitaille blocked Gregory in the back of the knee in the third quarter; Gregory missed all but seven plays the rest of the regular season.

One play later, SU defensive tackle John Dominic was ejected, following a brawl with Colgate's Brian Smith.

SU climbed a notch to No. 8.

29. What Orangeman ranks 1-2-3 in season sacks?

**GAME 8: NOT EXACTLY THE PITTS, BUT** … A 24-10 win at Pittsburgh wasn't pretty.

Craig "Ironhead" Heyward (24 for 141 yards) ran through an SU defense sans the injured Gregory and linebacker Terry Wooden.

"He was like a tank out there," said defensive tackle Paul Frase, who was a big 1987 contributor with 51 tackles and six sacks.

Still, SU was up by 21 at the half.

Kane had his third successive 100-yard receiving game.

**GAME 9: TRA-DI-TION, TRA-DI-TION** Not realizing the Brigade of Midshipmen always marches onto the field 1½ hours before home games, Coach Mac objected twice before finally agreeing to move his troops to the sideline.

Once back on the field, SU yielded 204 rushing yards to Navy's option ground game. Free safety Markus Paul had to make 15 tackles. Gregory's absence was painfully obvious.

But McPherson, who eclipsed his own season record for passing yards, tossed touchdowns to Deval Glover and Kane; the latter broke Mike Siano's season mark for receiving yards. After SU's 34-10 win, a scout pinned a little Sugar Bowl pin on Coach Mac. Sugar? Fiesta? Orange? Which would it be?

"We're 9-0 and still counting," said Mac. "We haven't got it done."

**GAME 10: WAKE-UP CALL**  The Dome was full. And the Orange bowl was filled with sugar cubes.

Sugar Bowl President Jerry Romig disclosed a week later, while making everything official, that No. 6 SU and the Sugar made a deal the week of the Boston College game that SU would be the bowl's at-large team if it beat BC.

A 12:10 p.m. kickoff caused the team to awake at 6:45 a.m.

Into the second quarter, it appeared the Orangemen were still yawning. BC led, 17-0.

"It took us some time to shake the cobwebs off," said Coach Mac.

But shake they did, the Orangemen scoring 45 unanswered points in a 45-17 romp. The barrage began with the same McPherson to Moore "eight-route" post pattern that initiated the Penn State rout — this a 46-yarder to set up the first of two touchdown passes to Kane, who broke Scott Schwedes' career touchdown reception mark (15, set the year before).

**GAME 11: 'THE DRIVE'**  The BC scare came early. The West Virginia game came down to a final march — 87 seconds in what had been a perfect '87 season — and a win-or-lose two-point conversion.

ESPN turned down a chance to televise it, so *Sports Illustrated* dubbed the classic, "The Best Game No One Saw." Except for a full house in the Dome.

The game had everything: each team scored five touchdowns, kicked a 30-yard field goal and ran 74 offensive plays. There were 966 total yards and nine turnovers (six by SU, including four interceptions thrown by Donnie Mc).

Four times, frosh quarterback Major Harris directed WVU to seven-point leads.

And when the Mountaineers took a 31-24 lead on Undra Johnson's 10-yard run and the point-after, with 1:32 to go, what was Dick MacPherson's sideline response?

"I'm linebacker coach, on the sideline," said Paul Pasqualoni, nearly a decade later. "Norm (Gerber, the defensive coordinator) is in the press box. I'm relaying plays in.

"They score, and the defense feels like we've lost the game; the season's down the tubes.

"Mac goes over to me — and he shocked me when he said it — he says, 'Good, I'm glad they scored that quick.

*30. Who's the only defensive back to lead SU in interceptions four years? (hint: he was a two-time finalist for the Jim Thorpe Award)*

*On the same day that the Orange football team played West Virginia, Syracuse's basketball team, ranked No. 1, suffered a 96-93 overtime loss to North Carolina in the televised Tipoff Classic. But the football team was able to shake off the ominous overtones and win, 32-31.*

*Tight end Pat Kelly (right) caught the touch-down pass that set up the biggest conversion in SU history …*

*… and Michael Owens (below) took a pitch left into the end zone for the two-pointer to beat West Virginia and preserve an unbeaten 1987 season.*

Now, we've got a chance to win the game!' "

SU, taking the ball at its 26-yard line with those 87 clicks holding history in every tick, marched with fast-break precision.

Donnie Mc hit Michael Owens for six, Deval Glover for 23 and, after an incompletion, Glover for 20 more yards.

SU stopped the clock, then McPherson to Pat Kelly gained eight. Another incompletion. Third-and-2 at WVU's 17-yard line.

Coach Mac'll never forget the rest:

"Donnie McPherson looked at (tight end) Pat Kelly, a high school quarterback now on Wall Street. 'I'm coming to you,' he tells Kelly. The defense left him wide open."

There was a defensive penalty, but no matter. Kelly scored, SU was down by one.

Assistant Jim Hofher researched two-point conversions. SU had its play. A season hung in the balance.

McPherson rolled left and … "Donnie almost held on too long," says Coach Mac.

The pitch went to No. 44, SU's numeral of greatness in its only other unbeaten season.

"Not a foot was there between the sideline and Michael Owens' left foot," says 1987's Coach of the Year.

SU, 32-31. Pandemonium! The comeback of comebacks had former Orange star/radio analyst Jim Ridlon exclaiming the same words over and over and … again and again and … oh, yes! Yes! Yes!

## ORANGE ·QUIZ·

*31. After Dave Sarette in 1961, who was the only QB until 1985 to throw more touchdown passes than interceptions in a season?*

**1988 SUGAR BOWL** Orange fanatics kept trying to devise a scenario by which their team could win a second national championship. There was none; as sure as Sugar Bowl MVP Donnie Mc wouldn't win the Heisman (he was second to Notre Dame's Tim Brown).

Still, No. 4 SU (11-0) and Southeastern Conference champ Auburn (9-1-1) provided an appealing New Year's Day matchup over which New Orleans visitors could respectfully disagree. The way the game ended, arguments in pubs along Bourbon Street, or Rue St. Pierre, raged into the wee hours.

SU won the stat battle — time of possession, first downs, total yardage.

Auburn couldn't run on Norm Gerber's defense; few could.

But SU never led the game, which was tied at three different times. With 2:04 left, the Orange having been stuffed on a third-and-1 and gaining a sub-par 174 rushing yards, MacPherson opted to break a tie. Vesling's third field goal gave SU a 16-13 edge.

Auburn moved quickly on the arm of Jeff Burger against a defense that was without Gregory the second

*Tim Vesling, whose PAT broke Alabama's NCAA record of 199 in a row, kicked three field goals in the 1988 Sugar Bowl.*

*Auburn's Win Lyle boots the tying field goal that left the Orange with a bittersweet taste of 1988 Sugar.*

**ORANGE ·QUIZ·**

32. *What foe wisely called it quits after going 0-25 against Syracuse by a collective score of 797-40?*

half. The Tigers moved 62 yards to SU's 13-yard line. The clock read :04.

A never-before-attained 12-0 record hung on one play. Do-or-die. Or tie?

"When Syracuse went up, 16-13, I relaxed; I thought I was done for the day," said Auburn placekicker Win Lyle. "Most of the offense wasn't satisfied; they wanted to go for the win."

What transpired left Dick MacPherson hot under the collar.

"Why the hell didn't he (Auburn coach Pat Dye) call timeout and ask the players what they wanted to do?

"I thought he was going to throw in the end zone three or four times at the end. Instead, they were farting around."

Called to action, Lyle was stunned. Auburn settled for a Win for a tie — his 30-yarder creating a 16-16 deadlock, first in Sugar Bowl history.

"What in the hell did they come here for in the first place?" MacPherson wondered. "In Syracuse, we don't play for ties."

SU fans won't forget the Tidy Bowl ... or Pat TieDye.

**A BOWL(ING) DOUBLE?** The 1988 season had more open dates than losses, so you know the Orangemen were very good.

The big question mark was quarterback. Fifth-year senior Todd Philcox had spent most of his career on the sidelines, other than holding for placements and attempting 10 passes. Strong-armed, ballyhooed Billy

# A SEASON TO REMEMBER

Don McPherson led the nation in passing efficiency in 1987, throwing for 2,341 yards and 22 touchdowns. He won the Maxwell and Davey O'Brien awards.

McPherson was a unanimous first team All-American, noseman Ted Gregory — though missing four games — a consensus pick.

Tommy Kane set a scoring mark for receivers, and his 22.0 per-catch average eclipsed Lonnie Allgood's 13-year standard.

The defense had 31 takeaways. And even the SacMacPac had to hail everyone's Coach of the Year.

But before the 1988 season began, Mac looked back on the final minute of '87, saying:

"It's my fault. In my own mind, I sold something so much to my kids that I believed it myself. … You go after 'em; that's defensive strategy. I'm just keeping 'em out of the end zone.

"That's what I have to live with. I told the kids, 'That's my fault, because I should have known.' You never guess what your opponent is gonna do."

*Fullback Daryl "Mooooose" Johnston (32) often led the way for quarterback Don McPherson to operate the option running game.*

*Fifth-year senior Todd Philcox had the 1988 Orangemen armed to record the school's first consecutive double-figure win seasons.*

*SU played in front of its largest crowd ever (89,768 at Ohio State) in a losing effort to the Buckeyes (26-9) in 1988.*

Scharr was heir apparent to McPherson.

SU accepted a bowl invite to play Jan. 2, 1989, in Tampa, Fla. For the first time in 29 years, back-to-back bowl games.

Philcox was the big story; so unheralded, an unknown quantity, he completed 60.2 percent of his passes for more than 2,000 yards and 16 touchdowns for the season.

Aground, homegrown Rob Drummond's career yardage surpassed that of Jim Brown.

Moore and Glover became SU's first pair of 40-plus receivers in the same season.

Nearly everyone, except All-America selectors, acknowledged Daryl Johnston — a crushing blocker, 5.0 yards per carry, 20 receptions — as the nation's premier fullback.

Kevin J. Greene extended SU's collegiate mark of consecutive PATs to 260.

And All-American Markus Paul (a record 19 interceptions, eclipsing Tommy Myers' career mark) spearheaded a seasoned secondary and overall defense that allowed two touchdown passes all season … none in the final 38 regular-season quarters, plus the bowl game!

Was Louisiana State a match for the Orange?

Michael Owens was not among those suited up; he'd

Rob Drummond produced mirror-image stats in 1987 and '88, capping his career with a Hall of Fame performance (122 yards, two touchdowns) against LSU.

been suspended for repeated failure to adhere to "team guidelines."

SU ran 12 times in a 14-play, 80-yard opening drive.

The Tigers tied it at 10 in the third quarter. But bowl game MVP Drummond (23 carries for 122 yards) dashed in from short yardage for the second time, and Philcox to Glover nailed down the win.

Greene missed the PAT, but bowl game stats don't count and the streak was alive.

For the first time, Syracuse (10-2) had double-figure wins in consecutive seasons.

**CENTENNIAL SEASON** The 100th year of SU football was a curious one.

Rob Moore became the first single-season 1,000-yard receiver, and he and Notre Dame transfer Rob Carpenter combined for 94 catches in 1989.

Scharr had his moments, most notably against Rutgers, when he became the fifth quarterback (third in as many years) to toss four touchdown passes. His passing efficiency rating was higher than Philcox. But he was

SU's Centennial poster

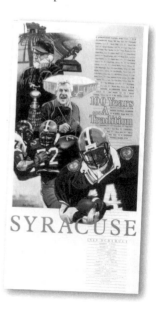

*Rob Thomson's seven interceptions in 1989 is tied for second on the single-season list.*

*SU's Hall of Fame Bowl shirts included a "103" patch, which was worn in memory of the Dec. 21, 1988, crash of Pan Am Flight 103 over Lockerbie, Scotland, in which 35 Syracuse students perished.*

inconsistent, and with eligibility remaining, he didn't return to play in 1990.

Rob Thomson picked off seven passes, one shy of Myers' season mark set in '71.

Freshman Qadry Ismail made an impact with a record 738 yards returning kickoffs.

Michael Owens rebounded from his Hall of Fame Bowl suspension to become the fifth individual to rush for 1,000 yards in a season. Still, there were those who felt his 2,000-yard career fell short of all it might have been.

That might be said of the '89 Orange, too, though they did earn SU's third consecutive bowl berth, a first for the program.

This was a team at 2-0 that lost three in a row — by seven at Pitt, by 31 to Florida State (ending SU's 16-game Dome winning streak) and 22 to Penn State. After winning the next four, the Orangemen lost their third Dome game of the season, by seven to West Virginia.

A closing win over Louisville in Tokyo left SU with a 7-4 mark, its fans less than delirious over making the trip to Atlanta for the Peach Bowl.

**1989 PEACH BOWL** The Orangemen outgained the Bulldogs by 276 yards and had 15 more first downs.

Still, it took John Biskup's 26-yard field goal with 25 seconds remaining to eke out a 19-18 victory over Georgia.

MVP Owens (116 yards) made the game's biggest reception — down the sideline for 29 yards on a fourth-and-5 from the Orange 43-yard line, keeping alive a game-winning drive that began at SU's 27-yard line with 3:37 to go.

The pass was delivered by Mark McDonald, who spelled starting quarterback Scharr with the Orange trailing, 18-7, and completed 10 of 13 passes.

SU shut down the running of Rodney Hampton (15 for 32, negative yardage after the first drive), and limited the Dawgs to four second-half first downs.

**NEW DECADE, NEW LEADERS**  With the 1990s came an attitude that Syracuse was back, not an elite program yet, but among the heavyweights.

But in '90, there was plenty of regular-season frustration.

Freshman quarterback Marvin Graves ran the show, and accounted for 1,866 yards total offense in 10 games. His best was still to come.

Carpenter caught 52 passes and Shelby Hill set a frosh mark grabbing 33.

For the third season in a row, SU completed better than 61 percent of its passes.

Dan Conley and Glen Young were at the heart of a defense that needed to mature.

But inconsistency gripped this team all season.

**SAY IT AIN'T SO, JOE**  Joe Paterno said it was over; no need for the Fat Lady to sing.

The largest crowd ever to witness a Syracuse-Penn State game (86,002) crammed Beaver Stadium on Oct. 13, 1990.

An all-sports conference plan quashed, Paterno wanted to change the face of the home-and-home series, tilting it in Penn State's favor. Orange Athletic Director Jake Crouthamel would have none of that.

MacPherson said the Nittany Lion alums, who expressed displeasure with the death of the series, shouldn't allow it to happen.

It did, with that day's game: Nittany Lions 27, SU 21.

Series: Penn State 40, Syracuse 23 (five ties).

Each program would go its separate way, finding a conference home.

Eastern football was changed forever.

**1990 ALOHA BOWL**  Despite a modest 6-4-2 ledger, the Orangemen were invited to the Aloha Bowl in Honolulu, where they stuffed Arizona, 28-0.

Graves sandwiched touchdown passes of 47 yards to Terry Richardson and six yards to tight end Chris

*One notable fact from the 1989 season was a missed point-after by John Biskup in the season-opening win at Temple, ending an NCAA-record run that began in 1978, and included kickers Dave Jacobs, Gary Anderson, Russ Carpentieri, Don McAulay, Tim Vesling, Kevin J. Greene and Biskup. That record of 262 consecutive PATs by kick still stands.*

*The 1990 season saw the start of what would become The Series, a 33-7 loss at Miami (first trip there since 1979).*

*Joe Paterno*

Gedney, the local product of Liverpool High, between his pair of 5-yard touchdown runs. For Marvelous Marvin, who took snaps from consensus All-American center John

# MAC PACKS

Richard Frederick MacPherson, 11th of 12 children and son of a plumber, once thought life's best job was in the PCF Paper Mill in a small town in Maine. In 1987, he found out it was coaching Syracuse University.

He never forgot a face, a name — even after a chance meeting. His craggy face looked as if it wore the road map of a Maine shoreline. Mac's New England twang and penchant for malaprops made him an endearing part of the Syracuse landscape, after permanently escaping the clutches of the SacMacPac.

His 66-46-4 record in 10 seasons left him second in victories to Ben Schwartzwalder.

The time to wrap himself in a security blanket came in 1990.

"Ben had a couple of chances to go (to the NFL); the Patriots, the Rams. Me, I was 60 years of age," Mac said, reflecting on his departure to take the head coaching job of the New England Patriots in January of 1991.

"It was financial security. … We (Mac and his wife Sandra) could see our way home."

MacSpeak remained. Like the time he said of the SU football program:

"I wouldn't have come here when Frank Maloney took the job. But now, the support systems are in place. To me, it was very easy for it to happen here. They put up the Carrier Dome. All the talk's done, it's done. That's it!"

Or when he spoke of the guy

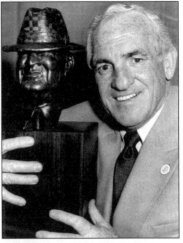

*Dick MacPherson received the 1987 Paul "Bear" Bryant Award as Coach of the Year, selected by the Football Writers Association of America.*

called "Mooooose":

"Daryl Johnston came to us as the No. 1 kid in his class of 290. His mother, Ann, gave him to me, and I made a beer-drinking, woman-chasing, 2.6 student out of a class valedictorian."

Or the Sugar Bowl, a tie which bugs him still:

"We knocked the living crap out of 'em!"

Or how the Dome clock couldn't seem to stop one afternoon:

"I remember Foge (Fazio) brings Pitt here in '86. They're on our 12 (SU up, 24-20) and throw an end zone pass (incomplete). Two seconds left. 'Oh, s- - -!' Next time I look up, there's zero-zero on the clock. … Let's get out of here!"

Flannery, there was Aloha Most Outstanding Player honors. It wouldn't be his last such postseason accolade.

The whitewashing was the first time in 19 years a shutout had been tossed at the Wildcats, who failed to penetrate SU's 28-yard line all day. The shutout, spearheaded by Rob Thomson and Dan Conley, was SU's first in its bowl history.

# PAUL PASQUALONI

*Years coached at SU: 1987-present; head coach since 1991*
*SU record (through 1995-96): 42-15-1*

Among the least-publicized assistants, certainly not flamboyant, Paul Pasqualoni provided a comfort zone for Crouthamel in selecting a successor to MacPherson.

"I watched the staff very closely and when Mac left, I talked with all the members of the staff for input," said the Orange athletic director.

"It became clear in my mind. Paul was the guy who'd won."

The linebackers coach kept winning as head coach.

Though he'd never run a program above the Division III level (Western Connecticut State), the former walk-on and later letterman at Penn State, was — and is — a tireless worker.

Literally, the 47-year-old bachelor eats and sleeps football.

Assistants have come and gone. Opportunity knocked. But in some instances, there were rumblings

## ORANGE ·QUIZ·

33. Who's the highest-ranking all-time rusher not to reach 1,000 in a season?

*Paul Pasqualoni*

# A LEAGUE OF THEIR OWN

The Big East Conference was born in 1979, a basketball league that rapidly rose to national attention in the 1980s with back-to-back national champions.

Its football counterpart, born in 1991, is comprised, for the most part, of traditional Eastern rivals. Boston College, Miami, Pittsburgh, and SU have been full members since 1991. Rutgers and West Virginia became full members on July 1, 1995. Temple and Virginia Tech are football-only members of the league.

The Big East established its own regional football television package before the conference played its first game.

In 1996, the Big East was in the first year of five-year contracts with CBS and ESPN, assuring a conference game will be telecast virtually every week through 2000.

Under Commissioner Mike Tranghese, its position in the changing alliance of bowls is as powerful as any league in the country.

A Big East team had a shot at claiming a national championship on New Year's Day the first four years of the league's exsistence.

*34. In what year did SU set its attendance record, averaging 49,325?*

the staff felt overworked.

Coach P just grinned then ... and now.

"My perception of the program is that you roll up your sleeves and go after it. If you have good people, you're demanding.

"I haven't changed," said Pasqualoni, prior to the '96 season, his sixth at the helm. "Not one ounce.

"I can't!"

**OUT OF THE BLOCKS** The Pasqualoni Era began impressively.

Tony Montemorra took a fumble recovery 37 yards for a score as SU wiped out Vanderbilt, 37-10.

Special teams played a big role in Coach P's first road win. Pat O'Neill, whose career kickoffs were rarely returned, broke the single-game punting record by one yard with a 72-yarder at Maryland. Shelby Hill returned a punt 61 yards for a touchdown in SU's 31-17 victory.

The season ended at Tampa, Fla., in the '92 Hall of Fame Bowl, where Syracuse battled Ohio State.

*Now running backs coach on the Hill, David Walker (33) had the great balance and leg drive to splash his way for yardage in the 1990 Aloha Bowl win over Arizona.*

As he did the season before, Graves put on an MVP performance, throwing for a career-high 309 yards (18 of 31). He began and ended the scoring by hurling the two longest pass competitions in Hall of Fame history — a 50-yarder to Hill and 60-yarder to Antonio Johnson — as SU never trailed the Buckeyes.

Down, 17-3, in the third quarter, the Buckeyes knotted it at 17 on Carlos Snow's 2-yard run and a

recovery in the end zone of O'Neill's blocked punt.

Two minutes later, a play-action pass saw Johnson break free and Graves, who also scored on a 3-yard run, hit him for the game-winner.

John Lusardi (11 tackles) led SU's defense.

Coach P's first season was a resounding 10-2 success. Only twice in major college football annals had a rookie head coach won more games.

**DEFENSE COMES THROUGH** Although SU wound up allowing the same number of points (183) as it did the year before, 1992 got off to a rocky defensive start, allowing 29 points per game in its first three contests.

But the Orangemen came around, as the defensive unit allowed no more than 10 points to Temple, Pitt, Virginia Tech or Boston College.

**BEASTS OF THE EAST** Since the Big East formulated its football conference, Miami has been the team to beat. And thus far, Syracuse hasn't done it.

But in 1992, the Orangemen came oh-so-close.

Just one more play … nine more feet.

SU came into the game with its longest single-season winning streak (seven games) since '87. The Hurricanes were a devastating defensive bunch and grabbed control at intermission; SU couldn't gain an inch.

The Orange rallied from 16 down, and trailing 16-10,

*In SU's first Big East game, David Walker's four rushing touchdowns in a 31-27 win at Pitt were the most by an Orangeman in 26 years. Walker would win the conference rushing title and gain 969 yards in 1991.*

*Stampeding Buffaloes are lined up in pursuit of quarterback Marvin Graves (5), who earned his third consecutive bowl MVP in the 1993 Fiesta victory over Colorado.*

*In 1992, Marvelous Marvin annihilated single-game records for aerial yardage (425, on 18 of 28 passing, three touchdowns) and total offense (476) in a 22-point win over Rutgers.*

were on a final march that would spell victory or defeat. SU had given Miami more than it expected.

Graves was knocked woozy, but tried to bring home what would have been a huge victory before a frenzied crowd and ABC television audience. On the game's final play, Graves hit tight end Chris Gedney, but SU's only unanimous All-American of the '90s was taken to the carpet on Miami's 3-yard line.

While Miami left knowing there was more than one heavyweight in the Big East, SU hasn't come that close since.

**1993 FIESTA BOWL** For a sixth successive season, Syracuse went bowling.

And what a matchup it was between No. 6 SU and 10th-ranked Colorado.

*Nose guard Kevin Mitchell (50), whose 64 solo tackles in 1991 is a record for SU down linemen, earned defensive player of the game honors in the '93 Fiesta Bowl.*

Colorado was directed by the nation's fifth-rated passer, Kordell Stewart. But defensive player of the game Kevin Mitchell harassed him all day in lousy field conditions, SU's nose guard making eight tackles, two sacks.

And when Mitchell wasn't making the stop, the terrific linebacking combination of Glen Young and Dan Conley (23 combined stops) were. Twenty-four of Stewart's 41 passes were incomplete or intercepted.

Trailing at halftime, 7-6, David Walker (16 for 80 yards) opened SU's 20-point third quarter with a 13-yard

touchdown run, a conversion pass failing.

Mitch Berger's 38-yard field goal narrowed SU's lead to 12-10.

Marvin Graves was selected offensive player of the game, though he had his least-impressive statistical performance in a bowl (64 yards passing). Still, his 28-yard touchdown dash and John Biskup's PAT made it 19-10.

Stewart's second touchdown pass tightened it at 19-16.

Then came the biggest play in SU's 26-22 Fiesta victory over the Buffs, who were led that day in Tempe, Ariz., by the running of James Hill (11 for 109 yards) and catching of Michael Westbrook (six for 83).

Kirby Dar Dar took the kickoff on the goal line and raced 100 yards — bowl marks for the Fiesta and SU. That proved to be the game-winner.

SU won its fifth bowl in as many years; only Florida State had a longer streak.

## DONNIE Mc & MARVELOUS MARVIN  Graves had departed after a mediocre 1993 season, and Orange fans could argue who was the best quarterback.

Donnie Mc had taken a program that had wandered aimlessly for nearly 20 years and brought them to the promised land. Graves broke most of his records and won three successive bowl game MVPs.

Graves, a four-year starter, threw for 8,466 yards and had 8,755 total offense. Both are SU standards.

McPherson, a three-year regular (hurt part of '84), threw for 5,812 and had 7,063 total offense, twice leading the Orange in rushing.

## PREMATURE EXULTATION  The 1994 and 1988 seasons were similar in that an unknown quantity — albeit fifth-year senior — was at quarterback.

Unfortunately, results were not the same.

To lay the blame on quarterback Kevin Mason for November's demise — taking a bowl-bound 6-1 squad to a stay-at-home 7-4 — would be unfair and inaccurate. Mason completed 56.1 percent of his passes, throwing for 1,627 yards and 10 touchdowns (seven interceptions). His passing efficiency rating was the seventh-best in 35 years.

## LOWER EXPECTATIONS  With three televised November '94 defeats by a 71-6 tally, few of the faithful expected big things in 1995.

The No. 1 preseason question: Who'd be quarterback?

Donovan McNabb's performance in the spring game was a hint. The staff kept any predisposition cloaked in mystery.

*Syracuse suffered back-to-back blankings at Miami (49-0) and at home to West Virginia (43-0) in 1993. ESPN viewers by the thousands clicked off those games. SU hadn't been blankety-blanked since Harry Truman was in the White House (Holy Cross, Penn State '47).*

*Perhaps the star performer of 1993 was Pat O'Neill, a straight-A student who holds SU punting marks for a game (55.2-yard average vs. Virginia Tech), season (44.3) and career (41.1).*

*In the 1994 opener SU and OU hooked up in an offensive barrage that included Kevin Mason's 78-yarder to Marvin Harrison. SU staged an incredible rally, but the Orange players' overzealous celebration drew a penalty flag. That shortened the Sooners' last-minute drive to a 30-29 victory.*

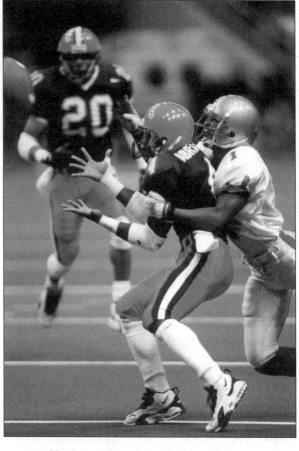

*The premier "cover" man in the Orange secondary in 1995 was diminutive Kevin Abrams, shown stepping in front of a Boston College pass.*

*The 1995 season was the year of McNabb to Harrison; touchdowns of 66 yards at Rutgers, 43 vs. Temple, a school-record 96 vs. West Virginia (Harrison caught nine for 213 yards to pass Shelby Hill in career reception yardage). On the season, Harrison caught 56 for 1,131, eight touchdowns, and returned two punts for scores.*

McNabb, the poised redshirt freshman from Chicago, quickly lit a fire under a team and its fans. "I made a few errors in judgment," he said of the ESPN-televised opener at North Carolina. And the offense, though balanced, was outgained by 162 yards. Two turnovers led to SU's first 10 points in a 20-9 come-from-behind win.

After McNabb tossed his first college touchdown pass and SU enjoyed a 21-0 lead over East Carolina, the No. 1 question mark the rest of the season became defense, despite the fact an improved secondary included the best back in man coverage in years, All-American corner Kevin Abrams.

ECU rode the record aerial show of Marcus Crandell (31 of 59 for 392 yards, four touchdowns thrown to different receivers). Disdaining a tying field goal on fourth-and-4 at the 12-yard line, a bad snap resulted in a fumble, and SU lost, 27-24, yielding 531 total yards — 360 the second half.

Syracuse went on to put together a five-game win

# RECEIVER U.

Known for its great running backs, Syracuse wide receivers have fashioned some impressive numbers since coming out of the cold to play home in the Dome.

Pasqualoni compared the best since joining the staff in 1987:

"Rob Moore ran the post route the best, and he could leap.

"Qadry Ismail had the greatest acceleration.

"Shelby Hill didn't have the senior year we'd hoped. He had a hamstring pull in the Big East track meet that spring; his 40 dash time was never quite the same. But from a catch-the-ball standpoint, he was fantastic.

"Marvin Harrison may be the all-time best. He had the whole package — quickness, precision, making cuts underneath, catching and flat-out speed."

*Qadry Ismail had trouble catching the ball early in his career, but caught 73 his last two seasons at Syracuse.*

*Record-smashing wide receiver Marvin Harrison recorded 135 catches from 1992 through '95.*

*It may not be wise to try and derail this locomotive! As a freshman, Rob Konrad ran for 130 yards, three touchdowns at Pitt.*

streak that was snapped in a 31-7 loss to Virginia Tech in Blacksburg.

McNabb, the all-conference quarterback and Big East rookie of the year, had a six-game span in which he completed 67.6 percent of his passes; overall he was .618 and his PER (162.3) was third in the nation.

**BURYING THE HATCHET** Never one not to speak his mind, Jim Brown healed some old wounds with his alma mater in 1995.

He told *The Syracuse Newspapers*, "There was a period when I was vicious on Syracuse.

"I'm very happy that I'm able to be an alumnus. Just an alumnus, not a guest."

And maybe, just the greatest running back of all time.

*Entering 1996, Syracuse (49-19-3 in the 1990s) was just one victory shy of its 600th. Coach Paul Pasqualioni's next bowl victory will make him SU's winningest bowl game coach.*

Brown returned again in the 1996 season, when a bust of Big Jim was placed outside the football wing of Manley Field House.

**1996 GATOR BOWL** What figured to be a hum-dinger New Year's Day in Jacksonville, Fla., turned out to be a ho-hummer.

In the most lopsided of the 51 Gator Bowls and the biggest margin of victory in SU's 16-game bowl history, Syracuse (9-6-1 record) cruised to a 41-0 demolition of Clemson to complete a pleasantly surprising 9-3 season.

*Coach P and Donovan McNabb: Orange leaders on the sideline and the field talk it over. McNabb was one of the most exciting players in the Big East in 1995, and he was only a redshirt freshman.*

MVP McNabb threw for 309 yards, three touchdowns, and ran for another. Harrison sustained a broken thumb, yet caught touchdown passes of 38 and 56 yards, 173 yards in all. Malcolm Thomas ran it in twice. Sean Reali boomed a record 73-yard punt.

And after a 20-0 first quarter, there was little doubt Coach P's bowl record would be 3-0.

That left Syracuse with a 49-19-3 mark for the '90s entering the 1996 season

# 1900-76
# **Basketball**

They have trudged through knee-high whiteness of winter, head bowed against the biting wind as a fullback might lower his helmet into a 300-pound tackler, to see the game.

The fans have been Syracuse basketball's supporting cast for decades. Taken for granted and, yes, even maligned at times during an incredible 11-year run in which SU was the national gatekeeper.

Come to the home of hoops, they have. To Archbold Gym, Jefferson Street Armory, Fairgrounds Coliseum, War Memorial and — in a sense, with the rebirth of a program born, chronologically, at the turn of the century — willing to taste the dust rising from the floor, some in anticipation of fries at Jabberwocky.

And since Manley Field House was "officially closed" by John Thompson's Hoyas, the faithful — more than 6,000,000 of 'em — have journeyed to the Carrier Dome.

But no building a program makes. Not a conference, nor a rivalry as healthy as Georgetown's, though surely they play a part.

SU's coaching has been stellar … Jim Boeheim's greatness withstanding tests of time and duress.

And yet, Syracuse basketball has won and lost, risen, fallen and rose again, because of players.

The Reindeer Five … Roy's Runts … Sweet D and the Brothers Lee.

Vic Hanson to Vinnie Cohen … Bouie 'n Louie to The Pearl … Coleman and Owens to Moten and Wallace.

They've taken the Orange and its followers on Cinderella rides to San Diego and, 20 years later, the Meadowlands. And, in between, a National Championship that was just "The Shot" away from being ours.

At the heart of it all, however, there is one performer who took what was the nation's worst program, loser of 27 consecutive games, and brought it back to life.

Nearly 35 years have passed since Fred Lewis coaxed a slender kid from Washington, D.C., away from more than 200 collegiate suitors.

Others, playing more games, have scored more points. None has done it with such grace.

Because of Dave Bing, Syracuse basketball has never had to rise again from the ashes.

**IN THE BEGINNING** With the turn of the 20th century, men's basketball — two winters after the women began

*35. What made the 1913-14 basketball team unique?*

*36. Which hoops opponent deprived the 1925-26 Helms Foundation National Champions of an undefeated season?*

play on the Hill — first courted the Syracuse scene.

A 21-8 loss to Rensselaer Polytechnic Institute was the first of more than 2,100 games that have been contested.

In the early years, fanfare was nil, support minimal.

For three seasons, there was no coach.

The first decade ended with SU a modest 65-53.

# ED DOLLARD

*Years coached: 1911-24, 13 seasons*
*Record: 148-56*
*1917-18 Helms Foundation National Champion*

Ed Dollard was a freshman on a 1904-05 team whose center was 5-foot-4. John A.R. Scott, the athletic director, was in the second of what would be an eight-year stint volunteering his services as coach.

Dollard's SU playing career began with a 15-7 season and ended with an 11-2 record in 1907-08.

Following a terrible season in 1909-10, SU's Athletic Governing Board sensed the urgency to hire a full-time coach if the sport was to be retained.

Dollard took over in 1911. The first season, Dollard was paid $75. The following year, he was rehired for $87.50 and an additional $12.50, providing the season was successful.

Dollard received his $100.

And in 1913-14, Syracuse was unbeaten, led by All-

*Lew Castle (seated, with ball), captain in 1914, was SU's first Helms Foundation All-American.*

American center Lew Castle.

A fine all-around student-athlete, Castle stroked the 1913 crew to victory at the Intercollegiate Rowing Association Regatta at Poughkeepsie, was a three-year football letterman at halfback, student body president, ragtime pianist/songwriter and, in 1961, Helms Foundation College Basketball Hall of Fame inductee.

The faculty limited the team to a 12-game schedule, starting Jan. 10. SU (12-0) claimed the national championship, unofficial though it was.

Joe Schwarzer, an end on the 8-1-1 football team that fall, was the star of the 1917-18 basketball team. John Barsha, whose son, Jerry, logged a good many years as a broadcaster in Syracuse, was a starting guard.

Dollard rated Schwarzer and Castle the best players he coached at SU.

The lone defeat came in the finale at Archbold. SU had beaten Penn in Philadelphia.

Many years ago, Schwarzer — an All-American — recalled his last game:

"They had a fellow by the name of Sweeney from Buffalo who was playing guard for them. In those days, one man shot all the fouls, and he shot 15 out of 16, and they made one field basket, and they beat us, 17-16 … can you imagine going through a whole college game — and a good game — and the team only making one field goal, and winning?"

Still, Helms Foundation recognized the Orangemen

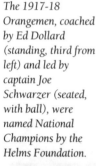

*The 1917-18 Orangemen, coached by Ed Dollard (standing, third from left) and led by captain Joe Schwarzer (seated, with ball), were named National Champions by the Helms Foundation.*

(16-1) as national champions.

SU continued having winning seasons, posting a decade record of 112-32 (106-21 the last nine years). But following two losing campaigns, Dollard bowed out in 1924. A disciple of the short passing game, Dollard's winning percentage and that of his successor are nearly identical.

# LEW ANDREAS

*Years coached: 1924-50, 25 seasons*
*Record: 355-134, .726*
*1925-26 Helms Foundation National Champion; 1946, 1950 NIT*

*A legendary all-around athlete in the 1920s, Vic Hanson was the Helms Foundation's National Player of the Year in 1927.*

While Ed Dollard had played the game collegiately, Lew Andreas had not; he played football and baseball on the Hill.

Early practice sessions leading up to the 1924-25 season were run by Andreas, who was eventually named head coach. He'd also coach football and serve SU as athletic director longer than anyone in history.

His coaching legacy is basketball, his greatest of many stars Vic Hanson, who led teams from 1924 through 1927 that won 48 of 55 games.

The 1925-26 team (19-1) was Helms Foundation National Champion.

An analysis of a half-century of college basketball was done for a national wire service, and the 1925-26 squad was ranked No. 5 during the decade of the 1920s.

Just as he was in football, Hanson was the school's greatest basketball player of the first half-century. Of the many Hanson tales that are spun, his performance in the fourth game of the 1925-26 season stands out above all others.

SU played Pennsylvania during holiday break, and after 40 minutes it was deadlocked at 25; Hanson had scored 21.

In a 30-25 overtime victory, Hanson's 25 points matched Penn's total.

That season, Hanson's 282 points (a lofty 14.1 average) were 42 percent of SU's production.

With a 15-0 record, SU journeyed to Penn State without its coach; Andreas' tonsillitis turned into an ear infection that didn't allow him to travel. SU lost by six.

Charley Lee, one of the "Three Musketeers" (Hanson, Lee and "Gotch" Carr), was quoted years later in Rod Macdonald's *Syracuse Basketball 1900-1975* as saying, "… we walked the campus there almost all night long crying. Our hearts were just broken."

*Lew Andreas-coached SU, led by All-American Vic Hanson (seated, with ball, in front of Andreas), was the 1925-26 Helms Foundation National Champion.*

Back on Piety Hill, where the players lived a spartan life at Pneumonia Hall (no heat, no hot water, one light in the ceiling, slept on cots), SU would avenge — in 29-12 fashion — its lone loss in the next-to-last game of the season.

Hanson, a master ballhandler who was national Player of the Year in 1927, once recalled his farewell to Andreas, at practice the night before his final game as a senior:

"I went over and shook hands with Andreas and said, 'Well, Coach, I've mixed emotions. I've really enjoyed playing under you for three years, and we certainly had our share of victories.' ... He looked at me and growled out, 'Take a hundred foul shots before you go down to the showers.' "

That was Gloomy Lew.

**RUN, REINDEER, RUN** While the 1925-26 season was a crowning moment for the Orangemen, Andreas admitted "the one I may have enjoyed the most was the team they called the 'Reindeers.' "

Four average-sized juniors and 6-foot-3 sophomore "Slim" Elliott were the starters. The star was Ev Katz, who felt the annual back-to-back games played against Creighton were the toughest because "they were as fast as we were."

Because of the travel expense, the teams would play consecutive games at alternating sites from 1929 through 1932.

In the 1929-30 season, SU's only losses in a 20-game season were at Creighton by four and at Columbia by three.

The hallmark victory came against Pitt, led by three-time All-American Charlie Hyatt. More than 3,000 were packed to the rafters in Archbold for that one. Katz scored 15, Dan Fogarty and top sub George Armstrong held Hyatt to six and SU won by 11, breaking Pitt's 19-game winning streak.

But Pitt (23-2) played five more games than the Orange (18-2); the Panthers were crowned National Champions.

The "Four Reindeer" — Katz, Fogarty, Tuppy Hayman and southpaw Kenny Beagle, the captain — went out in style, closing the 1930-31 season (16-4) with a 16-point win over Colgate.

The decade record: 127-54, an even more impressive 85-19 under Andreas.

**HOME COOKIN'** The Class of 1935 never lost a home game in three seasons, the .880 winning percentage (44-6) among the best in SU history.

It was the depression, but Lou Alkoff, who'd gone from walk-on to captain of the 1934-35 squad, was no longer "peeling potatoes up at Sims Hall for my food and tending a furnace for my room."

The high scorer was Johnny DeYoung, known as the "Passaic Wonder" for his legendary scoring as a New

*They were called the "Reindeer Five." Left to right: Tuppy Hayman, Dan Fogarty, "Slim" Elliott, Ken Beagle and Ev Katz ran a lot of opponents into the ground.*

Jersey high school phenom.

The year before, one of the starters was Ronnie Phillips. In later years, Phillips — an FBI man — would team with Syracusan Johnny Lynch to officiate Colgate and Cornell games here. As a whistle-blower, Phillips used the name John Hamilton.

In those days, the home athletic director selected officials. And many of Andreas' buddies — Larry Russell, Ed Kearney, Win Power — worked most home games. There was rarely a problem; that's just the way it was done.

**"S-MEN"** The late 1930s stood out for the great number of stars whose last name began with the letter S.

Ed Sonderman ... Johnny Simonaitis ... John Schroeder ... Bobby Stewart ... Wil Sidat-Singh.

And the best non-S was Billy Thompson, kid brother of 1,000-point Bobby Thompson, also a Passaic, N.J., phenom who matriculated at SU but never played a varsity minute because of a heart murmur.

For all his legendary feats on a football field, Sidat-Singh was no slouch on the court.

"(He) had probably the quickest reactions of any athlete I've ever seen," said Les Dye, a star end in football who was a frosh basketball player during Singh's senior year. "I think he actually had more quickness than Dave Bing."

Just as Sidat-Singh was forced to sit out a football game at Maryland because of the shameful racial policies of the day at some institutions, so it was with the 1939 Navy game in basketball. But he led the team in scoring

*The "S-Men" of the late 1930s were (left to right) Wilmeth Sidat-Singh, Bobby Stewart, Billy Thompson (a non-S Man) and John Schroeder, along with Ed Sonderman and Johnny Simonaitis (not shown).*

that season.

The late 1930s also included such players as '36 captain Marc Guley, who'd later coach the Orange; '38 center Don MacNaughton, who'd rise to the chairmanship/CEO of Prudential; and Philadelphia Phillies Whiz Kid Jim Konstanty, who'd beat SU in the '40s playing for Sampson Naval Training Station.

A decade of consistency, in which only the 1931-32 squad lost more than five games, produced an overall record of 135-43.

**"BULLET" & THE WAR YEARS** The 1940s saw Andreas endure his first losing season (8-10 in 1942-43). But that season, a freshman named Billy Gabor flashed on the scene.

He was the first frosh scoring leader on the Hill. The game would change that decade, and offense — at SU and elsewhere — would never be the same.

Basketball was suspended the following winter because of World War II, and many of Andreas' players performed military duty.

Gabor, an Air Force bombardier, didn't play basketball for the 2½ years he was gone. Returning in October, too late to start classes at SU, he enrolled at University College and was eligible for the 1945-46 season.

The team was a mix of kids such as starting guard Ed Stickel, 17, and hardened older guys. Artillery veteran Andy Mogish, who returned for the second semester, was 26; Roy Peters parachuted into France on D-Day; Larry Crandell flew 35 missions over Italy as a bombardier.

Mogish was at the heart of everything — the team's best rebounder, calling plays, defending the opponent's top player. But Gabor was the star.

"Bullet," they called him, because he could motor. SU had never scored 80 points in a game, but against Oswego State, the Orange put up 100; Gabor scored a record 36.

The 1945-46 highlight was a 52-43 win over St. John's, a 10-point favorite led by future pros Max Zaslofsky and "Hightower Harry" Boykoff, in front of a sold out Madison Square Garden doubleheader crowd. "Long John" Ludka, 6-foot-10, and 6-8 Royce

*His speed earned him the nickname "Bullet," and 1940s star Billy Gabor was the greatest scorer in SU history until the mid-1960s.*

*His playing days were interrupted by World War II duty, but Andy Mogish was always physical under the boards before beginning a lengthy coaching career on the Hill.*

*Royce Newell was a tall drink of water and effective man in the pivot following WWII.*

Newell held Boykoff to six points.

Gabor got hot at the end of the Temple game at Archbold, and SU won by one — a victory that keyed the team's selection to the National Invitation Tournament, which at that time was *the* postseason tournament.

One of the officials was not so lucky. An irate Owl belted the ref, knocking him out.

SU, ranked in the Top 10 and seeded No. 3, was upset by Muhlenberg, 47-41. The 23-4 record was SU's winningest.

Gabor, who scored 395 points, became the first to reach the 400 mark (409) the following year. The Orange went 19-6, narrowly missing another postseason invite when it lost to City College of New York, 61-59, in an NCAA District II playoff game at the Troy armory.

In January 1947, Archbold Gym burned down, and a team Andreas felt could have been one of his strongest was not.

SU had to practice downtown at the armory or at Central High or the west side, or wherever a court was available.

That 1947-48 team faced Michigan State with future Phillie Whiz Kid Robin Roberts, Yale with All-American/accordion-playing Tony Lavelli, and Colgate led by future New York Knicks Carl Braun and Ernie Vandeweghe.

Again, there was an NCAA district playoff game with CCNY at Troy. Gabor labored with a charley horse, and a set play for him on the final possession saw the shot miss; SU lost by one.

Gabor's senior year was nothing short of disappointing for the Orange, which began 6-1 and wound up 11-13. Seven losses were by a total of 15 points.

Gabor, SU's first 1,000-point man (his four-year total of 1,344 wasn't surpassed until Bing's senior year), went on to have a great NBA career with the Syracuse Nationals.

**MY CAPTAIN, MY COACH** Andreas' last two teams were a combined 36-16. SU could again practice in the gym, but games remained at the State Fair Coliseum.

*Big Ed Miller was a gawky kid who improved under the tutelage of Lew Andreas, poured in a record 40 points against Canisius and led Marc Guley's 1952-53 team in scoring.*

Royce Newell felt the 1948-49 team (18-7) his senior year was better than the 23-4 club in 1945-46, based on a much-improved schedule and despite the fact "we bombed in the Garden (nine first-half points vs. New York University)."

The Orange overcame Hillary Chollet's Coliseum-record 37 for Cornell, as Ed Stickel became SU's second 1,000-point producer. It was not Stickel's biggest night; he scored 38 against Canisius.

The rising star was sophomore Jack Kiley (31 vs. Iowa State, 26 in a season-ending win over Colgate, in which

*Airborne Ed Stickel scores two of his 38 points in a 1949 win over Canisius at the Coliseum.*

Newell contained Vandeweghe).

The next year, Andreas had done wonders developing big, gawky Ed Miller. And his improvement keyed SU developing into an NIT team (18-9).

SU displayed no Garden jitters in upsetting fast-breaking CCNY, which would go on to win both the 1950 NIT and NCAAs, a singular accomplishment in the annals of those tournaments. CCNY would later be victimized by a point-shaving scandal.

In the NIT, the Orange shot down the Long Island University Blackbirds, then trailed the nation's No. 1 team, Bradley, by a point at halftime. SU lost by 12 in what may have been the best game of that year's NIT.

Kiley (39 points in the NIT) set a new season scoring mark with 439.

And at the half-century, Andreas — athletic director since 1937 — chose to exit the bench after 25 seasons,

37. *How many points did Jim Brown score in the 1957 NCAA East Regional final against North Carolina?*

18 consecutive winners, 22 overall and 355 victories in 489 games.

Not bad for a guy who never played college basketball. But plenty good enough to be enshrined in the Helms Foundation Hall of Fame in 1948.

Andreas' hand-picked successor was his varsity assistant and 1936 captain. Marc Guley was given a one-year contract to replace a Hill legend.

# MARC GULEY

*Years coached: 1950-62, 12 seasons*
*Record: 136-129, .513*
*1957 NCAA East Regional Final; 1951 National Campus Tournament Champion*

There were more ups and downs in Marc Guley's dozen years as the helm than a roller coaster at the State Fair.

But the end was so far down, it dulled the memory of some very fine seasons.

It all began so smoothly, the 1950-51 team led by Jack Kiley. The Orange was battle-tested in New Orleans, losing by eight to All-American Gene Melchiorre-led Bradley and 10 to Adolph Rupp's Kentucky, featuring 7-footer Bill Spivey.

SU needed a seven-game winning streak to earn a berth in the National Campus Tournament in Peoria, Ill., where the Orangemen beat Toledo and Utah by 17 apiece and faced host Bradley in the title game.

The Braves jumped out to a huge double-digit lead. (Later, Melchiorre would be implicated in a point-shaving scandal that wrecked a few college basketball programs.) Bradley self-destructed as the Orange rallied to win the title game, 76-75, and Kiley joined the 400-point club (403).

*Jack Kiley was a three-year scoring leader and the only Orangeman until 1957 to score more than 400 points in each of two seasons.*

The following season (14-6) saw the Orange move home games to the downtown War Memorial and Archbold Gym. The winter's top performances were Ed Miller's 40 points in a win over Canisius and Frank Reddout's 34 rebounds in a victory over Temple at Philadelphia's Convention Hall.

Then came four uneventful campaigns, producing a collective 41 wins and 38 losses. Still, 1955-56 set the table for what was to come. Despite the loss of Manny Breland (the Central High product forced to sit out the season with a case of tuberculosis), SU went 14-8.

Vinnie Cohen, who'd led the team in scoring as a sophomore, did so again as a junior (401), and for the first time three players scored at least 300 points (Jim Snyder 326, Gary Clark 308). All five starters scored in double figures, including a muscular football star named Jim Brown (249), who had been second in scoring to his roommate, Cohen (314), in 1954-55.

*Frank Reddout led the 1952-53 Orangemen in scoring, a year after grabbing 34 rebounds against Temple.*

Brown didn't like not starting as a junior and chose not to play basketball his final year.

"They basically didn't want to start more than two blacks," Brown claimed, "although nobody could outrun, outjump or outshoot me."

Breland conceded that because of a lack of depth, "we could sure have used him that year."

Even sans Brown, 1956-57 would be a hallmark season, the grandest of the Guley years.

**THE BIG DANCE** Guley felt he had a winner going into the 1956-57 season, saying his team "has more potential than any team I've coached here since 1950-51."

He was correct, though his statement was put to an early test after the Orange opened with a 15-point loss to Canisius and dropped a 71-70 thriller to Columbia, led by All-American Chet Forte, who went on to a great career in network television.

A Christmas round-robin tournament included North Carolina. SU so impressed Tar Heels' coach Frank McGuire, he told SU freshman coach Andy Mogish he "felt

*The 1956-57 team was SU's first to gain an NCAA Tournament berth.*

darn lucky the pairings worked out the way they did."

SU-UNC would meet later, on a larger stage.

The Orange would run off a string of eight wins, and later even survive a charter flight to Penn State in a converted World War II plane.

SU was 13-3 at one point, but closed the regular season 16-6, good enough to earn the school's first NCAA bid.

*Jim Brown (30) was more than just a great running back, he was a double-figure scorer, too.*

The Orange rallied from a double-digit deficit to beat Connecticut by six, part of a Madison Square Garden tripleheader. Then, in the Palestra, the Orange squandered a healthy lead and taxed its front-line players, needing forward Gary Clark's 34 points (still an Orange

*Jim Snyder battles North Carolina's Danny Lotz for a rebound in the 1957 NCAA East Regional final at the Palestra in Philadelphia. The Tar Heels won, 67-58.*

NCAA Tournament record) to get by Lafayette by four.

That — and not having a Jimmy Brown — cost SU in the East Regional final against Carolina. The Tar Heels won, 67-58, and went unbeaten, defeating Wilt Chamberlain and Kansas by one point in triple overtime for the national championship.

Vinnie Cohen had a record-setting season for the Orange (18-7), scoring 605 points (24.2 ppg). But he had a terrific supporting cast in Clark (17.8 ppg/10.8 rpg, .829 free-throw percentage), the center combination of Jim Snyder (10.2 ppg/7.9 rpg) and sophomore Jon Cincebox (9.9 ppg/11.8 rpg), and a backcourt trio of Vinnie Albanese, Larry Loudis and Manny Breland.

Cohen (1,337) departed seven points shy of Billy Gabor's all-time scoring total. But 40 years later, only two players — Dave Bing and Bill Smith — have surpassed his career scoring average of 19.7 per game.

Guley called Cohen "the greatest ballplayer he had ever coached."

He would never have another player or team of that caliber.

*Vinnie Cohen was the greatest scorer in Syracuse history until a guy named Bing came along.*

*Southpaw Pete Chudy was the second player in Orange history to average better than 20 ppg in a season.*

*A consistent double-figure scorer and floor leader, Eddie Goldberg was a terrific guard on Marc Guley's last three winning clubs.*

**A DECLINE TO DISASTER** Guley's fall from near the top of the mountain wasn't sudden. The next three years produced a creditable overall mark of 38-27.

Cincebox was the big man inside; he averaged 19.1 ppg/16.4 rpg as a junior and 19.0 ppg/15.9 rpg as a senior. His 1,004 rebounds topped SU's career list for nearly 30 years, and his 14.6 career average remains No. 1.

Top gun in the backcourt was Eddie Goldberg, who averaged 15.5, 17.6 and 15.5 ppg his three varsity seasons. As a sophomore in 1957-58, he outscored Pitt All-American Don Hennon, 21-12.

Goldberg, southpaw Pete Chudy and Tom Mossey led the 1959-60 team, but then the cupboard was bare — except for Chudy's last hurrah.

Guley, battling personal problems and with a team lacking talent, got some help in 1960-61 from footballers Ernie Davis, John Mackey and Don King. Davis averaged

10.2 ppg/9.6 rpg. It wasn't enough. Even Chudy's 20.8 ppg (including a school-record 41 vs. Alfred) couldn't help a team that dove to a 4-19 record.

**A WALK-ON'S BIG THRILL** "It was the greatest privilege of my life to play for Syracuse," said Terry Quigley, a hometown, pint-sized guard.

"I loved playing one-on-one in practice against Pete Chudy. He competed so hard.

"And I remember getting a start in the War Memorial against St. John's. They had LeRoy Ellis (son LeRon later transferred from Kentucky to Syracuse), and I scored the first eight points.

"Then, I got to room with Ernie Davis on the road, when John Mackey broke his nose and couldn't go with us. ... And to be an honorary pallbearer at Ernie's funeral, representing the basketball team," said Quigley, who later coached SU forward Mark Wadach at Bishop Ludden High School.

"What a thrill for a 5-8 kid from the Parochial League!"

**ROCK BOTTOM** The 1958-59 season was worse, so bad that it seemed the only people watching SU games at the War Memorial were sports information types, a few drunks wandering in off the street to get out of the cold ... and a couple of hoop junkies who appreciated the effort of Carl Vernick (16.5 ppg).

This was America's worst team. WORST ... as in 22

*Basketball hit the skids in 1960-61, but football stars Ernie Davis (24), John Mackey (35) and Don King (25) tried to help buoy coach Marc Guley's sinking ship.*

*Carl Vernick*

consecutive losses, an NCAA-record 27 in a row over two seasons (a subsequent Rice team wiped Syracuse from an infamous spot in the record book).

Guley announced his resignation in February; SU was 0-16 at the time.

A season-ending New England trip produced wins at Boston College and Connecticut. SU wound up 2-22, outscored by 17.5 ppg, outrebounded by 11 rpg.

Guley's 12-year record slid to 137-131, but it had been 131-90 before a 6-41 free fall those last two dismal winters.

# FRED LEWIS

*Years coached: 1962-68, six seasons*
*Record: 91-57, .615*
*1966 NCAA East Regional Final; 1964, 1967 NIT*

With Fred Lewis at the helm, it didn't take long for Syracuse basketball to regain respect.

Who knows how much longer it would have taken if a trip to Washington, D.C., didn't produce stunning results.

"It was a miracle of recruiting in my judgment," Jim Boeheim said of Lewis convincing Dave Bing of the value of building a program.

It didn't take much to get Boeheim to Syracuse; he

39. Who was the first Orangeman to score 1,000 career points?

*With the opening of Manley Field House in 1962 came new coach Fred Lewis. His big man on the 1963-64 and '64-65 teams was West Point transfer Chuck Richards.*

entered in 1962 as a walk-on. Bing was the recruiting coup.

Those two would wind up together in Raleigh, N.C., playing for the East Regional crown and a berth in the Final Four. Curiously, it was Bing's poorest performance in an otherwise brilliant, All-American, program-building collegiate career.

Lewis had come from Southern Mississippi, where his last two editions ranked third and second, respectively, among small colleges. But he was a big city boy, a New Yorker who had played for Clair Bee's championship teams at LIU and, after the war, was a small college All-American at Eastern Kentucky. Rookie of the Year in the old National Basketball League, he'd had a fine pro career before going into coaching.

While Boeheim never had any problems with his mentor, he admitted Lewis "was difficult to play for, hard on his players."

Bing's presence meant the freshman team was better than the 1962-63 varsity. They scrimmaged daily, "and we beat the hell out of them every time," said Boeheim.

Lewis played the hand he was dealt — Carl Vernick, Phil Schoff, Herb Foster, Mannie "Klutch" Klutschkowski — and won eight games, twice as many as either of the two previous winters of discontent on the Hill.

Fans came to new Manley Field House to watch Bing & Co. (the freshman squad) win 13 of 17 that season. Bing, wearing uniform No. 22, averaged 25.7 ppg.

"He's the best freshman player I've ever seen here at Syracuse," Athletic Director Lew Andreas said.

Lewis, a masterful recruiter in the Metropolitian New York area, brought in more than Bing. And with the addition of 6-8 West Point transfer Chuck Richards, the Orange would catapult from national embarrassment to National Invitation Tournament in two years.

**THE HOUSE THAT BING BUILT** Dr. George L. Manley was the benefactor of the Manley Dome. It was built primarily as an indoor practice facility for Ben Schwartzwalder's autumn gladiators, in need of a bad-weather place to drill for late-season games and bowls.

Basketball was more of an afterthought. Lewis and Bing changed that ... with the rapidity of an Orange fast break.

The 1963-64 squad (17-8) featured the first pair of 500-point scorers on one SU team. Bing (22.2 ppg) and Richards (22.0) combined for a record 1,084 points, topping the two-man total of Vinnie Cohen/Gary Clark (1,049 in 1956-57).

"I'm going to ask (AD) Frank Carver to find a reason to break relations with Syracuse until Bing graduates," said Pittsburgh coach Bob Timmons.

## ORANGE ·QUIZ·

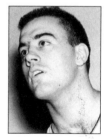

*40. Name the old oar (above) who later entered the coaching ranks and political arena, and the former major league right-handed pitcher (below), both of whom donned Orange uniforms.*

Along the way to the NIT, there were two nail-biters over Cornell, the first on Richards' basket after SU rallied from 17 down. Sam Penceal held Princeton All-American Bill Bradley to 20 points under his average in the Hurricane Classic, and SU won in overtime in the Classic final over All-American Rick Barry-led Miami on a basket by Bob Murray, whose layup had ended SU's 27-game losing streak two seasons before.

SU lost to NYU by nine in the NIT. But the top nine scorers returned, and everyone expected big things in 1964-65.

**THE PROMISED LAND** Even before the 1964 NIT invite, Bing had promised SU's tournament in 1965 would be the NCAAs.

*No. 22 is to Syracuse basketball what No. 44 is to football. And in case you don't recognize the lithe leaper wearing 22, he's Dave Bing, the greatest player in Orange history.*

He was one year off.

Although Syracuse won 11 of its final 13 games, a 1-6 start (six straight losses) quashed postseason tourney hopes.

Bing scored a record 45 points against Colgate and averaged 23.2 ppg/12.0 rpg for a team with a per-game rebounding margin of 11.3.

Disappointment turned to delirium in 1966-67.

**SCORING MACHINE**  Bing pointed the way to the NCAAs, his performance consistently great … scoring 30 or more 13 times, at least 20 every game until his last … fifth in the nation averaging 28.4 ppg, scoring 794 points (both still records in 1996) … he boarded (10.8 rpg) … glided down the lane and found the open man (7.6 apg).

*Vaughn "Kangaroo Kid" Harper (40) could sky for rebounds, and was later a successful disc jockey in New York.*

"He hangs up in the air so long that you think he's never coming down," said Pitt's Timmons.

George "Blond Bomber" Hicker averaged 15.9 (32 on television vs. West Virginia, 25 in a half vs. Army) ... Boeheim 14.6 (27 vs. Cornell, 28 vs. Niagara back-to-back) ... 6-foot-6 center Rick Dean 12.1 (30 vs. Colgate, a record 13 of 13 field goals) ... Vaughn "Kangaroo Kid" Harper was second to Bing on the boards.

Defend the Orangemen? They ran, ran, ran their way to 99 points per outing, an NCAA mark. They needed 124 points in the regular-season finale, but scored "only" 122 against Colgate. Fourteen times they scored 100 or more.

And, yes, they allowed 82.5 ppg — also more than any team in SU history — because they played up-tempo, all over the floor.

*He had sharp elbows and played in the shadows of Dave Bing, but Fred Lewis called Jimmy Boeheim his catalyst.*

Excitement was SU's middle name.

And "Duke" Bing was The Man. Of his play in the Los Angeles Classic, Mitch Chortkoff of the *Los Angeles Herald Examiner* wrote at the time:

"(Bing has) uncanny court demeanor, incredible jumping ability and a fine team approach to the game."

Bing scored a record 46 vs. Vanderbilt in the L.A. Classic, in which SU lost its opener to Vandy (All-American Clyde Lee had 39) but Bing would become SU's all-time scorer, average 36.3 in the three-game tournament and be named the MVP.

His 39-point, 25-rebound performance against Cornell ranks as one of the most memorable under the Manley Dome.

In a 94-78 NCAA win over Davidson, in which Hicker scored 22, Bing came up with 20 points and outplayed All-American Dick Snyder.

**DUKE DOWNS SIX IN DOUBLES** "We were a good, but small team," Boeheim said of the squad that faced favored Duke for a spot in the Final Four.

The Blue Devils were led by Jack Marin and Bob Verga. And while SU put six in twin figures and had Duke on the ropes, SU was bedeviled by Bing's off-game.

"They didn't guard some other guys," Boeheim said.

Fred Lewis would say, "The greatest catalyst on that club was Jimmy Boeheim."

For a program that was pathetic just a short time before, 22-6 and 1966 East Regional finalist was a considerable accomplishment.

*A rock in the middle during the mid-1960s was center Rick Dean, a .550 career shooter from the field.*

**TRANSITION PERIOD** In the future, SU would lose its brightest star and, often, not skip a beat. But Bing had been more than a cut above the rest; the Orange would be good, not great, for quite awhile.

Lewis fielded another 20-game winner with great

# SIMPLY THE BEST

Dave Bing was an elegant player, an all-purpose All-American.

"He was the greatest player … to ever play here," former teammate and current SU coach Jim Boeheim said in the 1970s, repeated in the 1980s and 1990s.

The greatest, not just because of 1,883 points (in three seasons, still No. 5 all-time) and 24.8 scoring average, which has never been threatened. But because he led his team by every statistical measure, a proud leader on and off the court.

"Bing reminds you of Oscar Robertson, when Oscar was in college," coach Fred Lewis once said.

The three years before Bing, SU was 14-54. During his three seasons, the Orange was 52-24.

His uniform No. 22 was retired in 1981; 1920s star Vic Hanson and SU's most electrifying player of the 1980s, Dwayne "Pearl" Washington, are the others to have their jerseys retired.

In the ensuing years, just as Floyd Little has done for football, Dave Bing has been a source of strength for Syracuse basketball … and his old roomie, Jim Boeheim.

*In 1990, the Man of Steel — Bing Steel exec/Syracuse University and Detroit Pistons great Dave Bing — was enshrined in Basketball's Hall of Fame at Springfield, Mass.*

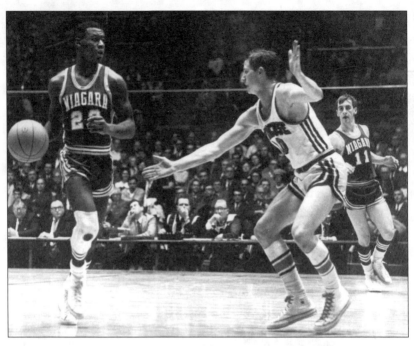

*Niagara's Calvin Murphy put on more than one memorable performance under the Manley Dome. Here, he's being checked by playmaker Richie Cornwall, SU's career free throw-shooting leader (.861).*

scoring balance. The "Hicker Flicker" produced 18.6 ppg from long range, although George Hicker's springtime auto accident had cast a dark cloud on the 1966-67 campaign. Rick Dean (17.9), Vaughn Harper (16.3) and Richie Cornwall (14.7) were the major contributors.

SU warmed up to the Motown sound and Harper's pregame ballhandling act, which wowed crowds at Manley.

But a 66-64 opening-round NIT loss to New Mexico (on a questionable foul vs. Dean) abruptly ended postseason play.

It would be four years before the Orange would return.

**CHANGE AT THE TOP** Dr. Fred Lewis had to fight to elevate basketball's status at a football school. In so doing, he irritated some administrators.

Lewis, himself, seemed more interested in a business venture — an exercise machine called "Exergenie." It was the final year of his six-year contract. He was leaving, though it wasn't public knowledge at the time.

"It's not worth the aggravation," he would say.

Freshman coach Roy Danforth became more of a vital cog during practices. His yearlings (15-1) boasted a powerful inside duo of Bob McDaniel and Bill Smith, who combined for 45.8 ppg.

Lewis' last road win was a skillful slowdown at Niagara, 50-49 in overtime; Calvin Murphy (the Niagara star who scored 50 in a 116-107 win earlier in the season) was he held to his collegiate low.

SU closed a disappointing 11-14 with a Manley win over Colgate. Lewis resigned, moving to Cal-Sacramento State as athletic director.

A masterful recruiter, he had recruited Bing and transformed an abyss into an NCAA team in four years.

# ROY DANFORTH

*Years coached: 1968-76, eight seasons*
*Record: 148-71, .676*
*1975 NCAA Final Four; 1973, 1974, 1976 NCAA; 1971, 1972 NIT*

As freshman coach, Roy Danforth's Tangerines were 55-8 overall, and 31-1 the last two years, including a 25-game win streak.

Succeeding Lewis, for whom he played at Southern Mississippi, Danforth's first two Orange editions (9-16, 12-12) were of little note beyond the fact that 6-foot-11 Bill Smith was the tallest talent SU had ever had.

"But he didn't have the work ethic," said Jim Boeheim, then the frosh coach.

And Smith's temper got him suspended on Valentine's

41. *When SU began its two-year, 27-game losing streak, who was the team's leading scorer?*

*Left-hander Bob McDaniel might have been one of SU's finest forwards, but his off-court habits led him to give up basketball on the Hill.*

Day in 1970, after an ugly fracas at West Virginia. Bob McDaniel, an even more talented forward with bad habits who was ineligible in 1968-69, had 36 points against LaSalle in 1969-70, when heralded guard Ernie Austin (19.3 ppg) was finally able to play a full season. McDaniel had 14 points and 14 boards in the 1970-71 opener, then he quit the team.

The 1960s, even with the Bing years (52-24), had produced a record of 118-126, SU's only losing decade in its basketball history.

With the 1970s came the start of a 22-year, national pace-setting postseason tournament run … a Cinderella team's Final Four journey … another coaching change … an official closing of Manley … and a decade mark of 217-61.

*Tommy "JoJo" Green played point guard for Roy Danforth, coached on his staff and later assisted in Danforth's hiring as athletic director at Fairleigh Dickinson, where Green is head coach.*

It began with "Roy's Runts."

Mike Lee and Mark Wadach were mini-forwards at 6-foot-2 and 6-1. Boeheim said of them, "They embarrassed those other guys into working harder. … They turned the whole thing around."

Manley became the "in" place to be, fun for the faithful, hell for the foe, home for The Zoo.

Far from gaining the national spotlight of 1987 or 1996 Final Fours, or countless nationally-televised games in between, those early 1970s might have been the most delightful of all.

**"WICH" WAY TO THE NIT** This was a time when the Orangemen outhustled opponents, diving for loose balls, beating bigger guys for rebounds. The fans loved it.

Chuck Wichman was a slender sub who, Danforth claimed, "had the quickest first step in college basketball." Well, he did step up against Niagara and Fordham, making baskets that propelled SU into the 1971 and 1972 NITs.

*Twice, reserve Chuck Wichman made the big play to lead the Orangemen into the NIT in 1971 and 1972.*

Observing the quiet leadership and hard play of Lee and Wadach, Bill Smith once told Boeheim, "I've got to play hard or else I feel ashamed." As a senior, Smith put up big numbers (22.7 ppg/14.5 rpg/.606 shooting) and a school-record 47 points against Lafayette (Tracy Tripucka had 41).

It was the first year assists were kept as an official statistic. Tommy "JoJo" Green was the floor leader; he'd later coach under Danforth at Syracuse and Tulane, then become head coach at Fairleigh-Dickinson, where he helped Danforth get hired as athletic director.

The 1971 NIT team (19-7) lost to Michigan by six, with Smith scoring 27.

**"THE KID"** Greg Kohls might have led the nation in scoring if there had been a three-point shot at the time.

*Big Bill Smith sprawls on the floor, but his shot is about to fall through the hoop as teammate Bob Kouwe flies by overhead.*

"Kid" came over mid-court armed for a clothesline jumper.

"Finest shooter in the East," Danforth said of Kohls, who went from sophomore benchwarmer (38 points all season) to averaging 22 points as a junior and among the national leaders at 26.7 ppg (748 points, 30 or more seven of SU's first 11 games) in 1971-72. He's still second to Bing in single-season scoring.

"Best I played with in college," said backcourt mate Dennis DuVal (15.8), who hit the Holiday Festival buzzer-beater against Duke.

That season (22-6) produced an NIT win over Davidson, SU's first postseason victory since 1966, and a

**ORANGE QUIZ**

*42. What guard started in the 1960s, but chose to forego his senior year for his studies?*

*Has Syracuse ever had a better long-range shooter than Greg "Kid" Kohls, who scored 1,322 of his 1,360 points in his junior and senior years?*

six-point loss to a strong Maryland team.

"Roy's Runts" were Lee, Wadach, DuVal, Kohls and 6-5 center Bob Dooms. Outrebounded, of course, but never outfought.

And outshot? Not with "Kid" Kohls tossing it up 610 times.

**"SWEET D" AND THE BROTHERS LEE** "Getting Mike Lee, it was us and St. Bonaventure," said Boeheim. "(Younger brother) Jimmy never wanted to go anywhere else because of Mike.

"But Dennis DuVal was a big recruit for us, best in New York. He took us to the Final Four club."

Not to the Final Four; he was gone.

He amazed Manley crowds with his own brand of pregame ball wizardry. It happened by accident, he claims.

"We had this drill, and I got caught screwing around by Roy," DuVal said. "We thought he wasn't looking. We weren't allowed to throw those passes.

" 'Seeing you want to do that, you'll do it from now on,' he told me. So, I'd get on the foul line, they'd cut off me and I'd throw those (behind-the-back, between-the-legs) passes. We did it all three years."

DuVal was a stylish player, one of the best guards ever at Syracuse.

He led the team in scoring as a junior (19.5) and senior (20.6 as a senior), leaving as SU's No. 2 all-time scorer (1,504 points). A career-high 37 came against

*Dennis DuVal was drafted after his junior year by Denver (ABA), along with Marvin Barnes of Providence. "Sweet D" opted to return for his senior year, averaged 22.2 ppg, and wowed the Manley faithful with his pregame ballhandling routine.*

*Mike Lee still holds the school record for most consecutive free throws in a season (34 in 1970-71).*

Bucknell (his 18 field goals and 30 attempts remain SU home-court records), a game he'll never forget because Danforth promised to join the student section — called The Zoo — in cheering if SU got ahead by 50.

"I couldn't believe he said it," said DuVal. "But he did, so I guess he had to do it."

The Bucknell coach? Jim Valvano, so furious after the game he shouted at Danforth all the way into the dressing room.

For DuVal, Boeheim was his security blanket.

"Roy and Jimmy would argue over which plays to call. Jimmy's plays seemed to work ... he was the tactician, Roy the politician — not that he couldn't coach, he could. But I'd go with Jimmy's plays, knowing he'd back me up."

His one-game memory? "Well, there was Mike Lee (a big-game performer who always took the tough opposing forward) fouling out against St. John's on a blocking call. Disgusted with the call, he grabbed the ball and kicked it into the stands ... and the officials never saw it.

"But the win over Furman in the (1973) NCAAs was great. They were huge (four starters 6-8 or taller). Our press killed 'em," said DuVal. "We had too much speed.

"We didn't play the next game for a week. Roy said be in bed by 11. We were out (on the town) before he was."

This team was dubbed "Roy's Runts Plus One," because frontline player Hackett moved in for departed guard Kohls.

SU bowed out of the NCAAs to a Maryland powerhouse, but beat Pennsylvania by one in a regional contest to become SU's winningest team (24-5) … until the current coach took over.

Drafted after his junior year by Denver (ABA), DuVal returned and ended his career scoring 28 in a 1974 NCAA overtime loss to Oral Roberts, when Rudy "Rag Man" Hackett (0-for-6 at the free-throw line) missed two free throws with 17 seconds remaining in regulation.

That team (19-7) was led by DuVal, Hackett (16.8 points/11.6 rebounds), Jimmy "Rat Man" Lee (13.7 ppg) and defensive stopper/rebounder Fred Saunders, a transfer eligible after 10 games. Better than 1975? Personnel-wise, yes … but you couldn't tell that during March Madness.

**"RAT," "BUG" & DIVINE PROVIDENCE** The ball was dished from "Rag Man" to "Rat Man." From 18 feet and five seconds away from history, it flew.

Shock spread along Tobacco Road. Syracuse 78, North Carolina 76.

Trailing by one, its last timeout called, seven-point underdog Syracuse sought Divine Providence in the Civic Center, site of the 1975 NCAA East Regional.

"We wanted to start out on the left side and run the 'High Three' (which the week before dumped LaSalle in an overtime opening-round gem in Philadelphia). They had it cut off," said "Rag Man" Hackett, "and we finally

*A shot that will live in infamy along Tobacco Road: Jimmy "Rat Man" Lee's jump shot was a touch of Divine Providence as the Orangemen upset North Carolina in 1975, en route to their first Final Four.*

*Jimmy "Don't Call Me Bug" Williams (dribbling ball) kept the dream alive in '75, had seven steals in the Final Four consolation game with Louisville, then led SU scorers the next two seasons.*

# ORANGE
## ·QUIZ·

43. Who was Dave Bing's freshman coach (1962-63 season)?

had to swing the ball inside to me."

Hackett had been blanketed by Tar Heels the entire game.

"I saw Phil Ford and the boys coming. So I threw it right out to 'Rat' (Lee).

"I knew he'd be there," Hackett told *The Syracuse Newspapers*. "He's been there for three years."

The game had belonged to the backcourts. UNC's Phil Ford and Brad Hoffman combined to score 44 points, SU's Lee and Jimmy "Don't Call Me Bug" Williams scored 43. UNC shot .653, SU .583.

"I just happened to be open," said Lee.

"I didn't know how much time was left. But I thought there was more than that."

The Play … of The Game … of The Season.

Who would have thought the 1974-75 season would be packed with some of March's most memorable

As a junior, Rudy Hackett had 22 rebounds against LaSalle, 23 against West Virginia, and his senior total of 407 was surpassed only by Derrick Coleman's 422 some 14 years later.

moments when SU dropped consecutive regular-season home games to Rutgers and West Virginia, in which leads of 16 and 21 points were squandered?

And how could any game top the NCAA-opener in the Palestra, where 6-10 LaSalle ace Joe Bryant (father of millionaire prep-to-pro Kobe Bryant) had precisely the 5-foot left baseline jumper Paul Westhead wanted to end SU's season. Bryant's shot rimmed around and out; SU won in overtime, 87-83.

"We're making a step now we've never made before," Hackett said after the Carolina game.

Curiously, SU would again be faced with having to play Beat The Clock. And again, five seconds left. This time against Kansas State for the NCAA East Regional crown and Final Four berth in San Diego. K-State led by two on Regional MVP Chuckie Williams' bomb from deep in the left corner.

*Net cutting time, and super-sub Kevin King snips some twine after the Orange has played its way to the 1975 Final Four.*

**ORANGE ·QUIZ·**

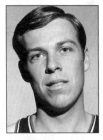

*44. Who is this former Orangeman (circa late-1960s), who barely elevated off the floor on his jump shot, but has had a lengthy career in the NBA in player personnel, scouting and coaching?*

A set play was called during a timeout. Roy Danforth told "Bug" Williams, his diminutive speed merchant, "You've got all the time in the world ... but we need a layup."

"We thought they (K-State) would be in a 'Red' — a man-to-man with someone playing in front of me," said Williams. "In that case, we have to set a screen so I can get free.

"But they didn't front me. So I just popped out to my right, got it, turned and went up the left sideline (like a blur).

"I knew I'd done my job when Rudy got the ball."

"I don't even know who was playing me," Hackett said. "I never looked up at the clock, because I knew 'Bug' could get there in time. 'Bug' hit me from about 25 feet away. I fumbled it, but fortunately was able to put it in the basket."

The teams headed into overtime locked at 76. The Orange dominated and won, 95-87.

"I think this is the greatest moment in Syracuse basketball history," said Danforth.

It was ... and it remains among the greatest.

The hometown reception was, well, let Jim Boeheim describe it:

"That whole experience … and the airport was the most unique thing I've ever seen."

**CALIFORNIA DREAMIN'** UCLA, Kentucky and Louisville; a Who's Who of college hoops in the 1970s.

And Syracuse (23-7). Cinderella, still wearing the slipper.

"I've been going there (to the Final Four) for 15 years," Danforth said. "I always told myself that some day I'd have a team here.

"Now, I have one."

A one-and-only … but one more than most coaches.

After one more season (20-9, one-and-done in the NCAAs with one frosh and two sophomore starters), Roy Danforth would leave after seven seasons with two years remaining on a three-year pact at $27,000 per year. He would take the Tulane job.

Leaving Syracuse, one can surmise, cost him a ton of money had he remained at the helm until the Big East, Carrier Dome and television bucks changed the financial picture.

*Doggone it! The bench is tense and Roy Danforth shows his displeasure. But Coach Roy lived the dream and took Syracuse to its first Final Four.*

But he accomplished what none before had done in 75 years of Orange basketball.

A coach's dream had been realized.

**PASS THE BLINTZES** That first Syracuse Final Four squad was the media darling of San Diego.

Danforth, who had his hair parted in more places than any coach in America, was cracking one-liners, such as:

"I'm not in favor of the 30-second clock. I don't know if he (6-9 wide-body center Earnie Seibert) can get from one end of the floor to the other in that time."

One scribe suggested Seibert had been locked in a blintz factory. Another suggested SU's wide-body "looks as if he was recruited in a tavern."

But Seibert was the game's top rebounder in the upset of Carolina.

"Bug" Williams wore dark sunglasses onto the court for practice in San Diego. Kentucky players called him "Stevie Wonder."

Yet who in the Final Four but Williams could have played Beat The Clock, and won?

Hackett (22.2 ppg/12.7 rpg) and Lee (17.2 ppg) were Mr. Inside and Mr. Outside, combining for 1,259 points that senior season.

*Nottingham High's Chris "Rocket Man" Sease scored 18 points in the 1975 Final Four loss to a huge Kentucky team.*

*The long-defunct Saltine Warrior leads Rudy Hackett and the Orangemen onto the court at Manley, a wild and woolly place in the mid-1960s and '70s.*

Homegrown Chris "Rocket Man" Sease (12.1 ppg) was a 6-4 leaper who had skied so high, battling Carolina despite a throbbing toe injury.

And Kevin King was the primary pinch hitter off the bench.

"That team did an unbelievable job to get to the Final Four," said Jim Boeheim.

"We were not really to that level yet."

Syracuse couldn't overcome Kentucky's tremendous height and bruising strength. In a less-than-artistic semifinal, the Wildcats clawed their way to a 95-79 win, advancing to face UCLA in what would be John Wooden's final coronation and last game.

In the third-place game, the Orangemen displayed all the heart that had gotten them to the Final Four … none of that diminished by a 92-88 overtime loss to Louisville, which had taken UCLA to the last shot in the other semifinal.

Trailing by as much as 18, Syracuse put on a comeback that made Louisville's legs buckle with a second-half press and half-court trap. The Cards had 33 turnovers.

Lee's potential game-winning, foul-line jumper bounced off the rim, ending regulation at 78-all.

"Their overall strength took us in overtime," said Lee, an all-tourney selection and the only Syracuse player ever to lead the NCAA Tournament in scoring.

*45. What national basketball tournament did SU win, and when?*

## *1976-Present*
# Basketball

When Roy Danforth resigned to take the job at Tulane, Syracuse wisely didn't open up the coaching vacancy to outside applicants.

Jim Boeheim, a native Central New Yorker from Lyons, could have had the University of Rochester job … but six hours after Danforth resigned on April 3, 1976, James Arthur Boeheim, 31, was named SU head coach.

"Ever since I came to Syracuse, I have wanted to be the coach. Today, my dream has come true," Boeheim said.

When the 1979-80 season ended (SU was 217-61 in the 1970s), and Manley was officially closed, Boeheim had already won 100 games.

Apparently, Syracuse had made a wise decision.

## JIM BOEHEIM

*Jim Boeheim's first staff (from left): Rick Pitino, Mark Meadors and Bernie Fine, who has remained Coach Jim's right-hand man ever since.*

*Years coached: 1976 to present, 21 seasons*
*Record: 483-159, .752*
*1987, 1996 NCAA Runnerup; 1989 Midwest Regional Final; 17 NCAAs; 1981 NIT Final; two NITs*

What would Boeheim have done, if not coach basketball?

"Probably been an undertaker (his father was) or golf pro," said the slender, bespectacled coach who twice in a

row won the National Association of Basketball Coaches golf tournament.

But Boeheim bled Orange basketball so long, he was where he belonged.

He had already put his stamp on the program, convincing Danforth to play 2-3 zone defense and influencing the offense. Then, in 1976 the program was Boeheim's.

His first coaching hire was a University of Hawaii assistant.

"It's our wedding night. We're in our hotel room.

"I married a nice Italian girl and, well, it's a pretty big deal," said the young bridegroom.

"The phone rings; it's Jim. He's downstairs; wants to talk, now.

"I tell my bride I'll be back right away … About two hours later …"

Boeheim had an assistant, and Rick Pitino's coaching career was about to take off.

And Joanne Pitino? She got even on April Fool's Day in 1996, when Rick's Kentucky Wildcats beat Jim's Cinderella Orange for the National Championship.

**ACT I: CAN YOU TOP THIS?** "When Roy left, the whole thing hinged on getting Roosevelt Bouie," said Boeheim. "St. Bonaventure or us.

## ORANGE
### ·QUIZ·

*46. "Classrooms make me nauseous." Which Orange shooting guard made that statement?*

*Career shot-blocking leader Roosevelt Bouie went on to have a lucrative pro career in Europe.*

"Louis (Orr) was a gift." Not even Gale Catlett, then at the University of Cincinnati, wanted the skinny Cincinnati Kid.

Boeheim inherited "Bug" Williams from the Final Four starting lineup. Williams (14.1) led a balanced attack, in which six players averaged more than nine points.

Bouie provided a defensive presence in the middle.

Marty Byrnes, Dale Shackleford (who started as a

*A man for all positions, that was Dale Shackleford. Career-wise, he ranks seventh in steals (and first to record 200), 10th in assists, 11th in rebounding and tied for 15th in scoring.*

frosh the year before, and could play all five positions) and Ross "The Boss" Kindel were returning starters, with Kindel splitting time in the backcourt with Larry Kelley.

Boeheim's career began with the winningest season in SU history (26-4).

The Orange beat Old Dominion, then upset Tennessee's Bernie & Ernie Show in the NCAAs. Bernard King and Ernie Grunfeld led the favored Vols, but Kelley scored 22 and Notre Dame transfer Billy Drew tossed in seven during overtime in a 93-88 thriller.

Cornbread Maxwell and North Carolina-Charlotte's long-armed perimeter defense were too much for SU to handle in a 22-point loss.

Still, some beginning for a rookie head coach!

**THIS MAGIC MOMENT** "We were so fortunate with those early guys we had. Great kids, great work ethic," said Boeheim.

"Only one guy we had who wasn't; we cut him. ... I was tougher in those days."

Seasons came and went as if mirror images ... 26-4, 26-4, 22-6, 26-4.

*Erich Santifer jumps out on the shooter, others go to the glass, as Bryan Warrick of St. Joseph's plays Beat The Clock and guns down SU in the 1981 Carrier Classic final. The Orange hasn't lost a CC game since.*

*In 1978, forward
Marty Byrnes was
SU's initial NBA
first-round pick
(Phoenix Suns) since
Dave Bing in 1966.*

## ORANGE
### ·QUIZ·

*47. John Wallace
was the only
Orangeman named
to the 1996 Final
Four All-
Tournament team.
True or false?*

There were the Coneheads (or was it CohenHeadds) — guards Hal Cohen, who had shot his way into the Hall of Fame as a scholastic free-throw shooter, and local product Marty Headd, who would shoot down Georgetown. And "Fast Eddie" Moss, as good a defensive guard as SU's ever had. Another 6-11 player, Danny Schayes, was the homegrown son of Syracuse Nats Hall of Famer Dolph Schayes and himself still an NBAer.

The 1977-78 season featured a title-game win over New Mexico in the Lobo Classic (Kindel's career game, 23 points).

Boeheim said The Pit in Albuquerque "was the noisiest arena I've ever been in."

When you'd spent half your life in Manley, that's saying something.

That season also saw the birth of a December four-team tourney at SU, the Carrier Classic. The host has won 17 of 19 titles, 36 of 38 games, losing only to Maryland and St. Joseph's in 1980 and '81. A kid named Earvin Johnson came with Michigan State in '77, and when Magic was named MVP after the Orange beat the Spartans by eight in the championship game, Boeheim burned.

Marty Byrnes should have gotten it; an MVP comes from the championship team, Boeheim declared ... conveniently forgetting Dave Bing in the L.A. Classic, when Bing and Boeheim were seniors.

For a week, Boeheim vs. the media was all you heard. The next home game at Manley was St. Bonaventure, at which the media was greeted with a huge banner that read: "Boeheim 1, Media 0."

Would the vote have been reversed after SU lost its NCAA-opener by one in overtime to a less-than-overwhelming Western Kentucky team?

"In the NCAA Tournament, everybody loses to somebody they're not supposed to," said Boeheim, having won 27 of 44 NCAA games, 20 of the last 29.

After another 26-game winner in 1978-79 ended with an NCAA loss to Pennsylvania, the curtain was pulled on the Bouie 'n Louie Show and the door at Manley closed ... but not before Dave Gavitt's brainchild gave Eastern basketball schools — Boston College, Connecticut, Georgetown, Providence, St. John's, Seton Hall, Syracuse the initial members — a league of their own.

**'WE'LL LOSE HOME-COURT ADVANTAGE'** That was Jim Boeheim's concern, moving to the $28 million Carrier Dome.

"But if we average 15,000 a game, I guess it'll be worth it," said Boeheim.

SU averaged more than 16,000 the first season, and

*Manley closed when the Carrier Dome was ready, after the 1978-79 season. More than 33,000 fans were on hand for SU-Georgetown during the 1989-90 season. The next year, 33 more folks squeezed in, setting a new NCAA on-campus attendance mark (33,048) that still stands.*

# MOVIN' ON UP

The final season in Manley, 1978-79, was bittersweet, but memorable for so many reasons:

✔ Syracuse smashed Seton Hall at Manley, SU's first game in the fledgling Big East Conference.

✔ Rosie Bouie stuffed All-American Joe Barry Carroll's shot and SU won at Purdue on national television, 66-61; Bouie was NBC's MVP, but it should have gone to Eddie Moss, who forced Boilermaker point guard Brian Walker to commit 10 turnovers.

✔ The Orangemen (14-0) knock on No. 1 in the polls, but a tip-in at the buzzer — hadn't time elapsed? — dealt them a 68-67 loss at Old Dominion.

✔ SU had won 190 of 217 Manley encounters when it put a 57-game home winning streak, tops in the nation, on the line. That appeared secure at halftime; Georgetown had

*The Bouie 'n Louie Show catapulted Jim Boeheim to 100 victories in his first four seasons.*

*Purdue's Joe Barry Carroll was cut down to size by Rosie Bouie in a nationally-televised game won by the visiting Orangemen.*

just 16 points. But the Orange didn't put the ball up in the second half, and when Louie Orr's last-gasp long jumper didn't fall, SU did, 52-50.

Towel-draped/milk carton-in-hand, John Thompson declared: "Manley Field House is officially closed!"

"Georgetown; it is, probably always will be, the best rivalry," says Boeheim.

✔ Orr's driving layup at the buzzer beat St. John's, 72-71.

✔ SU bowed out of the NCAAs by 11 to Iowa (Boeheim two technicals).

✔ Bouie left as the school's career shot-blocker (327, still unmatched). Orr outboarded Bouie their senior year. (They're still among SU's Top 20 all-time scorers.)

The Bouie 'n Louie Show ended. Their 100-18 record produced the highest four-year winning percentage (.847) in SU history.

*Point guard Eddie Moss, hero of the 1980 Purdue game that gave SU a 14-0 record, remains the single-season leader in steals (85 in 1980-81) and second career-wise (230).*

more than 20,000 ever since 1982-83. The Orange led the nation at the gate 11 years running beginning in 1984-85, topped by the NCAA record (29,919 average, 1989-90) and single-game on-campus mark (33,048 vs. Georgetown, 1990-91).

Syracuse basketball would usher in its 7,000,000th Carrier Dome fan in 1996-97.

"I would have liked to have played in the Dome," said 1970s star Dennis DuVal. "But I lost one home game in college (UConn, snapping a 36-game Manley streak). Nobody wanted to come here to play in those days.

"I'm glad I played in Manley Field House ... that was our Dome then."

**THE GREATEST GAME?** On ... and on ... and on, it went. Overtime, double OT, triple ... and the longest game was tied at 80. The game was Syracuse against Villanova for the 1981 Big East Championship, and what the Manley

*In what is arguably the greatest collegiate game ever played in Syracuse, Leo Rautins' tip-in won the 1981 Big East Tournament crown in triple overtime over Villanova.*

*In the 1980 Carrier Classic final, Maryland's Buck Williams appears to be playing footsie with SU's Danny Schayes, whose 23 rebounds against Georgetown later that season remains a Dome record.*

faithful assumed would be an NCAA bid.

Erich Santifer's 12-footer missed, but Leo Rautins tipped it in with three seconds to play. Villanova called a timeout when none remained.

Danny Schayes' free throw iced it.

Syracuse won, 83-80, in triple overtime.

"That first overtime, when we were down six, was the first time I ever thought we were out of a game," Boeheim said.

"I'm not disappointed in Coach, that he thought we were out of it," Santifer said. "He'll know better next time."

But SU was out of the NCAAs; 11 losses can do that, the NCAA Selection Committee decided. So SU rescued what had been a 15-11 disaster into a 22-win season, taking Tulsa to overtime in the NIT final at the Garden.

**A RECRUITING GEM** After a 16-13 season in 1981-82 (Boeheim's only non-20-game winner) that ended in an NIT loss to Bradley in the Carrier Dome, 1982-83 figured to be much stronger. Tri-captains Santifer, Rautins and Tony "Red" Bruin were seniors.

*48. Why did John Thompson pull his Georgetown players off the floor during a game at the Dome?*

Recruiting guru Howard Garfinkel dubbed scholastic All-American Bruin "the greatest swingman since Benny Goodman."

But this group didn't quite live up to its press clippings. Though winning 21 and getting into the NCAAs after a two-year hiatus, the Orange couldn't play its way back to the Dome for the East Regionals, losing instead to "Granny" Waiters and Ohio State by five in Hartford, Conn.

The program needed a shot in the arm. It got it when Boeheim landed Dwayne "Pearl" Washington, the nationally-sought, flashy guard from Brooklyn.

"The Big East, Carrier Dome, Pearl, 1987 and this year," Boeheim said in 1996, ticking off the biggest events in the first 20 years of his coaching career.

"I'm not a practice player," said Washington. "When the green light goes on, I'll be ready."

The green light went on one incredible night for guard Gene Waldron, who averaged 9.2 ppg in 1983-84. On Dec. 4, in the finals of the Carrier Classic vs. Iona, Waldron scored 40.

The green light — and bright lights just off Broadway — never gleamed brighter for "The Pearl" than the 1984 Big East Tournament.

It was a performance unlike any other he had, as Gene Waldron accepts plaudits from the crowd after his 40-point barrage against Iona in the 1983 Carrier Classic final.

The league had added Pitt, after Villanova, and numbered nine in double round-robin format.

In consecutive games, "Pearl" wrecked Rollie Massimino's multiple defenses, then John Thompson's multiple defenders, scoring 30 and 27.

There hasn't been a better back-to-back Big East tourney performance before or since.

Earlier in the season, he'd tossed in a 45-foot buzzer beater and never broken stride all the way to the dressing room to beat Boston College by two, sending the Dome into a frenzy and forever etching his flair into Big East highlight films. He had 18 assists at St. John's.

SU (23-9) lost that Big East title game to the Hoyas and bowed out of the NCAAs to Virginia.

Next season brought record ticket sales.

**STILL A QUICK OUT** Although SU had a 71-24 record during the Pearl Era, the Orange continued to make an early exit from the NCAAs. Not since the '75 Final Four had an Orange edition won more than one NCAA game.

Georgia Tech was the out in '85, Navy (beaten by 22 in the Carrier Classic) in '86 in the Dome.

There had been more magic from "The Pearl" … his game-winning shot vs. Georgetown as a sophomore, the

## ORANGE ·QUIZ·

49. Why was Jim Boeheim involved in a chair-raising experience at Madison Square Garden?

*One half of the A-Team: Soft-spoken Wendell Alexis really stepped up as a senior, and was second in scoring (15.2 ppg) and rebounding (7.4 rpg).*

*Just call Kay Root of Baldwinsville "The Dome Knitter." You'll find her in the first row at the Dome, cheering ... and knitting.*

Dome crowd spilling onto the floor ... a Big East Tournament MVP performance as a junior, albeit in a one-point title-game loss to St. John's.

He bypassed his senior year for first-round NBA loot from the Nets, but his effect on national recruiting was immeasurable.

Gone, too, from a 26-game winner was the A-Team — No. 2 all-time scorer Raf Addison (1,183 points) and Wendell Alexis.

When a team loses three 1,000-point scorers, it cannot anticipate the March Madness that was to follow.

# 1986-87: NCAA RUNNER-UPS

"The Dome Knitter" has been on the edge of her seat a lot of times. She had plenty of company during the dream season of 1986-87, when questions were answered and balance showed the way.

The NCAA Rules Committee tossed in a new wrinkle, the three-point shot. There should have been a grace year for coaches to recruit long-range bombers; there wasn't. Who would shoot the trey? Greg Monroe hit .439 beyond the arc.

Could Sherman Douglas handle the ball? "The General" broke Dwayne "Pearl" Washington's single-season assist mark with 289 and, surprised even himself by leading five twin-figure scorers (17.3 ppg).

Even at 15-0, second-best start in SU history, some of the faithful wondered if a soft early slate spelled another postseason downfall.

Coming out of the Big East Tournament finals with its third loss to Georgetown, the Orange felt it could be an NCAA force.

There was senior leadership (former reserves Monroe/Howard Triche were more than mere role players). Rony Seikaly and frosh Derrick Coleman were shot-blocking/rebounding interior forces. Douglas ran the show. Stevie Thompson was first off the pines.

First, Georgia Southern fell ... then, Western Kentucky (four score 20 or more) ... Florida (Seikaly poured in 33, eating Dwayne Schintzius for lunch) ... North Carolina (Seikaly again; 26, bye-bye J.R. Reid) ... say, isn't that Rick Pitino joining Boeheim in New Orleans?

*Corcoran High's Howard Triche scored a career-high 31 against Northeastern and grabbed a personal-best 11 rebounds in the Final Four against Providence his senior year.*

**GET SMART!** After beating Rick Pitino's Cinderella Providence Friars by 14 in one semifinal, it was time to tangle with Bobby Knight's Indiana Hoosiers for the national crown.

"We outplayed 'em. We didn't have the game won ... but we were close," Boeheim said in 1996, looking back 10 seasons.

Close enough that Derrick Coleman, who hauled down 19 rebounds in the championship game and 73 total in

*Just a shot away — the one that fell for Indiana — from a crowning moment in 1987, this team remains the winningest in Orange history.*

those NCAAs, could have iced it at the foul line. He didn't.

Indiana, down one, needed a shot to fall. The ball went inside-out, to guard Keith Smart, loose by a half-step for a 16-footer from the left side.

Howard Triche stretched as far as he could … but not far enough to deflect Smart's jumper.

The final tally: Indiana 74, Syracuse 73.

Douglas, Seikaly, Monroe, Coleman, Triche. All scored more than 400 points, a first at SU. And no other Orange team has won 31 games.

So why couldn't that shot have spun out, as Joe Bryant's did to start Cinderella on a magic ride in 1975?

"Sometime, it'd be nice to win it all," Boeheim said. "I don't think I'd be a better coach if that shot hadn't gone in, though."

"The General" and "DC" make the NCAA all-tournament team.

### KNOCK, KNOCK, KNOCKIN'

"From '86-87 to '90, we were there," Boeheim said of his team's annual competitive status come March Madness.

In '88, a 26-game winner bows out of the NCAAs by three to Rhode Island. Douglas was sick. "He probably shouldn't have played," said Boeheim.

"If he's healthy, we win."

Seikaly had 27 points and 10 boards in his final game. That season, he broke Jon Cincebox's 29-year career

*Sherman Douglas is No. 4 on the all-time point parade, but it was his command of the court that made "The General" the assist king; his 22 against Providence in 1988-89 set an NCAA record.*

rebounding standard.

The 1988-89 team — last to win 30 games — made a strong postseason run.

"We'd gotten Billy (Owens), the No. 1 or 2 recruit in the country (along with Georgetown's Alonzo Mourning). … But Missouri took a lot out of us," Boeheim said of SU's three-point win in the 1989 Midwest semifinals.

One thriller after another, but Illinois — instead of Syracuse — advanced to the Final Four by three.

SU's five starters — Douglas, Stevie Thompson, Coleman, Owens and homegrown Matt Roe (who would then transfer to Maryland) — scored more than 400 points and averaged in double figures, the second and last time that has happened. The Orangemen reached the century mark 11 times that season, the most since Bing and Boeheim 23 years before.

But "The General" left after the season. He had turned alley-oop into an art form — passing to Coleman, Owens, Thompson, the athletic open-court performer who departed a year later as No. 3 on SU's all-time scoring list (1,956, now fourth).

Douglas became an Orangeman, unwanted by others including John Thompson and SU's fourth choice to replace "The Pearl," with a funny-looking shot. He left as the program's first 2,000-point scorer (2,060 to surpass Dave Bing's 23-year standard), the NCAA career assist leader (he's now No. 2), and SU's all-time No. 1 in assists/steals (that record still stands).

The decade of the 1980s (243-90) would end in the Superdome, where a crowning moment had been a shot away three years before. A 26-game winner fell by seven to Minnesota in the 1990 Southeast semifinals.

First-team All-American Coleman had stayed his senior year and made it pay on NBA Draft day. He left as the school's all-time scorer (2,143, now No. 2 on the point parade) and remains the career rebounding leader (1,537).

"Derrick ushered in that four years of Final Four and near-Final Fours," said Boeheim. "His success rate was higher than anyone — 113 wins (31 losses), a lot of those wins (11) in the NCAAs."

**STORM CLOUDS GATHER**  The sun did not set Orange on March 4, 1990, when the book *Raw Recruits* arrived in Syracuse bookstores and an excerpt was printed in *The National*.

Recruiting violations were alleged.

For so many decades, so many, many years, never even an NCAA letter of reprimand to the Syracuse basketball (or football) program. And now …

"There are a lot of conclusions drawn without a single

*Fayetteville-Manlius grad Matt Roe set existing SU marks by making 83 three-pointers and shooting .474 beyond the arc as a junior in 1988-89, then transferred.*

## ORANGE ·QUIZ·

*50. Can you name the only Orangeman who was not a full-time starter until his senior year, yet still is a member of the 1,000-point club?*

*Although exonerated by a university report sighting possible NCAA violations, months prior to the NCAA Committee on Infractions' findings, Jim Boeheim told a 1992 press conference: "It's like when you lose a game. Who's responsible? Me."*

fact," Boeheim said in a March 5, 1990, news conference.

The heat intensified dramatically with the *Post-Standard's* two-part series, Dec. 20-21, 1990. Recruiting paid a heavy price while rumors of an NCAA penalty hung over the program.

The case was decided by the NCAA Committee on Infractions Aug. 8, 1992. Announcement of the results was not forthcoming until Oct. 1, 1992.

SU was hit with a two-year probation, one year ban on postseason play, loss of one scholarship for the 1993-94 seasons and some recruiting limitations.

"We believed," said SU Chancellor Buzz Shaw, a career .831 free-throw shooter and 12.9 ppg scorer at Illinois State, "it could never happen here. ... Clearly, we were wrong."

"We've been hurt, losing one or two recruits who

*Need an Orangeman of the 1990s to dive on the floor, come up with a bloody elbow and a loose ball? Mike Hopkins is your man. Now, he's passing that on to the current Orangemen.*

would have been all-Big East," Boeheim said. "… teams have fallen apart after being ruled ineligible for the NCAAs. N.C. State completely collapsed. Missouri, Illinois — they went to hell.

"But the Syracuse kids are winners."

Quarterbacked by frosh point Adrian Autry, the 1990-91 team won 26, but tasted an embarrassing four-point NCAA loss to a 15th seed, Richmond.

All-American Billy Owens scored 744 points, the third-highest single-season total ever, and left for the NBA with a year's eligibility remaining.

In 1991-92, Miami became the Big East's 10th member. That year, the Orange was led by Dave Johnson, who averaged 19.4 and 19.8 ppg his last two years, and freshman Lawrence Moten. SU finished with 22 wins and an overtime loss to Massachusetts in the NCAAs — after the Orange beat Georgetown by two for the Big East tourney title.

Despite being scorched by Seton Hall in its 29th and last game, the 1992-93 squad — banned from postseason play — reached the conference tourney final and kept Boeheim's 20-win season streak alive.

Mike Hopkins, now a Boeheim assistant, put fire in the belly of a team whose primary offensive weapon was Moten.

Years later, Boeheim would look back on those painful months turned into years and remark:

"I don't know if you ever fully recover."

**THE ROAD BACK TO THE FINAL FOUR** The next two years took their twists and turns.

A 23-game winner in 1993-94 was second in the conference, the strongest showing since 1990-91. The Orange featured a backcourt of Moten and Autry, the latter playing brilliantly the second half of his fourth season (16.7 ppg/6.1 apg) as the floor leader. SU took Missouri into overtime in the NCAA West semifinals before losing by 10.

The next year, the Orange "reopened" Manley Field House. The nagging question: Could SU survive at the point without Autry?

Michael Lloyd, who played one season in SU's backcourt before being declared ineligible by the NCAA, literally came off the floor to send the opener into overtime. But George Washington pulled off the shocker, winning by seven.

After the Orangemen ran off 14 consecutive wins, the last 15 games slid their way down a 6-9 path to a 20-win season.

But in a terrific NCAA game, SU and Southern Illinois each shot lights out before the Orange won by four.

**ORANGE ·QUIZ·**

*51. "I probably have more freedom than any assistant in the country. … I guess I'm at the point where I'm kind of like Radar O'Reilly (the character from M.A.S.H.). When (he) goes to say something, I know what he wants before he says it." Who made that statement in 1995?*

**ORANGE ·QUIZ·**

*52. Two players among SU's top 12 all-time point producers never led their team in single-season scoring. Who are they? (Hint, they were classmates).*

## ORANGE
·QUIZ·

53. What
cheerleader was
injured in 1982 —
fortunately, not
permanently —
falling to the Dome
floor from the top of
a "human pyramid"
during the first half
of a Big East game?
And what team was
SU playing?

And the season finale was, well …

"Arkansas would have been one of the great wins in Syracuse history," Boeheim said of the 1995 Midwest semifinal in Austin, Texas.

SU was a seventh seed (the lowest since 1985).

Down 12 in the second half, SU grabbed the lead and the ball — on a steal of an inbounds pass with 4.3 seconds remaining. But SU was whistled for a technical foul for calling a timeout it didn't have.

The Hogs, defending national champs, sent the game to overtime at the charity stripe, then went on to win by two en route to a return trip to the championship game (where they would lose to UCLA).

Moten surpassed Derrick Coleman as SU's top career scorer (2,334 points) and also became the conference all-time scoring leader.

With Moten, Lloyd and athletic Luke Jackson gone, countless questions would be asked of John Wallace & Co. going into the 1995-96 season.

# 1995-96: MAGICAL RUN

There was good chemistry in '95-96, with John Wallace and Lazarus Sims leading the way.

"He's taken this team on his shoulders; you just cannot deny this," Boeheim said of Wallace's final campaign, in which the 6-foot-8 forward broke the single-season scoring record (845, topping Bing's 30-year mark of 794).

And the playmaker, Sims?

"I really thought he could do that," Boeheim said of his point guard's steady floor play. "But I didn't think Final Four."

Sims' credentials were minimal, because he'd always been a bit role player; his career norms were 1.9 ppg, 1.6 apg prior to getting the ball his senior year.

"Z" averaged 7.4 apg, had a 2.3-to-1 assist/turnover ratio and chipped in 6.3 ppg. He had the team's only triple double (17 points/11 rebounds/10 assists at St. John's).

## ORANGE
·QUIZ·

54. All five starters
on the 1995-96 team
played in all 38
games. True or
false?

But Sims was more than numbers; he was a choreographer on the court, the catalyst for the proper chemistry between roommate Wallace and the rest of the Orangemen.

"There were a lot of stories involved on this team," said Boeheim, who also got big-time performances from undersized center Otis Hill (12.7) and athletic swingman Todd Burgan (12.1).

In the NCAAs, Hill came up big. He had 19 points and 11 boards against Georgia, and he was instrumental in attacking Kansas' big front line and then Mississippi State in the Final Four. Burgan was Syracuse's top

*Two of the great performances of the 1996 NCAA Tournament were turned in by SU career scoring leader John Wallace: 30 points/15 rebounds vs. Georgia, 29 and 10 vs. Kentucky. Wallace scored in doubles his final 46 games, 67 of the last 68. His double-doubles match his uniform number.*

rebounder in the NCAAs (8.5 rpg).

The shooting guard spot had its ups and downs, but Jason Cipolla stepped up in the postseason (17 vs. Georgia, in which he kept the dream alive) and Marius Janulis hit some big three-pointers early in the season.

Inside, J.B. Reafsnyder was an effective hammer to wield coming off the bench.

Wallace was the go-to-guy, never more so than when he rained down on Georgia.

"The Georgia game (after SU had disposed of Montana State and Drexel in Albuquerque, N.M.) was such a classic … really one of the great tournament games ever," Boeheim said.

SU and the Bulldogs met in the West Regional semifinals in Denver. Cipolla slid on the seat of his pants into the bench after hitting a corner jump shot that sent the game into overtime. Then, Wallace (30 points and 15 rebounds) dribbled across mid-court and let go an overtime last gasp that spelled an 83-81 victory.

"Georgia," said Boeheim, "made up for (the disappointment of) Arkansas."

A three-point win over Kansas, which many picked to be a Final Four member, meant SU was best in the West.

On to the Meadowlands. Mississippi State, which had beaten Kentucky in the SEC Tournament, fell by eight in the national semifinals.

## ORANGE ·QUIZ·

*55. Which 1996-97 returnee has scored the most points in a game?*

*Shown fending off Mississippi State giant Erick Dampier, Otis Hill's low post moves improved dramatically his junior season. Hill averaged 12.7 ppg, 16.0 in the NCAAs through the Final Four semifinals, then hauled in 10 rebounds in the National Championship game.*

Wallace scored 50 in the Final Four. His career ended with 29 in the National Championship game: Kentucky 76, Syracuse 67.

Four-time rebounding leader Wallace and Derrick Coleman are the only Orangemen in the top four in career scoring, rebounding and blocked shots. Wallace's figures: 2,119 points (third), 1,065 rebounds (third), 209 blocks (fourth).

And he had Kentucky, a huge favorite, perhaps one basket away from buckling after a second Orange rally from a double-digit deficit.

His was an all-tourney performance, SU's a maximized effort.

"Not many times has a team not picked in the top 40 gotten to the Final Four," said Boeheim. "This year (29-9), it was more fun just getting this team there."

**I'VE DONE IT MY WAY** Regrets, he's had a few. But James Arthur Boeheim remains his own man.

Well read … opinionated … at times, stubborn.

No one can argue with the record over time … or two

national championship games in 10 years. For that, Boeheim paid his dues. Walk-on to scholarship, grad assistant to head coach. He's worn Orange on his sleeve for 35 years.

"You don't go into coaching for the money. I got $2,000 as golf coach and grad assistant; for five years, I lost money coaching golf.

"The next few years (under Roy Danforth), I was making $12,000," Boeheim said.

Those days are long ago and seem far away from today's contract … lucrative Big Orange Basketball Camp, sneaker contract and television/radio shows.

But there's also the charitable side of Boeheim, particularly his work for the Kidney Foundation.

"I never claimed to deny who I am. I don't disclaim my personality," said Boeheim, perceived as whining and negative by some, to others a coach whose door has always been open.

"You do it your way," he said.

The winning way.

## ORANGE
### ·QUIZ·

*56. The 1996-97 staff is the first Orange coaching staff since Manley Field House was built that has all SU grads. True or false?*

*It's all business on the sidelines, but some victories deserve a little jubilation and arm-swinging.*

# Lacrosse

*For three seasons, from 1932 through 1934, SU was a combined 23-5-1. In 1932, the team was invited to the Olympic playoffs.*

*Hall of Famer Oren Lyons led the nation in 1956 with 220 saves.*

It's been 80 years since the old Indian game of baggataway was first played at Syracuse. The sport was given collegiate life by Dr. Laurie D. Cox in 1916. And for all these years, stewardship of the game has been in the hands of three coaches — Cox, Roy Simmons Sr. and Roy Simmons Jr., each a Hall of Famer, among 15 Syracusans so enshrined.

To some, whose memories are short, Syracuse lacrosse is defined by the Gait brothers, Gary and Paul. For good reason, perhaps; they brought a panache from western Canada not seen before or since on a collegiate lacrosse field. With it, came three consecutive national championships (1988 through '90).

SU has been in 10 NCAA finals and won a record six NCAA crowns, all under Roy Jr. Now, when collegiate lacrosse is spoken, the conversation begins with Syracuse.

For 66 years, a Simmons has coached SU lacrosse. Theirs is a story of a family intertwined in a genuine love affair with the ol' stick game.

That enduring saga — along with those of Jim Brown, still regarded by many lacrosse buffs as the greatest to ever play the game — is among those to unfold in ensuing pages. But first, let's begin at the beginning.

### DOCTOR IN THE HOUSE?

On a day given little fanfare in 1916, a sport later dubbed "The Fastest Game on Two Feet" by Baltimore scribe W. Wilson Wingate was born at Syracuse. Dr. Cox, who had played the game at Harvard, organized and coached a team at SU's School of Forestry.

Syracuse 3, Syracuse Lax Club 2 — final score of the first game ever played at SU.

### NOW, IT WAS LEAGUE-AL

In its first year in the United States Intercollegiate Lacrosse League (1920), SU's squad included Hall of Fame football guard Joe Alexander. The year is best remembered for the first athletic meeting with Cornell, ending a 30-year feud between the schools.

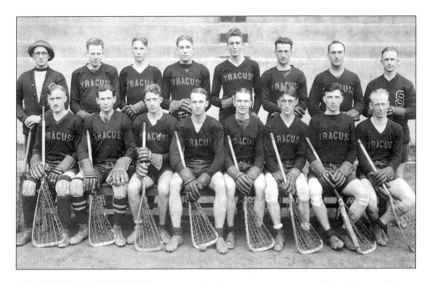

## COX'S CROWNING MOMENT
Victor "Chief" Ross was SU's first national scoring champion (40 goals in 1921).

The 1922 team (17-0) was declared USILL champion; it would be 35 years before another perfect season and 61 until the Orange again ruled as king of collegiate lacrosse, although SU was USILL co-champion in 1924 and '25.

Ross won a second scoring title (27 goals) for the 1922 team, captained by '60 Hall of Fame inductee Irving Lydecker.

Defensemen Paul Lowry and George Dickson joined Ross — who played "in home" and won a third national scoring title with 23 goals in 1923 — as SU's initial first-team All-America selections.

## DOC'S LAST GREAT TEAM
A 3-2 loss to the Crescents, a fabled club team from Brooklyn, cost SU a perfect season in 1926, when the league (USILL) which existed since

*Coach Laurie Cox (standing, far left) took the 1922 team to an unbeaten record.*

*Syracuse's 1926 team (12-1) lost only to the Crescent A.C. by a goal.*

57. Which school has the highest all-time winning percentage in NCAA Tournament play?

*During World War II, Simmons served in the Navy. Fred Schermahorn was interim coach in 1942. The sport was inactive from 1943-45 because of the war. Upon his return, Simmie remained in the Naval Reserve, rising to the rank of Commander.*

1906 was replaced by the United States Intercollegiate Lacrosse Association (USILA). An official rating system had difficulty determining whether unbeaten Johns Hopkins or Navy, or SU (12-1), was No. 1. The Orangemen wound up No. 2.

The 1926 squad completed a great five-year run under Cox, during which SU was twice undefeated and compiled an overall record of 67-4-3.

**LAURIE'S LEGACY**  The father of lacrosse at Syracuse meant more to the game than an oustanding winning percentage (.739), one outright national crown and three others shared in a six-year period.

During his lengthy stint on the SU sideline, Dr. Laurie Davidson Cox introduced changes in rules and equipment that would help stimulate the growth of collegiate lacrosse. He also initiated selection of All-America teams in 1922. Except for one year, Cox edited the "Official Guide" from 1922 through 1934.

Dr. Cox, who became the first president of New England College in Henniker, New Hampshire, where he also coached, would be the first from Syracuse to be inducted in the Hall of Fame (in 1957).

Important, too, was his turning over the reins to one of his defensive stars on the 1924 unbeaten team. In 1931, the Roy Simmons era began.

**THAT GAME WAS FOR THE BIRDS!**  Roy Simmons Sr. would coach the ol' stick game on the Hill for 40 years. But in just his second game as successor to the legendary Cox, the man generations of Orange athletes would refer to as

# SIMMIE: MAN FOR ALL SEASONS

Few, if any, athletic figures at Syracuse have ever been held in as high esteem as Roy Simmons.

A Runyonesque character who was president of the city's Common Council and devoted to betting the nags (albeit one of the worst horse players of all time), he coached national champs in the boxing ring and was a devoted aide to Ben Schwartzwalder on the gridiron.

Simmie is a lacrosse Hall of Famer (1974) not as much for his impressive ledger (252 wins, .659 winning percentage) as the thousands of student-athletes who are the better for his caring, loyalty and wisdom.

Simmie passed away in 1994 at age 93. But the legacy remains, the program grows.

*Roy Simmons Sr.*

*Decades before SU played on a carpet, games were often played on a sloppy track.*

Simmie might have wondered if he'd last the season.

After losing his coaching debut by a goal to Penn State, Johns Hopkins slaughtered SU, 20-0. Never before or since that loss to the Blue Jays has Syracuse been whitewashed to that extent. And the 20-goal margin of defeat was matched just once — in the 913-game history of the sport on the Hill — a quarter-century later.

Still, Simmie's first club finished 7-4; his teams wouldn't suffer a losing season until 1959.

**POST-WAR YEARS** It took awhile to re-establish lacrosse at SU. The fact the game wasn't played by high school teams in the city in the late 1930s and '40s didn't help.

But Simmons' teams from 1948-54 were a combined 62-17. The best of those seasons was 1949, when two-time All-American midfielder Bill Fuller (an '82 Hall of Famer) led SU to a 14-1 mark. Simmie coached the winning North squad in '54.

**UNDEFEATED, UNTIED, UNCROWNED** Simmie's best and only unbeaten team, 10-0 in 1957, felt it was robbed of at least an opportunity to win the national championship.

"There was a rating system, done every three years," said Roy Jr., who played for his Dad. "We played one less 'A' team than Johns Hopkins. We were both undefeated; a coaches' poll decided it. ... We challenged 'em to a game, but ..."

The winner-take-all game never took place.

# ORANGE
## ·QUIZ·

*58. What year did the Orange defense hurl five shutouts and allow a total of 20 goals in 17 games?*

# ORANGE
## ·QUIZ·

*59. How many perfect seasons has SU had, and when were they?*

# A DAY TO REMEMBER

Jim Brown was the Jim Thorpe of his generation. The time-honored example was a spring day in 1957.

"In Archbold, there was a track meet at noon with Colgate, and (coach) Bob Grieve asked Dad if he could use Big Jim in the javelin," said Roy Simmons Jr. "Our faceoff with Army was at 3, also in the stadium. We were undefeated and it was our last game.

"Gets to be game time and no Big Jim. Dad tells the manager to go out and get him. Seems Grieve put him in three events; he got a couple of firsts and a second; 13 points. Syracuse won the meet by 13.

"So with his track shorts on, Jim puts on his lacrosse jersey and we beat Army to finish 10-0."

Brown had seven goals, five assists against Cornell and scored 43 goals in 10 games for a team that also featured 1993 Hall of Fame goalie Oren Lyons (only the second Native-American to be inducted and current Faithkeeper of the Onondagas) and Brown's gridiron mate, Jim Ridlon.

That Army game was Brown's last in Ancient Archbold. And he was the last player to leave the dressing room.

"Big Jim's all by himself, walking through the tunnel out to midfield," said Roy Jr., relating a story told him by then-Sports Information Director Arnie Burdick, who watched from his office window, unnoticed by Brown.

"Big Jim looks around, climbs the concrete steps, turns and waves ... to an empty stadium."

Years later, at a gathering of Syracusans prior to the College Football Hall of Fame dinner, Brown was asked what his favorite sport was. It was the ol' stick game. Why?

"There ain't no scratch in lacrosse," he said.

Brown, who turned down lucrative pro offers to play his final season for Simmons, did so for the love of the game.

*Midfielder Jim Brown is the only member of the Lacrosse, College Football and Pro Football Halls of Fame.*

**BIG JIM, GREATEST PLAYER EVER?** "There were those who claimed he carried an illegal stick," said Roy Jr., better known as "Slugger."

"It looked small in his hands, but it was perfectly legal. I know; I fixed Jim's stick when it needed fixing."

Because he's arguably the greatest running back of all time, recent generations don't realize that Jim Brown was perhaps the best lacrosse player the game has ever seen.

"The greatest player I've ever coached," Simmie said, before Big Jim put on a display of strength/speed in the '57 North-South game (five goals, two assists in one half) that's remained a part of lacrosse lore for generations.

"I played attack. But Dad made me a midfielder my sophomore year," recalled Slugger. "Every day in practice, I had to go against Big Jim. All those linebackers he knocked over on the football field? Well, he knocked me down more than any other athlete.

"I couldn't wait for Saturday."

On game day, Brown made SU opponents feel Slugger's daily pain.

**LIKE FATHER, LIKE SON?** Both honorable mention All-Americans as players, Roy Sr. and Roy Jr. have combined for 520 victories in an Orange coaching career spanning seven decades.

Slugger — the son — is unlike most mentors, no matter the sport. How many coaches are award-winning artists, displayed in galleries and museums across the country? How many are students of pre-Colombian Andean textiles and African art?

He's coached at SU 37 years (11 as Simmie's frosh coach/assistant) ... did what no SU coach in any sport has done by winning consecutive national championships (1988-89) ... made it a three-peat (1990, a lacrosse feat matched only by Johns Hopkins 1978-80) ... and won an unmatched six NCAA crowns.

While Simmie came by the sport as a collegian, when he picked up a lacrosse stick, mistaking it for a crabbing net, Slugger was born to the game.

**SILVER ANNIVERSARY DUO** Little did anyone know at the time, but when North Carolina State dropped lacrosse, Syracuse was to become a prime beneficiary.

"The stage changed," said Simmons, "when we got Tim Nelson (now coaching Dartmouth) from N.C. State."

Nelson set the NCAA career assist record (225, 187 of them at SU from 1983-85) and teamed with fellow three-time All-American first-teamer Brad Kotz to lead the '83 Orangemen to the first of six NCAA crowns. Nelson had eight points in the title game and a tourney-high 15

## ORANGE ·QUIZ·

60. Who was the winning coach in the 1954 North-South game?

*Artist/coach Roy Simmons Jr. played for his father, succeeded him as coach and is the only six-time winner of the NCAA Championship.*

*Tim Nelson, shown here playing against John Hopkins, still holds NCAA records.*

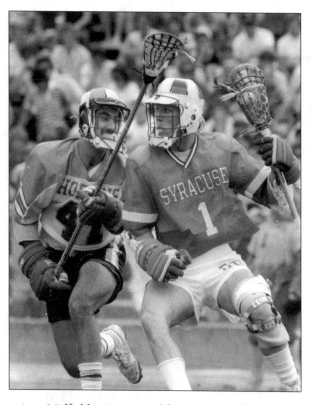

*The first of a record six NCAA crowns came in 1983.*

points. Midfielder Kotz netted five second-half goals as SU rallied from a 12-5 deficit in the third period to edge Johns Hopkins, 17-16.

Nelson was the Turnbull Award winner (nation's top attackman) each of his three seasons at Syracuse, the only Orangeman to win a national honor three times. In 1983, Kotz (Enners Award winner as the nation's top player) was SU's first Brine Award winner as Most Outstanding Player in the title game. In 1995, Nelson and Kotz were named to the NCAA 25th Anniversary Team.

**OH, CANADA!** SU returned to the championship game in 1984 and '85, losing to Hopkins. But the Orange was on the verge of sustained greatness in 1987, because the Canadian National Team coach felt he owed Slugger a favor.

"Before the World Games (Canada, England, Australia, USA), we scrimmaged the Canadians in Ottawa. Four years later," said Slugger, "they came to practice on our synthetic surface. (Canadian coach) Bob Allen said, 'I owe you a favor. There are two kids from Victoria,

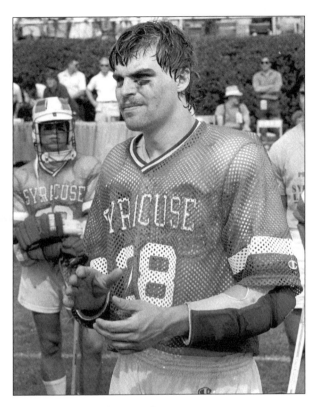

*Defensive stalwart Kevin Sheehan was a first-team All-America selection in 1985-86.*

representing British Columbia, coming to New Brunswick for the Canadian National Festival. You've got to see 'em play. Their name is Gait. They're twins.'

"It wasn't even field lacrosse. They play this game in an arena. Out come two guys who look identical. Gait and Gait. Well, they never even thought of going to college; hadn't taken the SAT. But they took them in November ... and they were on their way.

"They're passing behind their backs in practice. But our kids wouldn't talk to them. The team was going to rebel.

"So," said Slugger, "I didn't start either one of them the first game. But I had them right next to me. When I put Gary in, he electrified the crowd. 'Paul, come here!' "

  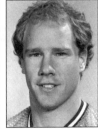

*Attackman Tim O'Hara (left) established the standard for points with 282 (124 goals, 158 assists) from 1977-80.*

*NCAA Silver Anniversary team selection Tim Nelson (middle), the Turnbull Award winner in 1983-85, holds the NCAA record for assists in a game (six), tournament (12) and career (27).*

*Midfielder Brad Kotz (right) was SU's first NCAA Tournament MVP in 1983.*

The rest is lacrosse history.

"I had Michael Jordan," Simmons said of Gary Gait. "And if Michael Jordan had a twin brother, I had him, too."

*Double trouble for opponents: Gary Gait (left) and twin brother Paul are both NCAA Silver Anniversary Team selections.*

*Air Gait: Gary goes over the top to score against Pennsylvania in the 1988 NCAA Final Four.*

## 1988: START OF A HAT TRICK
For the first time, the 1988 Orangemen were seeded No. 1 in the NCAA playoffs. After Gary Gait set a tournament record for goals (nine) and tied the point mark (12) in a rout of Navy, SU needed Paul Gait's goal with :03 left to nip Pennsylvania. That game was historic because it introduced "Air Gait" — Gary twice scoring by dunking over the top of the goal.

"They were nothing compared to what we'd seen in practice," said Simmons.

The title game with Cornell was a 10-1 rout, SU completing a 15-0 season (its first perfecto since 1957) by coasting to the crown, 13-8, in its Carrier Dome home.

Matt Palumb's 21 saves earned him tournament MVP honors.

## 1989: BACK-TO-BACK
Again seeded No. 1, having won 11 in a row after an opening loss at Johns Hopkins, SU beat Navy and host Maryland to earn a rematch with Hopkins. It was the fourth title game with the Blue Jays in the 1980s.

A record crowd of 23,893 saw the Orange rally from 8-5 and 11-9 deficits, Rodney Dumpson scoring the clincher in a 13-12 thriller. But it took Palumb turning away three shots in the last two minutes, one from point blank range in the closing seconds, to preserve SU's title defense. Paul Gait was named MVP.

## 1990: THREE-PEAT
Has there been a college lacrosse team before or since the equal of the 1990 Orangemen?

Five first team All-Americans, the only time in SU history ... A 13-0 season completed by an NCAA tourney demolition of Brown, North Carolina and Loyola by a playoff-record average of 10.3 goals ... Gary Gait's three consecutive five-goal games broke his own NCAA playoff record and earned MVP honors.

"We had kids coming off the bench who could have gone anywhere else and been stars," Simmons said.

Based on all the expertise available, they were the best. ... No Achilles heel, not a soft spot anywhere. The Gait-led Class of 1990 went an overall 42-1 in winning three straight national championships.

# ORANGE
## ·QUIZ·

61. Who was in goal making the most saves for the North in the most lopsided North-South game ever?

Matt Palumb (left), the 1988 NCAA Tournament MVP, is the Orange record-holder for most saves in the NCAAs with 146 in 1988-90.

Two-time Turnbull winner John Zulberti (1988-89) could freeze a goalie with his over-the-shoulder shot.

Thrice an All-American first-teamer, Pat McCabe (right) is the only Orangeman ever named Schmeisser Award winner as the nation's top defenseman (1990).

**BROWN OR GAIT?** Who was the best to ever play the game? Even Simmons is uncharacteristically hesitant to say, perhaps because they played in different eras, marked by changes in equipment and playing fields.

"Big Jim was a physical specimen," said Slugger. "And what people don't know is that when he got here, he was already an accomplished player.

"Gary never missed a game. But what he brought was the uniqueness of his style."

**1990s: CONTINUED DOMINANCE** After losing in the Final Four in 1991, the '92 Orangemen scored eight straight fourth-quarter goals in the semifinals to beat Hopkins in the highest scoring playoff game in NCAA history, 21-16. In the title game against Princeton, SU dug its way out of an 8-2 hole to tie it on Tom Marachek's goal in the final minute, only to lose on a shot off the faceoff in the second overtime.

In the 1993 Final Four, SU dispatched Princeton in the semifinals and was deadlocked with top-seeded North Carolina in a championship game seemingly bound for overtime. But Charlie Lockwood's pass to Matt Riter produced the crowning goal with eight seconds left.

Goalie Chris Surran (20 saves in the title game) was tourney MVP as SU celebrated a fifth national

 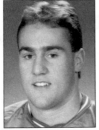 

*Goalie Chris Surran (left) won MVP honors in the NCAAs for the 1993 national champions.*

*Roy Colsey (middle), the 1995 McLaughlin winner, and defenseman Ric Beardsley(right) were stellar performers on two NCAA championship teams.*

championship, in College Park, Md.

Returning to the Final Four in College Park in '94, Virginia scored in the final minute to send that semifinal game into overtime, and the Cavs went on to win, 15-14.

Following a 15-11 Carrier Dome win over defending NCAA champion Princeton, SU took on host Maryland for the 1995 crown. The Orange remained the only team to win the NCAA title on its home field by beating the Terps, 13-9.

SU was king of college lacrosse an unprecedented sixth time. Of particular pleasure to Simmons was Frank Licameli's goal in the title game, not to mention his career-high four goals in the semifinals.

"I cut him the first year. He played summer ball and made the team the next year. But we could suit up 32 for the playoffs; Licameli was my 33rd guy," Simmons said.

"His junior year, no jersey again. But in his senior year, he scores four against Maryland and again in the championship game.

"The kid just had a lot of heart. He lived his dream. … I couldn't be a dream-buster."

Syracuse's dreams weren't realized in 1996. The team lost to eventual champion Princeton in the semifinals and ended an eight-year run of 12 wins or more.

But 1997 looks promising. Top-scoring, All-American attackman Casey Powell, wearer of Gary Gait's No. 22, will be joined by brother Ryan. The last time No. 22 and his sibling wore the Orange, there was a dynasty on the Hill.

As Yogi Berra might wonder, "Is this deja vu all over again?"

## ORANGE
## ·QUIZ·

*63. Who holds the Orange regular-season record for most goals in a game?*

# By the Numbers

The statistics, lists and records that appear in this chapter are taken from the Syracuse University media guides, which are produced by the Syracuse Sports Information Office.

## FOOTBALL
## SEASON-BY-SEASON

| Year | W | L | T | Coach | Captain |
|------|---|---|---|-------|---------|
| 1889 | 0 | 1 | 0 | (No Coach) | J. Blake Hillyer |
| 1890 | 8 | 3 | 0 | Bobby Winston | J. Blake Hillyer |
| 1891 | 4 | 6 | 0 | William Galbraith | William M. Fanton |
| 1892 | 0 | 8 | 1 | Jordan C. Wells | Sherman Rouse |
| 1893 | 4 | 9 | 1 | (No Coach) | George H. Bond |
| 1894 | 6 | 5 | 0 | George H. Bond | Robert B. Adams |
| 1895 | 6 | 2 | 2 | George O. Redington | Robert B. Adams |
| 1896 | 5 | 3 | 2 | George O. Redington | Robert B. Adams |
| 1897 | 5 | 3 | 1 | Frank E. Wade | Harry A. O'Day |
| 1898 | 8 | 2 | 1 | Frank E. Wade | Morgan A. Wilcox |
| 1899 | 4 | 4 | 0 | Frank E. Wade | Carl E. Dorr |
| 1900 | 7 | 2 | 1 | Edwin R. Sweetland | Hadden A. Patten |
| 1901 | 7 | 1 | 0 | Edwin R. Sweetland | Lynn B. Wycoff |
| 1902 | 6 | 2 | 1 | Edwin R. Sweetland | Ancil D. Brown |
| 1903 | 5 | 4 | 0 | Jason B. Parish | Frank H. O'Neill, Ancil D. Brown |
| 1904 | 6 | 3 | 0 | Dr. Charles P. Hutchins | Robert Park |
| 1905 | 8 | 3 | 0 | Dr. Charles P. Hutchins | David L. Tucker |
| 1906 | 6 | 3 | 0 | Frank J. O'Neill | James P. Stimson |
| 1907 | 5 | 3 | 1 | Frank J. O'Neill | Ford R. Park |
| 1908 | 6 | 3 | 1 | Howard H. Jones | Marquis F. (Bill) Horr |
| 1909 | 4 | 5 | 1 | T.A.D. Jones | Herbert H. Barry |
| 1910 | 5 | 4 | 1 | T.A.D. Jones | Harry H. Hartman |
| 1911 | 5 | 3 | 2 | C. DeForest Cummings | Preston D. Fogg |
| 1912 | 4 | 5 | 0 | C. DeForest Cummings | Rudolph W. Propst |
| 1913 | 6 | 4 | 0 | Frank J. O'Neill | Martin F. Hilfinger |
| 1914 | 5 | 3 | 2 | Frank J. O'Neill | James V. Shufelt |
| 1915 | 9 | 1 | 2 | Frank J. O'Neill | Walter S. Rose |
| 1916 | 5 | 4 | 0 | William M. Hollenback | Harold A. White |
| 1917 | 8 | 1 | 1 | Frank J. O'Neill | Alfred R. Cobb |
| 1918 | 5 | 1 | 0 | Frank J. O'Neill | Joseph Alexander, Joseph K. Schwarzer |
| 1919 | 8 | 3 | 0 | Frank J. O'Neill | Harold J. Robertson |
| 1920 | 6 | 2 | 1 | John F. Meehan | Joseph Alexander |
| 1921 | 7 | 2 | 0 | John F. Meehan | Bertrand L. Gulick |
| 1922 | 6 | 1 | 2 | John F. Meehan | Frank Z. Culver |
| 1923 | 8 | 1 | 0 | John F. Meehan | Evander G. MacRae |
| 1924 | 8 | 2 | 1 | John F. Meehan | Roy D. Simmons, Sr. |
| 1925 | 8 | 1 | 1 | C.W.P. Reynolds | James E. Foley |
| 1926 | 7 | 2 | 1 | C.W.P. Reynolds | Victor A. Hanson |
| 1927 | 5 | 3 | 2 | Lewis P. Andreas | Raymond J. Barbuti |
| 1928 | 4 | 4 | 1 | Lewis P. Andreas | Harold W. Baysinger |
| 1929 | 6 | 3 | 0 | Lewis P. Andreas | Albert W. VanNess |
| 1930 | 5 | 2 | 2 | Victor A. Hanson | Milton Berner, Warren Stevens |
| 1931 | 7 | 1 | 1 | Victor A. Hanson | George A. Ellert |
| 1932 | 4 | 4 | 1 | Victor A. Hanson | Thomas A. Lombardi |
| 1933 | 4 | 4 | 0 | Victor A. Hanson | Francis Tisdale |
| 1934 | 6 | 2 | 0 | Victor A. Hanson | James Steen |
| 1935 | 6 | 1 | 1 | Victor A. Hanson | Edward S. Jontos, George Perrault |
| 1936 | 1 | 7 | 0 | Victor A. Hanson | Vannie M. Albanese |
| 1937 | 5 | 2 | 1 | Ossie Solem | Walter J. Rekstis, Parker Webster |
| 1938 | 5 | 3 | 0 | Ossie Solem | James M. Bruett |
| 1939 | 3 | 3 | 2 | Ossie Solem | Hugh H. Daugherty, William T. Hoffman |
| 1940 | 3 | 4 | 1 | Ossie Solem | Richard Banger |
| 1941 | 5 | 2 | 1 | Ossie Solem | Thomas J. Kinney |
| 1942 | 6 | 3 | 0 | Ossie Solem | Richard C. Weber |
| 1943 | (Suspended) | | | | |
| 1944 | 2 | 4 | 1 | Ossie Solem | Victor E. Merkel |
| 1945 | 1 | 6 | 0 | Ossie Solem | Angelo A. Acocella |

| Year | W | L | T | Coach | Captain |
|------|---|---|---|-------|---------|
| 1946 | 4 | 5 | 0 | Clarence L. Munn | Richard Whitesell |
| 1947 | 3 | 6 | 0 | Reaves H. Baysinger | Laurence R. Ellis |
| 1948 | 1 | 8 | 0 | Reaves H, Baysinger | Robert A. Schiffner |
| 1949 | 4 | 5 | 0 | Ben Schwartzwalder | James J. Fiacco |
| 1950 | 5 | 5 | 0 | Ben Schwartzwalder | Game Captains |
| 1951 | 5 | 4 | 0 | Ben Schwartzwalder | Edward Dobrowolski, John Donati |
| 1952 | 7 | 3 | 0 | Ben Schwartzwalder | Richard Beyer, , Joseph Szombathy |
| 1953 | 5 | 3 | 1 | Ben Schwartzwalder | Game Captains |
| 1954 | 4 | 4 | 0 | Ben Schwartzwalder | Game Captains |
| 1955 | 5 | 3 | 0 | Ben Schwartzwalder | Game Captains |
| 1956 | 7 | 2 | 0 | Ben Schwartzwalder | Game Captains |
| 1957 | 5 | 3 | 1 | Ben Schwartzwalder | Game Captains |
| 1958 | 8 | 2 | 0 | Ben Schwartzwalder | Charles D. Zimmerman |
| 1959 | 11 | 0 | 0 | Ben Schwartzwalder | Gerhard H. Schwedes |
| 1960 | 7 | 2 | 0 | Ben Schwartzwalder | Albert D. Bemiller, Frederick J.Mautino, Richard L. Reimer |
| 1961 | 8 | 3 | 0 | Ben Schwartzwalder | Richard B. Easterly |
| 1962 | 5 | 5 | 0 | Ben Schwartzwalder | Leon Cholakis |
| 1963 | 8 | 2 | 0 | Ben Schwartzwalder | Richard B. Bowman, James L. Mazurek |
| 1964 | 7 | 4 | 0 | Ben Schwartzwalder | G. William Hunter, Richard K. King |
| 1965 | 7 | 3 | 0 | Ben Schwartzwalder | Harris A. Elliott |
| 1966 | 8 | 3 | 0 | Ben Schwartzwalder | Floyd D. Little, Herbert W. Stecker |
| 1967 | 8 | 2 | 0 | Ben Schwartzwalder | James M. Cheyunski, Lawrence R. Csonka |
| 1968 | 6 | 4 | 0 | Ben Schwartzwalder | Anthony J. Kyasky |
| 1969 | 5 | 5 | 0 | Ben Schwartzwalder | Game Captains |
| 1970 | 6 | 4 | 0 | Ben Schwartzwalder | Paul L. Paolisso, Raymond C. White, Randolph C. Zur |
| 1971 | 5 | 5 | 1 | Ben Schwartzwalder | Joseph C. Ehrmann, Daniel L. Yochum |
| 1972 | 5 | 6 | 0 | Ben Schwartzwalder | Game Captains |
| 1973 | 2 | 9 | 0 | Ben Schwartzwalder | David A. Lapham, Steven J. Joslin |
| 1974 | 2 | 9 | 0 | Frank Maloney | Robert G. Petchel, John E. Rafferty |
| 1975 | 6 | 5 | 0 | Frank Maloney | Raymond N. Preston |
| 1976 | 3 | 8 | 0 | Frank Maloney | William J. Zanovitch |
| 1977 | 6 | 5 | 0 | Frank Maloney | Game Captains |
| 1978 | 3 | 8 | 0 | Frank Maloney | Game Captains |
| 1979 | 7 | 5 | 0 | Frank Maloney | Jim Collins, Bill Hurley, Craig Wolfley |
| 1980 | 5 | 6 | 0 | Frank Maloney | Jim Collins, Joe Morris, Dave Warner |
| 1981 | 4 | 6 | 1 | Dick MacPherson | Ike Bogosian, Joe Morris |
| 1982 | 2 | 9 | 0 | Dick MacPherson | Gerry Feehery |
| 1983 | 6 | 5 | 0 | Dick MacPherson | Blaise Winter, Brent Ziegler |
| 1984 | 6 | 5 | 0 | Dick MacPherson | Marty Chalk, Jaime Covington, Jim Gorzalski, Jamie Kimmel |
| 1985 | 7 | 5 | 0 | Dick MacPherson | Tim Green, Rudy Reed |
| 1986 | 5 | 6 | 0 | Dick MacPherson | Pete Ewald, Jim Leible, Tim Pidgeon |
| 1987 | 11 | 0 | 1 | Dick MacPherson | Paul Frase, Ted Gregory, Don McPherson |
| 1988 | 10 | 2 | 0 | Dick MacPherson | Daryl Johnston, Markus Paul |
| 1989 | 8 | 4 | 0 | Dick MacPherson | Blake Bednarz, Dan Bucey, Rob Burnett, Michael Owens, Terry Wooden |
| 1990 | 7 | 4 | 2 | Dick MacPherson | John Flannery, Duane Kinnon, Gary McCummings, Rob Thomson |
| 1991 | 10 | 2 | 0 | Paul Pasqualoni | Andrew Dees, Mark McDonald, Tim Sandquist, Greg Walker |
| 1992 | 10 | 2 | 0 | Paul Pasqualoni | David Walker, Glen Young |
| 1993 | 6 | 4 | 1 | Paul Pasqualoni | Marvin Graves, Dwayne Joseph, John Reagan |
| 1994 | 7 | 4 | 0 | Paul Pasqualoni | Wilky Bazile, Eric Chenoweth, Dan Conley, Tony Jones |
| 1995 | 9 | 3 | 0 | Paul Pasqualoni | Cy Ellsworth, Marvin Harrison, Darrell Parker |
| Tot. | 599 | 390 | 49 | | |

# COACHING RECORDS

| Coach | W | L | T | Years |
|-------|---|---|---|-------|
| No Coach | 4 | 10 | 1 | 1889, 1893 |
| Winston, Bobby | 8 | 3 | 0 | 1890 |
| Galbraith, William | 4 | 6 | 0 | 1891 |
| Wells, Jordan C. | 0 | 8 | 1 | 1892 |
| Bond, George H. | 6 | 5 | 0 | 1894 |
| Redington, George O. | 11 | 5 | 4 | 1895-96 |
| Wade, Frank E. | 17 | 9 | 2 | 1897-99 |
| Sweetland, Edwin R. | 20 | 5 | 2 | 1900-02 |
| Brown, Ancil D. (co-coach) | 5 | 4 | 0 | 1903 |
| Parish, Jason B. (co-coach) | 5 | 4 | 0 | 1903 |
| Hutchins, Dr. Charles P. | 14 | 6 | 0 | 1904-05 |
| O'Neill, Frank J. | 52 | 19 | 6 | 1906-07, 1913-15, 1917-19 |
| Jones, Howard H. | 6 | 3 | 1 | 1908 |

| Coach | W | L | T | Years |
|-------|---|---|---|-------|
| Jones, T.A.D. | 9 | 9 | 2 | 1909-10 |
| Cummings, C.D. | 9 | 8 | 2 | 1911-12 |
| Hollenback, W.M. | 5 | 4 | 0 | 1916 |
| Meehan, John F. | 35 | 8 | 4 | 1920-24 |
| Reynolds, C.W.P. | 15 | 3 | 2 | 1925-26 |
| Andreas, Lewis P. | 15 | 10 | 3 | 1927-29 |
| Hanson, Victor A. | 33 | 21 | 5 | 1930-36 |
| Solem, Ossie | 30 | 27 | 6 | 1937-45* |
| Munn, Clarence L. | 4 | 5 | 0 | 1946 |
| Baysinger, Reeves H. | 4 | 14 | 0 | 1947-48 |
| Schwartzwalder, Floyd | 153 | 91 | 3 | 1949-73 |
| Maloney, Frank | 32 | 46 | 0 | 1974-80 |
| MacPherson, Richard F. | 66 | 46 | 4 | 1981-90 |
| Pasqualoni, Paul L. | 42 | 15 | 1 | 1991-present |
| **Totals** | **599** | **390** | **49** | **106 seasons** |

* No team in 1943

# BOWL RESULTS

Orange Bowl — Jan. 1, 1953, Alabama 61, SU 6
Cotton Bowl — Jan. 1, 1957, TCU 28, SU 27
Orange Bowl — Jan. 1, 1959, Oklahoma 21, SU 6
Cotton Bowl — Jan. 1, 1960, SU 23, Texas 14
Liberty Bowl — Dec. 16, 1961, SU 15, Miami (FL) 14
Sugar Bowl — Jan. 1, 1965, LSU 13, SU 10
Gator Bowl — Dec. 31, 1966, Tennessee 18, SU 12
Independence Bowl — Dec. 15, 1979, SU 31, McNeese St. 7

Cherry Bowl — Dec. 21, 1985, Maryland 35, SU 18
Sugar Bowl — Jan. 1, 1988, SU 16, Auburn 16
Hall of Fame Bowl — Jan. 2, 1989, SU 23, LSU 10
Peach Bowl — Dec. 30, 1989, SU 19, Georgia 18
Aloha Bowl — Dec. 25, 1990, SU 28, Arizona 0
Hall of Fame Bowl — Jan. 1, 1992, SU 24, Ohio St. 17
Fiesta Bowl — Jan. 1, 1993, SU 26, Colorado 22
Gator Bowl — Jan. 1, 1996, SU 41, Clemson 0

# TEAM OFFENSE RECORDS

* Former NCAA record

### POINTS

Game, all-time: — 144, Manhattan, 1904
Game, modern: — 71, Colgate, 1959
Season, all-time: — 405, 1904
Season, modern: — 390, 1959

### TOUCHDOWNS

Game: 10, Colgate, 1959
Season: 56, 1959

### FIELD GOALS MADE

Game: 5, Kent State, 1983
Season: 18, 1981

### FIELD GOALS ATTEMPTED

Game: 6, Navy, 1970; West Virginia, 1975
Season: 30, 1975

### TOTAL OFFENSE YARDS

Game: 675, Rutgers, 1992
Season: 4,843, 1987

### PLAYS

Game: 98, Kansas, 1959
Season: 835, 1979

### RUSHING YARDS

Game: 511, Colgate, 1956
Season: 3,136, 1959

### RUSHING ATTEMPTS

Game: 82, Virginia, 1975
Season: 656, 1979

### AVERAGE YARDS PER CARRY

Game: 8.5, Cornell, 1952
Season: 5.5, 1959

### PASSING YARDS

Game: 425, Rutgers, 1992
Season: 2,654, 1989

### PASSING ATTEMPTS

Game: 44, Cincinnati, 1993
Season: 297, 1993

### COMPLETIONS

Game: 29, Cincinnati, 1993
Season: 178, 1993

### COMPLETION PERCENTAGE

Game (min. 10 att.): 82.4, Navy, 1988
Season: 66.5, 1989

### PASSING YARDS PER ATTEMPT

Game: 19.2, Louisville, 1989
Season: 10.1, 1987*

### PASSING YARDS PER COMPLETION

Game: 26.9, Lafayette, 1949
Season: 18.1, 1987

### INTERCEPTIONS THROWN

Game: 6, Temple, 1948; California, 1968
Season: 26, 1982

### PUNTS

Game: 13, Dartmouth, 1946; Pittsburgh, 1975
Season: 88, 1939; 1948

### YARDS PUNTING

Game: 503, Pittsburgh, 1975
Season: 2,841, 1984

### PUNT RETURN YARDS

Game: 190, Miami, FL, 1970
Season: 662, 1941

### PUNT RETURNS

Game: 13, Holy Cross, 1968
Season: 51, 1941

### KICKOFF RETURN YARDS

Game: 230, Penn State, 1978
Season: 947, 1986

### KICKOFF RETURNS

Game: 10, Columbia, 1946
Season: 50, 1986

### FIRST DOWNS

Game: 36, Pittsburgh, 1994
Season: 258, 1992

### FUMBLES

Game: 11, Cornell, 1950
Season: 47, 1972

### FUMBLES LOST

Game: 7, Cornell, 1950; Wisconsin, 1972
Season: 28, 1972

# TEAM DEFENSE RECORDS

### MOST POINTS

Game, all-time: — 71, Union, 1891
Game, modern: — 63, Nebraska, 1983
Season, all-time: — 324, 1893
Season, modern: — 295, 1978

### FEWEST POINTS

Game: 0, 255 times, most recent vs. Tulane, 1991
Season, all-time: — 16, 1915
Season, modern: — 59, 1959

### MOST TOUCHDOWNS

Game: 9, Columbia, 1946; Alabama, 1952; Nebraska, 1983
Season: 40, 1979

### LOWEST AVERAGE TOTAL YARDS PER PLAY

Game: 0.3, George Washington, 1962
Season: 2.0, 1959

### HIGHEST AVERAGE TOTAL YARDS PER PLAY

Game: 9.8, Boston College, 1993
Season: 5.8, 1993

### FEWEST RUSHING YARDS

Game: -88, Boston University, 1959
Season: 193, 1959

### MOST RUSHING YARDS

Game: 455, Pittsburgh, 1973
Season: 2980, 1974

### LOWEST AVERAGE PER CARRY

Game: -4.0, Boston University, 1959
Season: 0.7, 1959

### HIGHEST AVERAGE PER CARRY

Game: 8.0, Pittsburgh, 1973
Season: 5.0, 1948, 1993

### FEWEST PASSING YARDS

Game: 0, Colgate, 1947; Colgate, 1948; Army, 1955; Army, 1989
Season: 487, 1941

### MOST PASSING YARDS

Game: 521, East Carolina, 1992
Season: 2,751, 1985

### FEWEST COMPLETIONS

Game: 0, Colgate, 1947; Colgate, 1948; Army, 1955; Army, 1989
Season: 35, 1955

### MOST COMPLETIONS

Game: 37, Navy, 1985
Season: 224, 1984

### LOWEST PERCENT COMPLETED

Game (min. 10 att.): 0.0, Colgate, 1947
Season: 33.3, 1939

### PASSES INTERCEPTED

Game: 6, Holy Cross, 1971
Season: 24, 1992

### SACKS

Game: 9, Rutgers, 1991
Season: 41, 1985

### FEWEST FIRST DOWNS ALLOWED

Game: 2, Maryland, 1959
Season, total: — 69, 1939, 1941
Season, rushing: — 27, 1959
Season, passing: — 21, 1949

### MOST OPPONENT FUMBLES

Game: 10, Colgate, 1959
Season: 37, 1972

### MOST OPPONENT FUMBLES LOST

Game: 8, Lafayette, 1951
Season: 24, 1951

# INDIVIDUAL RECORDS

## RUSHING YARDS GAINED, GAME

| | | | |
|---|---|---|---|
| 1. | 252 | Joe Morris vs. Kansas | 1979 |
| 2. | 216 | Larry Csonka vs. West Virginia | 1965 |
| 3. | 204 | Larry Csonka vs. California | 1967 |
| 4. | 203 | Joe Morris vs. Navy | 1978 |
| 5. | 197 | Jim Brown vs. Colgate | 1956 |
| 6. | 196 | Floyd Little vs. West Virginia | 1965 |
| 7. | 194 | Bill Wetzel vs. Boston University | 1952 |
| 8. | 193 | Floyd Little vs. Florida State | 1966 |
| 9. | 192 | Glenn Moore vs. West Virginia | 1980 |
| | 192 | Jaime Covington vs. Colgate | 1982 |

## RUSHING YARDS GAINED, SEASON

| | | | |
|---|---|---|---|
| 1. | 1372 | Joe Morris | 1979 |
| 2. | 1194 | Joe Morris | 1981 |
| 3. | 1127 | Larry Csonka | 1967 |
| 4. | 1065 | Floyd Little | 1965 |
| 5. | 1018 | Michael Owens | 1989 |
| 6. | 1012 | Larry Csonka | 1966 |
| 7. | 1001 | Joe Morris | 1978 |
| 8. | 986 | Jim Brown | 1956 |
| 9. | 969 | David Walker | 1991 |
| 10. | 951 | Jim Nance | 1964 |

## RUSHING YARDS GAINED, CAREER

| | | | |
|---|---|---|---|
| 1. | 4299 | Joe Morris | 1978-81 |
| 2. | 2934 | Larry Csonka | 1965-67 |
| 3. | 2704 | Floyd Little | 1964-66 |
| 4. | 2643 | David Walker | 1989-92 |
| 5. | 2551 | Bill Hurley | 1975-79 |
| 6. | 2386 | Ernie Davis | 1959-61 |
| 7. | 2188 | Jaime Covington | 1981-84 |
| 8. | 2164 | Robert Drummond | 1985-88 |
| 9. | 2091 | Jim Brown | 1954-56 |
| 10. | 2069 | Marty Januszkiewicz | 1969-72 |

## CARRIES

Game: 43, Larry Csonka, Maryland, 1967
Season: 261, Larry Csonka, 1967; Joe Morris, 1981
Career: 813, Joe Morris, 1978-81

## AVERAGE PER CARRY

Game (min. 8): 15.7, Ernie Davis, West Virginia, 1959
Season (min. 75): 7.8, Ernie Davis, 1960
Career (min. 200): 6.6, Ernie Davis, 1959-61

## TOUCHDOWNS

Game: 6, Jim Brown, Colgate, 1956
Season: 14, Floyd Little, 1965
Career: 35, Floyd Little, 1964-66

## AVERAGE YARDS PER GAME

Season: 124.7, Joe Morris, 1979
Career: 113.1, Joe Morris, 1978-81

## LONGEST RUSH

95, George Davis, Fordham, 1949

## PASSING YARDS, GAME

| | | | |
|---|---|---|---|
| 1. | 425 | Marvin Graves vs. Rutgers | 1992 |
| 2. | 361 | Marvin Graves vs. Cincinnati | 1993 |
| 3. | 336 | Don McPherson vs. Penn State | 1987 |
| 4. | 334 | Kevin Mason vs. Temple | 1994 |
| 5. | 329 | Bill Hurley vs. Penn State | 1977 |
| | 329 | Marvin Graves vs. East Carolina | 1993 |
| 7. | 318 | Marvin Graves vs. Pittsburgh | 1993 |
| 8. | 309 | Marvin Graves vs. Ohio State | 1991 |
| 9. | 308 | Donovan McNabb vs. W. Va. | 1995 |
| 10. | 295 | Marvin Graves vs. East Carolina | 1991 |

## PASSING YARDS, SEASON

| | | | |
|---|---|---|---|
| 1. | 2547 | Marvin Graves | 1993 |
| 2. | 2341 | Don McPherson | 1987 |
| 3. | 2296 | Marvin Graves | 1992 |
| 4. | 2076 | Todd Philcox | 1988 |
| 5. | 1991 | Donovan McNabb | 1995 |
| 6. | 1912 | Marvin Graves | 1991 |
| 7. | 1827 | Don McPherson | 1986 |
| 8. | 1711 | Marvin Graves | 1990 |
| 9. | 1627 | Kevin Mason | 1994 |
| 10. | 1625 | Bill Scharr | 1989 |

## PASSING YARDS, CAREER

| | | | |
|---|---|---|---|
| 1. | 8466 | Marvin Graves | 1990-93 |
| 2. | 5812 | Don McPherson | 1983-87 |
| 3. | 3398 | Bill Hurley | 1975-79 |
| 4. | 2661 | Todd Norley | 1982-85 |
| 5. | 2617 | Bernie Custis | 1948-50 |
| 6. | 2593 | Dave Warner | 1978-81 |
| 7. | 2116 | Pat Stark | 1951-53 |
| 8. | 2105 | Todd Philcox | 1985-88 |
| 9. | 1991 | Donovan McNabb | 1995- |
| 10. | 1989 | Rick Cassata | 1965-67 |

## PASS ATTEMPTS

Game: 44, Marvin Graves, Cincinnati, 1993
Season: 280, Marvin Graves, 1993
Career: 943, Marvin Graves, 1990-93

## PASS COMPLETIONS

Game: 24, Marvin Graves, Cincinnati, 1993
Season: 171, Marvin Graves, 1993
Career: 563, Marvin Graves, 1990-93

## PASS COMPLETION PERCENTAGE

Game (min. 10 att.): .909, Don McPherson, Colgate, 1987
Season (min. 100 att.): .633, Bill Scharr 1989
Career (min. 250 att.): .597, Marvin Graves, 1990-93

## PASSING EFFICIENCY

Season (min. 100 att.): 164.3, Don McPherson, 1987
Career (min. 250 att.): 142.5, Marvin Graves, 1990-93

## YARDS PER PASS ATTEMPT

Game: 22.2, Don McPherson, Colgate, 1987
Season: 10.2, Don McPherson, 1987
Career: 9.0, Marvin Graves, 1990-93

## YARDS PER PASS COMPLETION

Game (min. 6 comp.): 30.5, Bernie Custis, Lafayette, 1949
Season (min. 50 comp.): 18.1, Don McPherson, 1987
Career (min. 125 comp.) 15.8, Don McPherson, 1983-87

## TOUCHDOWNS

Game: 4, Pat Stark, Fordham, 1952; Jim Del Gaizo, Maryland, 1966; Don McPherson, Colgate, 1987; Todd Philcox, Rutgers, 1988; Bill Scharr, Rutgers, 1989
Season: 22, Don McPherson, 1987
Career: 48, Marvin Graves, 1990-93

## INTERCEPTIONS THROWN

Game: 5, Todd Norley, Penn State, 1982
Season: 16, Dave Warner, 1980
Career: 45, Marvin Graves, 1990-93

## AVERAGE YARDS PER GAME

Season: 231.5, Marvin Graves, 1993
Career: 196.9, Marvin Graves, 1990-93

## LONGEST PASSING PLAY

96, Marvin Harrison from Donovan McNabb (West Virginia, 1995)

## RECEPTIONS

Game: 14, Art Monk, Navy, 1977
Season: 56, Shelby Hill, 1993; Marvin Harrison, 1995
Career: 139, Scott Schwedes, 1983-86; Shelby Hill, 1990-93

## RECEIVING YARDS, GAME

| | | | |
|---|---|---|---|
| 1. | 249 | Scott Schwedes vs. Boston College | 1985 |
| 2. | 213 | Marvin Harrison vs. W. Virginia | 1995 |
| 3. | 193 | Tommy Kane vs. Colgate | 1987 |
| 4. | 191 | Marvin Harrison vs. Temple | 1994 |
| 5. | 188 | Art Monk vs. Navy | 1977 |
| 6. | 184 | Marvin Harrison vs. Minnesota | 1995 |
| 7. | 180 | Marvin Harrison vs. East Carolina | 1993 |
| 8. | 178 | Carl Karilivacz vs. Fordham | 1951 |
| 9. | 176 | Shelby Hill vs. Cincinnati | 1993 |
| 10. | 174 | Mike Siano vs. Kent State | 1985 |

## RECEIVING YARDS, SEASON

| | | | |
|---|---|---|---|
| 1. | 1131 | Marvin Harrison | 1995 |
| 2. | 1064 | Rob Moore | 1989 |
| 3. | 968 | Tommy Kane | 1987 |
| 4. | 937 | Shelby Hill | 1993 |
| 5. | 895 | Rob Carpenter | 1990 |
| 6. | 852 | Mike Siano | 1985 |
| 7. | 813 | Marvin Harrison | 1993 |
| 8. | 797 | Rob Moore | 1988 |
| 9. | 761 | Rob Carpenter | 1989 |
| | 761 | Marvin Harrison | 1994 |

## RECEIVING YARDS, CAREER

| | | | |
|---|---|---|---|
| 1. | 2728 | Marvin Harrison | 1992-95 |
| 2. | 2296 | Shelby Hill | 1990-93 |
| 3. | 2122 | Rob Moore | 1987-89 |
| 4. | 2111 | Scott Schwedes | 1983-86 |
| 5. | 1656 | Rob Carpenter | 1989-90 |
| 6. | 1644 | Art Monk | 1976-79 |
| 7. | 1574 | Mike Siano | 1982-85 |
| 8. | 1334 | Chris Gedney | 1989-92 |
| 9. | 1318 | Qadry Ismail | 1989-92 |
| 10. | 1307 | Tommy Kane | 1985-87 |

## AVERAGE YARDS PER CATCH

Game (min. 5): 31.1, Scott Schwedes, Boston College, 1985
Season (min. 20): 22.0, Tommy Kane, 1987
Career (min. 40): 20.7, Tommy Kane, 1985-87

## TOUCHDOWNS

Game: 4, Tony Gabriel, Miami, 1970; Tommy Kane, Colgate, 1987
Season: 14, Tommy Kane, 1987
Career: 22, Rob Moore, 1987-89

## AVERAGE RECEIVING YARDS PER GAME

Season: 102.8, Marvin Harrison, 1995
Career: 75.8, Rob Moore, 1987-89

## LONGEST PASS PLAY

96, Marvin Harrison from Donovan McNabb (West Virginia, 1995)

## TOTAL OFFENSE YARDS GAINED

Game: 476, Marvin Graves, Rutgers, 1992
Season: 2,696, Marvin Graves, 1993
Career: 8,755, Marvin Graves, 1990-93

## TOTAL OFFENSE PLAYS

Game: 58, Bill Hurley, Penn State, 1977
Season: 460, Don McPherson, 1986
Career: 1,377, Marvin Graves, 1990-93

## TOTAL OFFENSE AVERAGE PER PLAY

Game (min. 10): 15.2, Rich King, Richmond, 1963
Season (min. 100): 7.8, Ernie Davis, 1960
Career (min. 200): 6.8, Ernie Davis, 1959-61; Donovan McNabb, 1995-

## TOTAL OFFENSE AVERAGE PER GAME

Season: 245.1, Marvin Graves, 1993
Career: 204.7, Donovan McNabb, 1995-

## ALL-PURPOSE YARDS GAINED

Game: 300, Joe Morris, Miami, OH, 1980
Season: 1,990, Floyd Little, 1965
Career: 5,581, Joe Morris, 1978-81

## HIGHEST AVERAGE PER PUNT

Game (min. 3): 55.2, Pat O'Neill, Virginia Tech, 1993
Season (min. 30): 44.3, Pat O'Neill, 1993
Career (min. 60): 43.3, Sean Reali, 1993-

## PUNTS

Game: 12, Rich Panczyszyn, Penn State, 1968; Larry King, Pittsburgh, 1975
Season: 70, George Jakowenko, 1970
Career: 235, Jim Fox, 1983-86

## PUNTING YARDS

Game: 502, Rich Panczyszyn, Penn State, 1968
Season: 2,804, Jim Fox, 1984
Career: 9,518, Jim Fox, 1983-86

## PUNT RETURNS YARDS GAINED

Game: 172, Greg Allen, Penn State, 1969
Season: 436, Tommy Myers, 1970
Career: 876, Scott Schwedes, 1983-86

## PUNT RETURNS

Game: 9, Cliff Ensley, Navy & Holy Cross, 1968
Season: 31, Cliff Ensley, 1968; Scott Schwedes, 1986
Career: 82, Scott Schwedes, 1983-86

## AVERAGE PER PUNT RETURN

Game (min. 3): 43.0, Greg Allen, Penn State, 1969
Season (min. 18): 23.5, Floyd Little, 1965
Career (min. 25): 19.6, Floyd Little, 1964-66

## LONGEST PUNT RETURN

95, Floyd Little, Pittsburgh, 1965

## KICKOFF RETURNS YARDS GAINED

Game: 157, Dave Hodge, Navy, 1976
Season: 738, Qadry Ismail, 1989
Career: 2,290, Qadry Ismail, 1989-92

## KICKOFF RETURNS

Game: 7, Kirby Dar Dar, Miami, 1993
Season: 33, Qadry Ismail, 1989
Career: 105, Qadry Ismail, 1989-92

## AVERAGE PER KICKOFF RETURN

Game (min. 3): 46.7, Qadry Ismail, Florida State, 1991
Season (min. 15): 25.0, Qadry Ismail, 1991
Career (min. 20): 39.9, Floyd Little, 1964-66

## LONGEST KICKOFF RETURN

100, Lennie Burrell (Clarkson, 1903); Chet Bowman (William & Mary, 1923); Kirby Dar Dar (Colorado, 1992)

## POINTS SCORED

Game: 43*, Jim Brown, Colgate, 1956
Season: 114, Floyd Little, 1965
Career: 296, John Biskup, 1989-92

## TOUCHDOWNS

Game: 6, Jim Brown, Colgate, 1956
Season: 19, Floyd Little, 1965
Career: 46, Floyd Little, 1964-66

## TOUCHDOWNS RESPONSIBLE FOR

Game: 6, Jim Brown, Colgate, 1956
Season: 28, Don McPherson, 1987
Career: 65, Don McPherson, 1983-87; Marvin
    Graves, 1990-93

## FIELD GOALS MADE

Game: 5, Don McAulay, Kent State, 1983
Season: 18, Gary Anderson, 1981
Career: 57, John Biskup, 1989-92

## FIELD GOALS ATTEMPTED

Game: 6, George Jakowenko, Navy, 1970; Dave
    Jacobs, West Virginia, 1975
Season: 30, Dave Jacobs, 1975
Career: 101, Dave Jacobs, 1975-78

## LONGEST FIELD GOAL MADE

58, Dave Jacobs, Boston College, 1975

## LONGEST FIELD GOAL ATTEMPT

69, Dave Jacobs, West Virginia, 1976

## TOTAL TACKLES

Game: 42, Jim Collins, Penn State, 1979
Season: 229, Jim Collins, 1979
Career: 624, Jim Collins, 1976, 1978-80

## SOLO TACKLES

Game: 22, Jim Collins, Penn State, 1979
Season: 139, Jim Collins, 1979
Career: 389, Jim Collins, 1976, 1978-80

## ASSISTS

Game: 20, Jim Collins, Penn State, 1979
Season: 96, Tony Romano, 1982
Career: 266, Rudy Reed, 1982-85

## SACKS

Game: 4, Tim Green, Virginia Tech, 1985; Rob
    Burnett, Pittsburgh, 1987
Season: 15, Tim Green, 1984
Career: 45.5, Tim Green, 1982-85

# HONORS

## HEISMAN VOTING

1987  Don McPherson (2nd place)
      Winner — Tim Brown, Notre Dame
1967  Larry Csonka (4th place)
      Winner — Gary Beban, UCLA
1966  Floyd Little (5th place)
      Winner — Steve Spurrier, Florida
1965  Floyd Little (5th place)
      Winner — Mike Garrett, USC
1961  Ernie Davis (Winner)
1956  Jim Brown (5th place)
      Winner — Paul Hornung, Notre Dame

## NATIONAL COACH OF THE YEAR

1959  Ben Schwartzwalder*
1987  Dick MacPherson*
* consensus

## ALL-AMERICANS

(Named to at least one major first team)
1908  Marquis F. (Bill) Horr, tackle*
1915  Christopher P. Schlachter, guard
      Harold A. White, guard*
1917  Alfred R. Cobb, tackle*
1918  J.A. (Joe) Alexander, guard*
      Louis C. Usher, tackle*
1919  J.A. (Joe) Alexander, guard*
1920  J.A. (Joe) Alexander, center
      Bertrand Gulick, tackle
1923  Evander G. (Pete) MacRae, end*
1926  Victor A. Hanson, end*
1934  James Steen, tackle
1952  Robert R. Fleck, guard
1953  Robert R. Fleck, guard
1956  James N. Brown, halfback**
1958  Ronald M. Luciano, tackle
1959  Roger W. Davis, guard**
      Fred J. Mautino, end
      Robert E. Yates, tackle
1960  Ernest R. Davis, halfback*

1961  Ernest R. Davis, halfback**
1964  Patrick M. Killorin, center
      Floyd D. Little, halfback
1965  Charles E. Brown, defensive halfback
      Patrick M. Killorin, center
      Floyd D. Little, halfback
1966  Gary A. Bugenhagen, tackle
      Lawrence R. Csonka, fullback
      Floyd D. Little, halfback
1967  Lawrence R. Csonka, fullback**
1968  Anthony J. Kyasky, defensive halfback
1970  Joseph C. Ehrmann, defensive tackle
1971  Thomas P. Myers, defensive back
1975  Raymond N. Preston, linebacker
1979  J. Arthur Monk, receiver
1981  Gary Anderson, kicker
1982  Michael Charles, defensive tackle
1984  Timothy J. Green, defensive tackle
1985  Timothy J. Green, defensive tackle**
1987  Theodore Gregory, nose guard*
      Donald R. McPherson, quarterback**
1988  Markus Paul, defensive back
1990  John J. Flannery, center*
1991  Qadry R. Ismail, kick returner
1992  Christopher J. Gedney, tight end**
1995  Marvin Harrison, kick returner
      Kevin Abrams, cornerback
* consensus
** unanimous

# FOOTBALL LETTERMEN

**A** Abbott, Lafayette 1919-20; Abdo, Nicholas 1944-45-46-47; Abraham, Byron 1985-87; Abrams, Kevin R. 1994-95; Abrams, Prentice D. 1931; Acchione, Garry 1978-80; Ackley, Edward H. 1955-56; Ackley, Erie L. 1904 (Mgr.); Ackley, Willard D. 1918-19; Acocella, Angelo A. 1944-45-46-47; Adamcik, Christopher P. 1995; Adams, Kyle M. 1992-93; Adams, Raymond 1948-49; Adams, Robert B. 1894-95-96; Aebisher, Louis J. 1935; Ahern, Timothy P. 1975-77; Aikens, Lawrence M. 1928-29; Albanese, Vannie M. 1934-35-36-37; Albright, Edward M. 1953-54-55; Albstein, Arthur M. 1975-76 (Mgr.); Alexander, Joseph 1916-17-18-19-20; Alexander, Samuel W. 1952-53-54; Alford, Lynwood 1985; Alger, Doug 1944-45; Alkoff, Louis 1934; Aloise, Richard J. 1956-57; Allen, Edward B. 1965-66; Allen, Gerald T. 1982-83-84; Allen, Gregory 1969-72; Allen, Oley O. 1966-67; Allen, Philip H. 1937-38-39; Allgood, R. Lonnie 1973-74-75; Alther, Ernest 1942; Althouse, Donald H. 1952-55-56; Andelman, Edward J. 1948-49 (Mgr.); Anderson, Antonio K. 1993-94-95; Anderson, Gary 1978-79-80-81; Anderson, Harry D. 1905-08-09; Anderson, James E. 1957-58-59; Anderson, Richard F. 1956-58; Anderson, Willard 1920-21-22; Andreas, Lewis P. 1919-20; Ansley, Ernest C. 1911; Appelhof, David W. 1957-58-59; Arcade, Joseph D. 1964; Archer, David W. 1961-63-64; Archis, Lawrence J. 1975-76-77-78; Archoska, Julius 1924-25-26; Arkeilpane, Robert J. 1977-78-79-80; Armour, Sidney L. 1989-90; Armstrong, R.M. 1913; Arnold, Paul W. 1895; Ascherman, Ernest 1941; Atwater, David H. 1897-1900; Atwater, John C. ; Auld, Douglas C. 1970-71; Austin, Eugene C. 1950; Avery, George S. 1893-94-95; Avery, Robert H. 1974-75-76-77; Ayling, James A. 1910-11-12.

**B** Babbitt, Grover C. 1913; Babcock, Bruce 1978-79-80; Baccile, Nicholas J. 1956; Bachman, John H. 1923 (Mgr.); Bagley, Richard W. 1947-48-49; Bailey, Edward 1954-56; Baker, Arthur L. 1958-59-60; Baker, David L. 1957-58-60; Baker, Gerald 1938; Baldwin, Donald 1926; Balmer, Lester 1937-38-39; Bancroft, Robert N. 1967-68-69; Banger, Richard 1938-39-40; Banks, M. Beal 1905-06-07-08; Barbuti, Raymond J. 1925-26-27; Barclay, Robert J. 1969 (Mgr.); Barker, Kevin M. 1989-90-91; Barksdale, Lawrence 1963; Barlette, Robert 1972-73; Barlow, J. Brad 1985; Barnes, Christopher 1985-86-87; Barnes, Jamie 1982; Barowski, Sean M. 1989; Barradas, George 1945-46; Barry, Herbert H. 1906-08-09; Barsha, John 1916-17-18-19; Bartlett, Ronald A. 1957-58-59; Barton, Neil 1976-77; Bary, Ousmane S. 1989-90, 92; Bastable, S. Jeffrey 1968 (Mgr.); Batter, George 1924; Bauer, Kevin R. 1990; Baugher, Erie D. 1971; Bavaro, David A. 1986-87-88-89; Bayley, John M. 1924-25-26; Baylock, Victor 1935-36-37; Bayles, Eugene 1950; Baysinger, Harold W. 1927; Baysinger, Reeves S. 1921-22-23; Baysinger, Jr., Reeves S. 1944; Bazar, William 1942; Bazile, Wilky 1992-93-94; Beach, Gerald J. 1966-67-68; Beauregard, Joseph E. 1970; Bechara, Charles M. 1977-78; Beckom, Jon 1961; Bednarz, Blake K. 1986-87-88-89; Bednash, John 1985; Beehner, Kenneth 1939-40-41; Belcher, Harry B. 1904; Bell, Arthur 1946 (Mgr.); Bell, William G. 1985; Bellamy, Victor 1982-83-84; Bemiller, Albert D. 1958-59-60; Benecick, Alexander G. 1956-57-58; Benecick, William S. 1965-66; Benedict, Harry L. 1891; Bennett, James B. 1961; Benzel, Thomas F. 1962; Berger, Eugene 1939-40-41; Bergoffen, William W. 1929; Bernard, Michael E. 1988-89-90; Berner, Milford C. 1928-29-30; Berthold, Paul 1940-41-42; Bethmann, Mark 1981; Bevill, Bryce K. 1992-93-94; Beyer, Richard 1950-51-52; Bidlack, Richard A. 1967-68; Biggs, Carl S. 1923-24-25; Bill, Michael 1955-56-57; Bingham, Craig 1978-79-80-81; Bisgood, Byron T. 1909 (Mgr.); Bisik, Louis J. 1927; Biskup, John H. 1989-90-91-92; Blake, William H. ; Blatt, Dennis A. 1972-73-74; Blazek, John 1936 (Mgr.); Bletsch, Gary 1968-69-70; Blodgett, A. Burr 1937 (Mgr.); Blue, Daniel M. 1903;

Bodine, George H. 1970-71; Bogosian, Ike 1979-80-81; Bohannon, Kenneth E. 1970-71; Boland, Earl F. 1902-03; Bond, George H. 1891-93-94; Bond, Steven J. 1986; Boniti, Charles A. 1970-71-72; Bonstead, DeForest H. 1896; Borgognoni, Charles A. 1974 (Mgr.); Borton, Robert H. 1929; Bouchard, John 1944-45; Bouthiller, Fernand 1937-39; Bowers, Edward E. 1958-59; Bowman, Chester 1922-23-24; Bowman, Richard B. 1961-62-63; Boyer, David A. 1970-71; Boyer, Nathan P. 1975; Boynton, Laurence W. 1972-73; Brace, Donald B. 1961; Brandstadt, Fred E. 1958; Brane, DeForest 1902-03; Braney, Joseph P. 1915; Brannen, Gary P. 1993; Brazel, George 1960; Brennan, James G. 1975-76; Brennan, Joseph T. 1973-74; Brenneman, Neil E. 1951-52-53; Brickman, Herman 1916-17; Bright, Michael J. 1972-73-74; Brill, James N. 1954-55; Brokaw, Peter A. 1959-60-61; Brooks, David B. 1981; Brooks, E. Hawley 1915 (Mgr.); Brophy, J. Henry 1927-28-29; Brotzki, Robert 1982-83-84-85; Browchuck, Andrew 1950-51; Brown, Alban S. 1987-88-89; Brown, Ancil D. 1900-01-02; Brown, Sr., C.C. 1894; Brown, Charles E. 1963-64-65; Brown, Edward J. 1912; Brown, Ernest D. 1991-92-93; Brown, G. Edwin 1915-16-17; Brown, George D. 1946-47-48-49; Brown, James 1934-35-36; Brown, James N. 1954-55-56; Brown, Jerry 1947; Brown, John C. 1959-60-61; Brown, Matthew 1915-16-17; Brown, Michael A. 1995; Brown, Raymond 1938 (Mgr.); Brown, William 1955-56; Brown, William R. 1974-75-76; Bruckner, Nick 1982; Bruett, James M. 1936-37-38; Brunner, Raymond A. 1938 (Mgr.); Bryant, Christopher 1994; Bucci, Michael J. 1992; Bucey, Daniel H. 1987-88-89; Buchsbaum, Lee M. 1944-47-48-49; Buchwald, Clarence 1935-36; Bugenhagen, Gary A. 1965-66; Bulicz, John J. 1966-67-68; Bull, Charles J. 1992; Bullard, Donald A. 1965-66-67; Bullock, William 1942; Burch, Earl G. 1891; Burke, Edwin 1938-39; Burlingame, Menzo 1889; Burnell, Brian 1978; Burnett, Robert B. 1987-88-89; Burns, Bernard M. 1914-15; Burns, Mark C. 1977 (Mgr.); Burrell, Lennius O. 1903-04; Burrett, Adelbert P. 1927 (Mgr.); Burton, Robert E. 1907; Busch, George P. 1919; Buskirk, Jeffrey G. 1985-86-87-88; Butkus, Edward A. 1933-34; Butler, Michael R. 1995; Butzke, Herbert 1980-81-82; Butler, Clement 1954 (Mgr.); Byrne, Charles V. 1898-99.

**C** Cadigan, Robert E. 1905-06-07-08; Caldwell, Jr., Joseph J. 1924 (Mgr.); Cameron, John 1976-77-78-79; Camp, Samuel H. 1909-10-11-12; Campoleito, Leonard J. 1970-71; Canale, Leo P. 1939-40-41; Cann, Alan B. 1955-56; Cannon, Edward J. 1901-02; Capachione, John D. 1991; Cappadona, Joseph T. 1952-53-54; Caramanna, Pasquale J. 1959; Carey, III, John A. 1988; Carges, Roger C. 1990; Carley, Leon A. 1891 (Mgr.); Carlin, Jawood E. 1977; Carlson, Arne 1944; Carlson, Lyle S. 1953-55; Carpenter, Robert G. 1989-90; Carr, Harlan B. 1924-25-26; Carr, Lewis S. 1900; Carroll, Charles A. 1928; Carroll, Robert 1945; Carpentieri, Russ 1982; Carter, Charles A. 1975-76; Carter, Rodney 1982-83-84; Caruso, Joseph A. 1977-79; Cashman, Jerome F. 1954-55-56; Casmay, David E. 1965-66-67; Cassata, James R. 1965-66-67; Castle, John F. 1949; Castle, Lewis S. 1911-12-13; Castner, Lee C. 1968; Caswell, Frederick M. 1891; Chalk, Martin J. 1981-83-84; Champlin, Ernest G. ; Chapman, Kenneth 1941; Chapman, Preston G. 1905; Charles, Michael 1979-80-81-82; Cheney, Stephen 1938 (Mgr.); Chenoweth, Eric P. 1992-93-94; Cherundolo, John C. 1967-68-69; Cheyunski, James M. 1964-65-67; Chiari, Gerald 1967; Chlebeck, Michael C. 1968-69-70; Cholakis, Leon 1959-60-62; Chomyszak, Steven 1965; Christmas, William 1945; Christodulu, Gregory 1982-83; Chulada, Charles 1970-71-72; Chupaila, James W. 1967; Church, Hiram 1889; Ciervo, Daniel A. 1956-57; Cirillo, Ted 1981-82; Clark, Frank D. 1904; Clark, John M. 1908-09; Clark, Willis 1924-25-26; Clarke, Bradlee F. 1963-64; Clarke, Kenneth M. 1975-76-77; Clash, Harwood G.

1920-21; Cobb, Alfred R. 1915-16-17; Cobb, D. Raymond 1891; Cody, Bennett 1933-34; Cody, George F. 1949; Coffin, Edward T. 1956-57; Coghill, William J. 1967-70-71; Cogswell, Jack D. 1932; Cohen, Leon H. 1949-50; Cohen, Marvin 1944-45; Colceri, John 1950-51; Cole, George 1944; Colino, Peter 1963; Collins, James B. 1976-78-79-80; Collins, Wentworth B. 1914 (Mgr.); Colliver, Robert S. 1955-56 (Mgr.); Colvin, Paul 1975-76-77; Congdon, Fayette K. 1892; Congdon, John 1938-39-40; Conley, Danny L. 1990-91-92-94; Connolly, Robert A. 1977; Connor, Gregory J. 1967; Connor, John T. 1935 (Mgr.); Connors, Michael 1979; Conover, Frank J. 1988-89-90; Conron, Robert 1944; Consentino, Rudolph 1944; Constantine, Irving 1928-29; Conti, Edward P. 1962-63; Conway, John ; Cook, Charles F. 1925-26; Cook, Samuel H. ; Coon, Albert C. 1900 (Mgr.); Cooper, George 1935 (Mgr.); Cooper, Walter J. 1900; Cordisco, Ralph 1940-41; Cornish, Lorenzo D. 1900-01 (Mgr.); Cornwell, Ruland 1922 (Mgr.); Coslett, Mark A. 1975; Costello, Henry D. 1896-98-1900; Costello, William J. 1900; Cottrell, Dana R. 1993-94-95; Coughlin, Thomas 1965-66-67; Coulter, James A. 1905; Coulter, J.F. ; Coulter, J. Harvey ; Coulter, Stanley 1904; Coupe, Dennis A. 1970-71; Courtney, Gerald 1939-40-41; Covington, Jaime 1981-82-83-84; Cowell, Robert 1920; Cramer, Arthur R. 1929-30-31; Crane, Harley J. 1895-96-97; Crawford, William J.D. 1903; Cregg, Edward W. 1892-93-94-95; Cregg, Frank J. 1896-98-1900; Cregg, William F. 1894; Cripps, James E. 1962-63-64; Cross, Sr., Ladette R. ; Csonka, Lawrence R. 1965-66-67; Culver, Frank Z. 1920-21-22; Cumings, Orville E. 1906 (Mgr.); Cummings, C. DeForest 1898-99-1900-01; Cummings, James 1972; Cummings, James A. ; Cunningham, Charles 1924; Cunningham, J. Hart 1892; Cuony, Edward R. 1936; Curcuru, Joseph 1942; Curtis, C.E. 1904; Curtis, Harry A. 1903-04; Custis, Bernard E. 1948-49-50; Czekala, Adolph 1942.

**D** Dailey, John E. 1964; Dalrymple, Melvin I. 1972-73; Damon, Albert H. 1943 (Mgr.); Daniels, James E. 1972; Daniels, Wesley 1944 (Mgr.); Danigelis, Dean 1956-57-58; Danish, Jeffrey 1995; D'Antino, Angelo 1935; Darby, Jr., Samuel E. 1912; Darby, Walter A. 1908-09-10; Dar Dar, Kirby D. 1991-92-93-94; DaRin, James A. 1976; Darius, Donovin 1994-95; Darr, Richard L. 1955; Daugherty, Hugh H. 1937-38-39; Davis, Arthur E. 1900; Davis, Ernest R. 1959-60-61; Davis, George W. 1946-47-48-49; Davis, Patrick C. 1985-86-87-88; Davis, Roger W. 1957-58-59; Day, John L. 1911; DeBottis, David L. 1964 (Mgr.); Dees, Andrew W. 1988-89-90-91; DeFillip, Anthony W. ; DeFuria, Charles 1936-37; DeFuria, Edward 1932; DeLaCruz, Nelson 1991 (Mgr.); Delaney, Fred T. 1900-01; Delikat, Walter J. 1972-73; Delmonico, E. Joseph 1924; DeMaris, F.A. 1894-95; DeMoe, Joseph 1915; Dempster, Clarence B. 1903-04; Dempsey, James P. 1958; Denick, E.V. 1896; DeRiggi, Fred J. 1988-89; Detenback, Theodore 1935 (Mgr.); Deyermond, Jack 1938-39; Diange, Joseph 1946; Dieso, Stephen D. 1970-71-72; Dickinson, Thomas P. ; Dillon, John J. 1898-99-1900; Dillon, John P. 1942-46-47; Dino, Richard 1986; DiNunzio, Nicholas P. 1932-33-34; Distin, J. Arthur ; Dobrowolski, Edward 1950-51-52; Doherty, Gregg 1954 (Mgr.); Dolan, Edward V. 1944-45-46-47; Dolan, John A. 1905; Dolce, Stephen 1973-74; Dominic, Jr., John 1986-87; Dominik, Joseph W. 1953; Donati, John 1949-51; Donoghue, James 1973-74-75; Dooley, John M. 1918-19; Dorr, Carl E. 1897-98-99; Dorr, Donald H. 1967-68-69; Doubleday, Alan 1939; Dougherty, Terrence 1987-88; Douglass, Charles W. 1889-90-91; Dove, Wesley 1985-86; Downing, Keith 1995; Dragotta, Jr., James V. 1946-47-48-49; Drummond, Robert C. 1985-86-87-88; Dryden, William F. 1978-79-80; Dubey, Rick 1990 (Mgr.); Duckett, Nathaniel H. 1962-63-64; Dudley, John H. 1907-08; Dudley, Richard S. 1937-38-39; Dumoe, Joseph M. 1915; Dunlap, Samuel 1942; Dunlop, George B. 1930 (Mgr.); Dunn, Roderick ; During, William J. 1967; Durston, Edward 1897; Dutterer, Marlan I. 1963; Dye, Lester H. 1939-40-41; Dziekonski, Joseph A. 1964-65.

**E** Easter, Kylia 1992 (Mgr.); Easterly, Richard B. 1959-60-61; Eastwood, Robert 1983; Echert, Joseph 1974; Edsall, Randy 1979; Ehde, Mark R. 1982; Ehrmann, Joseph C. 1969-70-72; Ellert, George A. 1929-30-31; Elliott, David 1973 (Mgr.); Elliott, Harris A. 1963-64-65; Ellis, Jr., Lawrence R. 1942-46-47; Ellsworth, Cyrus J. 1993-94-95; Endieven, Anthony 1960; Engelhaupt, James N. 1968; Engren, George M. ; Ensley, Clifford J. 1966-67-68; Erbe, Warren 1946; Erickson, Daniel R. 1990; Erickson, Douglas 1949-50-51; Ericson, Kenneth B. 1959-60-61; Erwig, William 1918-19; Eschenfelder, William 1938-39-40; Esmond, Burton D. 1891-92; Evans, John F. 1931 (Mgr.); Evans, Nile R. 1969; Everett, Julius 1892; Everling, Gerald A. 1962-63-64; Ewald, Peter 1983-84-85-86.

**F** Fabian, Douglas B. 1973; Fabrizi, Kevin 1985; Faigle, Eric P. 1961 (Mgr.); Fair, George W. 1963-64-65; Fallon, Gary R. 1959-60-61; Fallon, Michael W. 1919-20; Fanton, William M. 1890-91; Farber, William J. 1912-13-14; Farmer, Ralph C. ; Farneski, David M. 1977; Farneski, Ronald V. 1976-77-78; Farnham, John H. ; Farrington, Harry W. 1905; Farrington, R.C. ; Faville, M. Roy 1899-1900; Federchuck, Robert A. 1957; Feehery, Gerald 1979-80-81-82; Feidler, Richard I. 1959-60-61; Feldman, David 1931; Feldman, Michael R. 1980-81; Fellows, Driscoll H. 1939-40-41; Ferrell, Kerry S. 1991-92; Ferri, Robert 1945; Ferris, Jesse L. 1928-29-30; Fetherolf, Brian G 1985-86-87-88; Fetterly, Kyle 1978 (Mgr.); Fiacco, Anthony 1949-50-51; Fiacco, James J. 1946-47-48; Finnegan, Dennis P. 1970-71; Finsterwald, Russell W. 1916-17; Fischer, Jeffrey L. 1979-80; Fish, Stephen 1978 (Mgr.); Fishel, Richard W. 1930-31-32; Fisher, Raymond M. 1910; Fisher, W. Claude 1905-06-07-08; Fitzgerald, William P. 1961; Fitzgibbons, Dennis M. 1965-66-67; Fivaz, William F. 1922-23-24; Flaherty, Todd D. 1969; Flanagan, Donald F. 1924-26; Flannery, J. Gordon 1916-17; Flannery, John J. 1987-88-89-90; Fleck, Robert R. 1951-52-53 ; Flournory, Henry 1987; Fogarty, Daniel C. 1956-57-58; Fogg, Preston D. 1909-10-11; Foley, James E. 1923-24-25; Foley, James R. 1947-48-49; Fornal, Charles 1946; Forsyth, Charles B. 1913-14; Foster, Fred F. 1920-21; Fox, Edwin 1941-42; Fox, James 1983-84-85-86; Francovitch, George M. 1959-60-61; Frank, Harry A. 1929-30-31; Frase, Paul 1984-85-86-87; Frawley, Joseph 1927; Fredericks, Gary J. 1967; Frederickson, Derek 1980-81-82; Freeney, R. Scott 1993-94-95; Frey, Frederick K. 1936; Friberg, Keith P. 1985-86-87-88; Friedman, Monroe 1933 (Mgr.); Friedman, Myles S. 1924-25-26; Frugone, James 1920-21-22; Frye, James A. 1910; Fuller, Jr., Robert A. 1988; Fusco, Andrew L. 1967-68-69; Fyfe, Charles W. 1980.

**G** Gabriel, Anthony P. 1968-69-70; Gabriel, Arthur 1939 (Mgr.); Gadson, Roderic 1994-95; Galaska, Chester 1944; Gardiner, Cooper S. 1985-87-88; Gardner, A.A. 1909; Gardner, Peter M. 1966; Garrett, John 1985-86-87; Garrity, Shawn 1986; Garvey, James 1938-39; Gaskins, James 1960-62-63; Gates, Gordon 1951; Gaughan, James 1986-87-88; Gayden, Jr., Harold 1982-83-84-86; Gazillo, Paul W. 1968; Gedney, Christopher J. 1989-90-91-92 ; Gendell, Richard B. ; George, James E. 1951-52-53; George, Peter P. 1949-50; George, Thomas C. 1946; Gerlick, Albert J. 1957-58-59; Giambatista, Nicholas 1942; Giardi, Augustine 1961-62-63; Gibbs, Stan K. 1995; Gibeley, Allen 1991 (Mgr.); Giewont, Lawrence M. 1970; Giffune, Frank P. 1973; Gilburg, Thomas D. 1958-59-60; Gilligan, Jack 1981-82; Gilmore, Eugene W. 1915; Ginter, Louis 1932-33-34; Gissinger, III, Andrew 1977-78-79-80; Glass, Edgar T. 1898-99; Glass, Joseph 1897; Glass, Walter L. 1915; Glickman, Martin 1936-37-38; Glover, Deval L. 1987-88; Godbolt, John M. 1968-69; Godfrey, Otis W. 1958-59-60; Goldman, Jonah 1926; Goldstein, Larry J. 1974; Goodman, Howard E. 1970-71; Goodrich, E. Fargo 1930 (Mgr.); Goodwill, James B. 1976-77-78-80; Goodwin, Clarence N. 1891-93 (Mgr.); Goodwin, Clinton E. 1897-98-99-1900; Gorecki, John 1935-36-37; Gorzalski, James 1982-83-84; Gould,

Spencer 1943 (Mgr.); Gouseff, Alexander 1966; Grabosky, H. Eugene 1959; Grader, George 1933; Graham, William H. 1929 (Mgr.); Grainge, Clarence R. 1922; Gramlich, Jr., J.E. 1933; Grant, Ulysses G. 1893-94-95 ; Graves, Marvin P. 1990-91-92-93; Graziano, Louis R. 1977; Greco, Matthew D. 1989-90-91-92; Green, Timothy J. 1982-83-84-85; Greene, Floyd S. 1948-49; Greene, George 1946; Greene, Kevin D. 1989-90; Greene, Kevin J. 1988; Greer, Alain 1987; Grefe, Frederick E. 1934 (Mgr.); Gregory, Theodore 1984-85-86-87; Greibus, Vito 1949-50-51; Griffin, Robin L. 1970-71; Griffith, C.B. 1904 (Mgr.); Griffith, John T. 1936; Grimes, Roland 1983-84-85; Groatt, George G. 1891; Gromniak, David 1984; Gronkowski, Gordon D. 1977-80-81; Groppe, Robert 1986-87 (Mgr.); Gross, Robert W. 1992; Grossman, Daniel 1944-45; Grosvenor, J. Robert 1991-92-93; Grubbs, James E. 1975; Grzibowski, Joseph K. 1947-48-49; Gubitosa, Louis 1967-68-70; Gugino, Frank J. 1927; Gulde, Russell M. 1916-17-19-20; Gulick, Bertrand L. 1918-19-20-21; Gutzman, Albert F. 1931; Gyetvay, Michael D. 1977-78-81.

**H** Habel, Eric W. 1977 (Mgr.); Hackett, Marcus 1980-82-83; Hadjis, Constantine 1951-52-53; Hagerty, Francis J. 1979; Haight, Clifford L. 1905 (Mgr.); Haley, Charles T. 1935; Hall, Jerome 1984-85; Halsey, William Mcd. 1898-99-1900-01; Hambleton, Brian E. 1971-72-73; Hamblin, Frank M. 1891; Hamilton, John A. 1889-90; Hamilton, Lloyd A. ; Hand, Christopher 1980-81-82; Handler, Alvin 1936-37-38; Hanners, George W. 1903; Hannigan, Hugh J. 1916 (Mgr.); Hanson, Scott R. 1992; Hanson, Victor 1924-25-26; Hares, George S.G. 1905; Harmon, John C. 1963; Harned, Harry ; Harrell, Wm. Alexander 1940; Harris, Kenneth M. ; Harrison, Marvin D. 1992-93-94-95; Harshbarger, Hubert 1952; Hart, John 1907; Hart, Robert B. 1958-59-60; Hartman, Dennis J. 1977-78-79-80; Hartman, Harry H. 1908-09-10; Hartwood, John ; Harwood, Oliver K. 1903-04-05-06; Harvey, Warren S. 1976-77-78-79; Haskins, Jr., William 1949-50-51; Hastings, George 1905 (Mgr.); Hatalsky, Lawrence 1971; Haviland, Clarence F. 1894-95; Hawkins, DeShawn A. 1976-77; Hawkins, Garland A. 1989-90-91-92; Hawkins, Kenneth J. 1989-91; Hazelton, Robert ; Hazzan, Anthony A. 1978-79-80-81; Heald, Robert 1939-40-41; Healey, Daniel 1966; Healey, Harvey J. 1954-55; Heater, William 1937-38-39; Heath, Bruce E. 1966; Heck, Charles A. 1959-60; Heck, Charles C. 1925; Hedgepeth, Bernard 1982-83; Hedges, Charles W. 1923; Heer, Charles 1937-38; Heers, Erwin A. 1920-21-22; Heffernan, Brian 1981; Helmstetter, Eliga E. 1912 (Mgr.); Hemingway, Stanton 1934-35-36; Hemsley, Nathaniel R. 1993-94-95; Henderson, Harvey N. 1899-1900-01-02; Henehan, John J. 1974; Henningsen, Peter L. 1959-60; Hensley, Gordon H. 1948-49-50; Henward, Howard B. 1928-29; Herbert, Harry 1920-21; Herlan, J. Scott 1967; Herlihy, John P. 1947-48-49; Hermanowski, Thomas A. 1967-68-69; Hershey, Gerald C. 1956-57-58; Hess, Linwood F. 1974-75; Hickenberry, R.N. 1899; Hilfinger, Martin F 1911-12-13; Hilfinger, Rober 1944; Hill, Shelby J. 1990-91-92-93; Hill, William 1985; Hilliard, L. Frederick 1959; Hillyer, J. Blake 1889-90; Hinkey, Benjamin 1908; Hinkle, Jack 1937-38-39; Hinton, Cedric S. 1978-79-80; Hnat, Robert J. 1961-62-63; Hoag, Bruce 1957-58-59 (Mgr.); Hobby, Ron 1981-82-83-84; Hobson, Edward A. 1992-93-94; Hocevar, Howard A. 1970; Hodge, W. David 1976; Hodge, William B. 1889-90; Hodges, G. Joseph 1978-79; Hodgin, Rush 1988; Hoffman, Mark 1952; Hoffman, William T. 1937-38-39; Hoffower, Paul M. 1957; Holmes, David R. 1985-87-88; Hollis, John 1928-29-30; Holman, Theodore W. 1946; Holzworth, John 1953 (Mgr.); Hooper, George 1937-38-39; Hoople, Howard C. 1916-17-18-19-20; Hoople, Theodore 1946; Hoornbeck, Christopher R. 1971-72; Hopkins, Eugene 1939-40; Hopkins, L. Jeffrey 1971-72; Hordines, John 1932-33; Horr, Marquis F. (Bill) 1905-06-07-08; Houle, Paul G. 1962-63-64; Houseknecht, Clarence 1905; Howard, Brian 1960-61-62; Howell, John

T. 1960; Hoyt, Chester J. 1889-90; Hoyt, Gordon W. 1889-90; Hueber, Brian V. 1916-17; Hueber, Joseph L. 1921 (Mgr.); Huettner, Henry J. 1961-62-63; Humphreys, John H. 1961-62-63; Hunter, G. William 1962-63-64; Hurley, Jr., William J. 1975-76-77-79; Hustis, Jefferds 1944-45; Huycke, Harold D. 1915.

**I** Iannicello, Louis 1956; Ingraham, Edgar B. 1911 (Mgr.); Ingram, Christopher B. 1985-86-87-88; Ishman, Brian K. 1976-78-79; Ismail, Qadry R. 1989-90-91-92; Isseks, Abram 1934-35-36.

**J** Jackson, Chester 1928; Jackson, Ernest E. 1957-58; Jackson, Ion A. 1892-93; Jackson, Karlos D. 1991 & 93; Jackson, Richard E. 1955; Jackson, Zachary N. 1975; Jacobs, David J. 1975-76-77-78; Jagiello, Kenneth 1982; Jajuga, Walter M. 1964-66; Jakowenko, George 1968-69-70; James, William 1974; Jamieson, John A. 1935-36-37; Januszkiewicz, Martin W. 1970-71-72; Jappe, Paul E. 1921-22-23; Jarosz, Raymond J. 1969-70-71; Jarzynski, Gregory 1983; Jaso, Michael 1950-52; Jenkins, Carl 1986; Jenkins, James 1974; Jenkins, Kenneth 1986; Jerome, James L. 1973-74-75; Jewell, Charles J. 1894-95-96; Jilleba, Christopher 1979-80; Johnson, Antonio D. 1991-92; Johnson, Carl S. 1940; Johnson, David L. 1968; Johnson, Louis I. 1913-14; Johnson, Murray W. 1966; Johnson, R. Sherwood 1932-33-34; Johnson, Robert 1995; Johnson, Rodney R. 1990; Johnson, Samuel G. 1951-52-53; Johnson, Stanley E. 1938; Johnson, Theodore R. 1914-15; Johnston, Daryl P. 1985-86-87-88; Joline, Jr., Ralph P. 1980-81-82; Jones, E. Raymond 1925-26; Jones, Jack C. 1966-67; Jones, Lawrence J. 1963; Jones, Marvin L. 1974-75-76-77; Jones, Michael L. 1975-76-77-78; Jones, R. Antonio 1991-92-93-94; Jones, Tebuckey S. 1995; Jontos, Edward S. 1933-35; Jordon, Allan L. 1892-93; Joseph, Dwayne 1990-91-92-93; Joslin, Steven J. 1970-71-73; Josselyn, Baxter S. 1948-49; Joy, Louis F. 1891; Justice, James 1973.

**K** Kallet, A. Harry 1909-10-11; Kaminski, David 1981-83-84; Kane, Edward T. 1935-37; Kane, John F. 1936; Kane, Thomas 1985-86-87; Kanya, Albert J. 1928-29-30; Karcich, Anthony 1968; Karilivacz, Carl 1950-51-52; Kartalian, George 1951; Kasmer, Todd A. 1991. Kaufmann, Peter 1981-82; Keiffer, Edward 1958; Kellogg, William 1920-21-22; Kelly, Patrick 1986-87; Kennedy, Francis A. 1931-32; Kerchman, John 1942-46; Kernaklian, Paul 1952-53-54; Kernan, James J. 1974; Kessler, George W. 1892-93; Kiernan, Scott 1995; Kiles, James J. 1974; Killorin, Patrick M. 1963-64-65; Kilpatrick, Gerald 1978-79-80-81; Kimmel, James L. 1980-82-83-84; Kimmel, Jerry M. 1982-83-84-85; King, Bernard 1882-83-84; King, David A. 1970-71-72; King, David T. 1972-73; King, Donald A. 1960-61-62; King, Larry E. 1974-75-76-77; King, Richard K. 1962-63-64; Kingsley, Grover C. 1913-14; Kinley, John W. 1977-78-79; Kinner, Hiram L. 1894-95; Kinney, Thomas J. 1939-40-41; Kinnon, Duane D. 1988-89-90; Kinsey, Kenneth J. 1973-74; Kirouac, Charles A. 1976-77-79; Kirkpatrick, W.D. 1909; Kish, Nicholas W. 1965-66; Kittle, Walter 1944; Kiviat, Jack 1956; Kleinback, Dennis K. 1967-69; Kmetz, Michael 1984-85-86; Knapp, A. Blair 1925 (Mgr.); Knauff, Jeffrey 1984; Knox, William T. 1968; Kobakof, Kosta 1974; Koban, Edward G. 1980-81-82-83; Kokinis, George J. 1970; Kokosky, Richard 1968-69-70; Koleser, Robert B. 1949-50-51; Kollar, Kenneth J. 1977-78-79-80; Konrad, Robert 1995; Kontrabecki, George A. 1965; Kopp, Hyman 1927; Korch, Michael G. 1931-32; Kornbluth, Arthur 1931 (Mgr.); Kosanovich, Peter 1966; Koski, Michael A. 1962-63-65; Kotz, Harold ; Kranack, Peter 1947-48-49; Krivak, Joseph J. 1954-55-56; Krok, John T. 1964-65-66; Krout, Charles W. 1936; Kruse, Russell M. 1969; Kubilius, Theodore J. 1947-48-49; Kuczala, Ferdinand A. 1955-56-57; Kuhns, Marshall 1973; Kukowski, Theodore 1953; Kyasky, Anthony J. 1966-67-68.

**L** Laaksonen, Donald C. 1953-54-55; LaBarge, Howard 1936; Laffey, James T. 1961; Lachowicz, Theodore A. 1969-70-71; Lake, Rush W. 1894-95-96; Lally, John

1979-80-81; Lamey, James 1959-60; Lane, Joseph T. 1902-03; Lang, Fred J. 1978-79; Langenheim, Scott P. 1992; Lapham, David A. 1971-72-73; Lapinski, David J. 1989-90; LaPorta, Luke 1945; Laputka, David R. 1972-73; Larkin, E.M. 1907; Lasse, Richard S. 1955-56-57; Lawrence, Gregory D. 1973-75; LeBaron, Brian P. 1989-90; Leberman, Robert W. 1952-53; Ledger, James R. 1994-95; Lee, Jr., Charles A. 1924-25-26; Lee, Marcus A. 1991-92-93; Lee, W. David 1982-83-84-85; Lehr, Thomas 1949-50-51; Leible, James 1985-86; Lelli, Robert L. 1961-62; LeMessurier, James T. 1966-67; Lemieux, Norman C. 1959-60; Leonik, Stanley P. 1956; Lessard, Peter 1950-51-52; Levay, Sidney 1924; Levy, Harvey S. 1924-25-26; Lewis, Grant W. 1927-28-29; Light, Charles W. 1965-66; Lipes, Myron D. 1897; Little, Floyd D. 1964-65-66; Livshin, Norman 1916-17; Lloyd, Richard 1928 (Mgr.); Lobon, John 1971; Lombardi, Thomas A. 1930-31-32; Lombel, Karl A. 1970-71; Longauer, Earl J. 1964; Longley, James G. 1971-72-73; Loomis, Leigh ; Loskamp, Alvin ; Loucks, Glenn D. 1928-29; Lowry, Raymond D. 1889-90-91; Lowther, Edgar A. 1901; Luciano, Ronald M. 1956-57-58; Lucier, H. John 1919; Ludington, George W. 1912; Lundberg, Arthur H. 1922; Lupo, William 1949-50-51; Lurie, Arnold D. 1947; Lusardi, John A. 1990-91; Lynch, John 1905; Lyon, James 1904; Lyon, J. Fred 1896-97.

**M** Mabie, Roger 1939 (Mgr.); Mace, Richard L. 1948-49; Machemer, Frederick E. 1931; Machosky, Stanley 1930-31-32; MacKenzie, Donald 1918; MacKenzie, E. Hillyer 1918 (Mgr.); Mackey, John 1960-61-62; MacLean, Bruce A. 1948-49; MacLeod, Michael 1974; MacRae, Evander G. 1921-22-23; MacWilliams, John J. 1919-20 (Mgr.); Maddox, Greg Deon 1994-95; Maddox, William 1968-69; Magee, Donald D. 1973-74-75-76; Magers, Norman P. 1965; Magoon, Herbert A. 1903-04-05; Mahle, Walley W. 1962-63-64; Mahley, Gordon H. 1924; Maines, Thomas L. 1940-41-42; Maister, Michael W. 1925; Malcovic, Stephen 1936-37; Malik, Edward C. 1936; Malone, John M. 1916-17-19; Mambuca, Frank B. 1959; Mammosser, W.H. 1933-34-35; Manchester, W.B. 1896; Manderino, John 1946; Mandeville, Kenneth 1978-79-80; Manfredi, Anthony R. 1972-73; Mangram, Jeffrey A. 1985-86-87-88; Mann, Wilfred 1927; Manning, Glenn E. 1928-29; Manning, Robert 1979-81-82; Mantie, Edmund E. 1965-66-67; Mare, Olindo 1994-95; Marcellino, Brian 1984; Marchiano, John F. 1972; Marchionne, Nicholas D. 1967; Marcus, Milton 1932; Marcy, Bert L. 1903-04-05; Markowski, Adam 1937; Marone, Frank J. 1980-81; Marques, Christopher E. 1993-94-95; Marrone, Douglas 1983-84-85; Marrow, Arnold M. 1950 (Mgr.); Marsella, Nicholas J. 1973-74-75; Martin, Edward 1894-95-97; Martin, Gerald J. 1974-75-76-77; Martin, Troy D. 1990; Marvil, C. Burns 1937; Marvin, Charles W. 1889-90; Masci, Leonard V. 1970-71-72; Mason, Donald 1946; Mason, Kevin M. 1992-93-94; Massis, John J. 1967-68-69; Matteo, Francis P. 1918; Matichak, Thomas 1978-79; Matthews, David B. 1897; Mautino, Frederick J. 1958-59-60; Mautino, Louis A. 1957-60; Mazejko, Francis R. 1941; Mazurek, James L. 1961-62-63; McAndrews, James 1979-80-81; McAulay, Donald 1983-84-85; McBride, John F. 1922-23-24; McCard, David C. 1967-68-69; McCard, Howard A. 1964-65; McClelland, Lester C. 1952-53; McCollom, John 1978-79-80-81; McConnell, Arden J. 1944-46-47; McCullough, Willie J. 1976-77-78; McCummings, Gary L. 1988-89-90; McCutcheon, Otto E. 1896; McDonald, Edward T. 1974; McDonald, Mark S. 1989-90-91; McDonough, John F. 1915; McElliott, Joseph J. 1913; McGill, Clarence E. 1968-69; McGuire, John 1965; McIntosh, Kyle D. 1995; McKee, Paul 1942-46; McMickle, Levi P. 1903; McManus, Timothy J. 1972; McNabb, Donovan J. 1995; McNamara, Howard 1926; McNeeley, Michael A. 1972-73; McPhail, Charles 1939-40-41; McPherson, Donald R. 1985-86-87; Meacham, Jr., Carl D. 1940 (Mgr.); Mead, Frank L. 1890; Meehan, John F. 1915-16-17; Meehan, Robert 1962-63; Meggyesy,

David H. 1960-61-62; Meeker, Howard 1930; Meier, Fred J. 1958; Meisner, William L. 1914; Mendell, Irving 1925; Merkel, Victor E. 1944-47-48-49; Merriman, Keith N. 1974-75; Merz, Henry 1933-34; Meyer, George F. 1910; Meyers, Jr., George W. 1994-95; Meyers, William 1961; Meyers, William L. 1914; Michael, Norman 1941-42; Michaelidis, John P. 1995; Michell, Willis 1899; Micho, William G. 1958; Mickey, LeRoy ; Miller, Burr C. 1890-91; Miller, John D. 1973; Miller, Richard 1983-84; Mills, Jason A. 1995; Mills, Raymond R. 1972-73; Mingo, Thomas S. 1961-62; Minko, Michael 1958; Minsavage, Joseph 1934-35-36; Mirabito, Frederick B. 1949; Mirabito, Salvatore 1940-41-42; Mitch, Robert L. 1973-74-75; Mitchell, Kevin D. 1990-91-92-93; Mitchell, Robert 1963; Moll, William J. 1953; Monk, J. Arthur 1976-77-78-79; Montemorra, M. Anthony 1990-91; Montgomery, James A. 1940; Moody, Keith M. 1972-74-75; Mooney, Harold 1927; Moore, Daniel L. 1959; Moore, Earl K. 1901-02-03; Moore, George O. 1937; Moore, Glenn 1980-81-82; Moore, Robert S. 1987-88-89; Moore, Thomas E. 1963 (Mgr.); Moran, Joseph E. 1930-31-32; Mordue, Norman 1964; Moresco, Timothy J. 1973-74-75-76; Moretti, Anthony 1991 (Mgr.); Morgan, Dulayne 1994-95; Morgan, Henry L. 1892-93; Morgan, Robert E. 1964; Morgan, Thomas W. 1972-73-74; Morgis, Dennis 1980; Morison, Arthur 1936-37-38; Morris, Horace W. 1946-47-48-49; Morris, Joseph E. 1978-79-80-81; Morris, Larry 1982-83-84; Morris, Leland A. 1940-41-42; Morris, Michael 1982-83-84; Morris, Myron B. 1901-02; Morris, Richard C. 1958; Morris, Terry E. 1994-95; Morrissey, Kevin P. 1973; Morrow, Peter 1942-45; Morton, Richard A. 1958; Moseley, Walter 1985-86; Moses, Benjamin B. 1921-23; Moses, Michael D. 1962; Mospaw, Jeffrey G. 1968; Moss, Kevin J. 1974; Moss, King J. ; Moutenot, Christopher P. 1968-69-70; Mozur, William 1939-41; Muessig, Lewis 1945; Muhlbach, Donald L. 1975; Mulholland, William S. 1894-95; Munson, Charles T. ; Murphy, James M. 1968-69; Murphy, Richard C. 1966; Murray, Eugene W. 1894-95; Murry, James 1921; Mustard, David E. 1964-65-66 (Mgr.); Myers, George H.; Myers, Thomas P. 1969-70-71.

**N** Nance, James S. 1962-63-64; Narsavage, David 1967 (Mgr.); Nash, Phillip L. 1995; Navaroli, Michael 1981; Neary, Michael P. 1958-59; Negroni, George E. ; Nett, Joseph M. 1980-81-82; Nettelbladt, Paul R. 1965-66; Neubert, Paul 1931; Neugebauer, Gary 1978-79-80; Nevins, Marshall S. 1932-33-34; Newberry, Claude H. 1915; Newman, Laurence S. 1977-78; Newman, Jr., W.A. 1927-28; Newton, Al 1968-69; Newton, Lewis W. 1929-30-31; Nicoletti, Eugene 1970-71 (Mgr.); Nicollello, Louis 1928; Nichols, John J. 1958-59-60; Nilsen, John M. 1991; Noble, James E. 1921-23-24; Nolan, James 1934-35-36; Nolletti, Natasha 1990 (Mgr.); Norley, Todd 1982-83-84-85; Novak, Stephen J. 1959; Novek, Joseph G. 1928-29; Novotny, Harry 1935-36; Nowak, Walter 1924; Nowicki, Edwin M. 1966-67-68; Noxon, James A. ; Nussbaum, Harry E. 1947-48-49.

**O** Obst, Henry 1928-29-30; O'Connell, David J. 1914-15; O'Connell, J.H. 1891; O'Connor, Charles J. 1928; Oday, Harry A. 1894-95-96-97; O'Donnell, Charles W. 1891; O'Donnell, John H. 1905; Oehler, Philip A. ; O'Hara, Kevin 1978; O'Leary, Terrence J. 1976-77-78; Olenik, George 1953; Olson, Harold V. 1921; O'Neil, Frank H. 1902-03; O'Neil, Harry 1949; O'Neill, Patrick J. 1990-91-92-93; O'Rourke, Patrick J. 1991; Orzehoswki, Joseph 1954; Orzolek, Mark S. 1975; Osborne, Naboth 1893-94-95; Owens, Michael L. 1987-88-89; Oyer, Ronald J. 1963-64-65.

**P** Paddock, A.F. ; Paddock, Frank E. 1892-94; Page, Ronald L. 1972-73; Paglio, John 1961-62-63; Paglio, Raymond J. .1965; Palmer, Charles L. ; Palmer, Harry J. 1896-97; Paltz, Leslie A. 1924; Panczyszyn, Richard C. 1967-68-69; Paolisso, Paul L. 1968-70; Parisi, Louis A. 1977; Park, Ford R. 1905-06-07; Park, Robert 1902-03-04; Parker, Darrell 1992-93-94-95; Parker, Edward L. 1894; Parker, H. Wallace 1919-20; Parker, Otto D. 1903-

04; Parks, Christopher 1988; Parrish, Frank C. 1966-67; Parrish, Jason B. 1898-99-1900-01; Paskevich, Anthony 1938-39; Patkochis, Bradley C. 1995; Patkochis, Charles A. 1962; Patten, Haden A. 1897-98-99-1900; Patterson, Jacob T. 1927; Patterson, John 1975-76-77-78; Paul, Alexander E. 1947; Paul, Markus D. 1985-86-87-88; Peach, Stephen M. 1982; Perlstein, Maurice C. 1936-37; Peckelis, Joseph W. 1972; Pellegrini, Gerald 1942-46; Pembleton, John G. 1901; Pendock, William J. 1980-81-82-83; Penny, Kenneth E. 1928; Pennypacker, Harvey A. 1994-95; Peppel, Larry E. 1964; Pepper, M. James 1947-48-49; Percey, Robert 1942; Perkins, Charles R. 1951-52-53-54; Perkins, Francis W. ; Perkins, William 1935-36-37; Perrault, George 1933-34-35; Perrin, Walter 1918-19; Perry, Joseph 1950-51-52; Perry, William 1942; Perry, William H. 1889; Petchel, Robert G. 1972-73-74; Peters, Howard 1937; Pfeifer, Rudolph 1936-37; Phelps, Deforest F. 1902 (Mgr.); Philcox, Todd S. 1987-88; Phillips, Edward J. 1970; Phillips, Jon 1960 (Mgr.); Pickett, Robert M. 1974; Picucci, Brian J. 1991-92-93; Pidgeon, Timothy 1983-84-85-86; Pierson, Frederick T. 1892-94; Pieto, Roger A. 1962; Pietryka, Peter J. 1968; Pietruszka, Walt H. 1957; Pina, Doug 1983-85-86; Pinder, Thomas F. 1910; Piper, Charles B. 1899; Piro, Henry W. 1938-39-40; Piro, John 1945; Pirro, Thomas S. 1976; Planck, Emerson ; Planer, Charles K. 1968; Podraza, James D. 1954-55-56; Pollino, Jr., Joseph A. 1955; Pomeroy, Gay 1962 (Mgr.); Ponds, Antwaune 1994-95; Pontera, Frank L. 1976; Powell, Arthur L. 1904-05; Praetorius, Robert J. 1975-76; Praetorius, Roger H. 1970-71-72; Prather, Peter 1976-77-78; Pratt, John W. 1913 (Mgr.); Preising, Glenn A. 1956-57; Prescott, Shelton J. 1994-95; Preston, Raymond N. 1972-74-75; Pritzlaff, James 1967-68-69; Propis, Joseph 1944-45; Propst, Rudolph W. 1910-11-12-13; Protz, John M. 1968-69; Pruitt, Jonathan A. 1980-81; Pulaski, Raymond 1938-39; Purdy, Frank L. 1891; Purdy, Ross C. 1894-95; Purello, Joseph A 1947.

R Rackiewicz, Daniel C 1960; Radivoy, Joseph J. 1966; Rafferty, John E. 1973-74; Rafter, William J. 1914-15; Rahal, Nicholas 1950-51-52; Raleigh, Phillip R. 1973-74; Ralph, George T. 1980; Rammi, August W. 1919; Ramsdell, Willard R. 1962; Randolph, E.E. 1892-94; Raner, Merton H. 1962; Ransler, Nicholas 1913-14; Ransom, Richard R. 1940-41-42; Raymond, Edwin 1927-28; Raymond, James H. 1969; Reagan, John D. 1991-92-93; Reali, Sean P. 1994-95; Reardon, Edward L. 1967; Rebar, David W. 1993-94-95; Reckmack, Raymond 1934-35-36; Redington, George O. 1891; Reed, Robert J. 1935; Reed, Rudy L. 1982-83-84-85; Reed, Vincent M. 1922; Reeve, George H. 1909-10-11; Regensburger, William 1944-45; Reid, Thomas 1985; Reidpath, Charles D. 1910; Reilly, Dennis J. 1963-64 ; Reimer, Daniel S. 1950-51-52; Reimer, Richard L. 1958-59-60; Rekstis, Walter J. 1935-36-37; Remo, Roger 1985-86; Rettig, David M. 1975; Revels, Frederick W. 1892; Reynolds, C.W.P. 1905-06-07; Rhodes, Michael 1946; Rice, E.G. 1904 (Mgr.); Rice, F. Seward 1903-04; Rice, Leon A. 1906; Rich, Robert 1951-52-53-54; Richards, Frank L. 1893-94; Richardson, Ronald 1976-78; Richardson, Roy S. 1890; Richardson, Terry J. 1991-92-93; Richardson, Thomas V. 1953-54-55; Richtmeyer, Stanley 1927; Ridlon, James A. 1954-55-56; Rigan, Joseph 1938-39-40; Ringo, James 1950-51-52; Ringo, Stephen 1956; Robbins, Howard W. 1913; Roberts, Melvin 1926; Robertson, Harold J 1916-17-19-20; Robertson, Miles E. 1911-12-13; Robinson, Edmund A. 1994; Robinson, Fay N. 1899; Robinson, Mandel R. 1976-77; Robinson, Roger 1945-46; Robinson, R. Scott 1971-72; Roche, Richard G. 1982-83; Rodiek, Edmund C. 1938-39-40; Roe, Terrell F. 1964-65-66; Roesch, Joseph 1931; Rogers, Earl A. 1889; Romaner, Samuel 1930; Romano, Anthony M. 1980-81-82-83; Ronan, Donald 1951-52; Rondeau, Andrew J. 1990 (Mgr.); Rooks, George D. 1988-89-90-91; Rooney, Frank M. 1889; Rooney, Harold A. 1963-64-65; Roos, John W. 1982-83-84; Rose, Joseph J. 1956; Rose, Walter S. ; Rosella, John A. 1970-71-72; Rosen, Richard 1975-76-77;

Rosengrant, Judson 1921; Rosia, Thomas E. 1966; Ross, Joseph 1981-82; Rossetti, Carlo 1995; Rotunda, L. Michael 1978-79; Rotunno, William A. 1949 (Mgr.); Roulin, Brian L. 1972; Rouse, Sherman 1890-91; Routses, Peter S. 1966; Rubin, J. Robert 1903 (Mgr.); Ruby, Edward J. 1923; Ruccio, Jerry A. 1966-67-68; Ruff, Guy 1978-79-81; Rugg, Augustus 1923-24-25; Ruggiero, Franklin D. 1971; Ruoff, Bernd A. 1971-73-74; Russell, Henry F. 1904-05; Rust, Robert E. 1967-69; Ruth, Harold 1937-38-39; Rutherford, Austin G. 1902-03-04; Rutherford, Walter 1936; Rutstein, Robert 1915.

S St. Peter, John P. 1969; St. Victor, Jose 1974-75-76; Salerno, John F. 1962-63; Salkin, Aaron 1992 (Mgr.); Sampson, Harold R. 1901; Sandquist, Timothy M. 1988-89-90-91; Sanfilipo, Carl C. 1975; Sanford, Lloyd N. 1934; Santoli, Frank A. 1961; Sapienza, David A. 1985-87-88; Sapp, Walter J. 1971-72; Sardinia, Thomas M. 1958; Sarette, David 1959-60-61; Sauerwein, Robert 1946; Sawyer, Herman 1919; Sawyer, Kenneth L. 1971-72-73; Saylor, James E. 1959; Schade, Fred F. 1902-03-04; Scharr, William P. 1989; Scharoun, Jeremy C. 1973-74; Schena, Matt 1995; Schiffner, Robert A. 1947-48-49; Schlachter, Chris P. 1914-15; Schmidlin, Carl E. 1923; Schmidt, Eugene I. 1941-47; Schmitt, Richard 1973-74; Schoonmaker, Robert J. 1968-70; Schoonover, William 1961-62-63; Schreck, Edward A. 1965-66-67; Schultz, Andress 1915; Schwarzer, Joseph K. 1916-17-18-19; Schwedes, Gerhard H. 1957-58-59; Schwedes, Scott 1983-84-85-86; Schwert, M. Peter 1953-54-55; Scibelli, Anthony J. 1963-64-65; Scipione, John A. 1969; Sciullo, Anthony 1985; Scoba, Michael J. 1947-49; Scully, John H. 1909; Scully, Stephen J. 1973-74; Seager, Raymond H. 1961-62; Sebo, Samuel E. 1927-28-29; Seeley, Wirt D. ; Segal, Harry L. 1916-17-19; Seibert, Thomas J. 1978-79-80-81; Seiter, Gordon 1944; Seketa, John B. 1960-61; Semall, Bruce D. 1976-77; Sessler, James P. 1975-76-77; Seymour, Richard D. 1912-13-14; Shaffer, Christopher L. 1976-77-78-79; Shale, Sheldon 1935; Shallish, Harry B. 1926 (Mgr.); Sharp, Jerry A. 1991-92; Shaw, Gregory A. 1993; Shaw, Lester A. 1909; Shaw, William F. 1925; Sheedy, James 1986; Shek, William 1939-40; Shekitka, Andrew 1946; Shemin, William 1922; Sheppard, Lucian H. 1891; Shimer, Mason C. 1909; Shreve, James R. 1948-49-50; Shufelt, James V. 1913-14; Siano, Michael 1982-83-84-85; Sickles, Joseph 1978-79; Sidat-Singh, Wilmeth 1937-38; Sidey, John 1939; Sidoni, Anthony T. 1973; Sidor, Anthony J. 1978-79-80; Silvanic, George 1947-48-49; Simko, Jack 1983-84; Simmons, Edward 1946; Simmons, Sr., Roy D. 1922-23-24; Simpson, Frank H. 1907-08 (Mgr.); Simpson, Scott 1991 (Mgr.); Sims, Jr., Turnell 1987-88-89-90; Sinceno, Kaseem 1994-95; Singer, Robert 1952 (Mgr.); Singer, Milton 1932-33-34; Singer, Walter 1932-33-34; Singer, Jr., William F. 1894; Sirowich, Kenneth C. 1991; Skonieczki, Gerald W. 1957-58-59; Skop, Michael 1952-53-54; Skurka, Joseph 1948-49; Skyinskus, William 1950-51-52; Slaby, Leonard 1961-62-63; Slade, Daniel 1942; Slater, Charles A. 1914-15; Slick, Paul I. 1952-53-54; Slovenski, Walter 1946-47-48-49; Smalley, Frank M. ; Smallwood, W. Martin 1892-93-94-95; Smallwood, W.T. 1896-97-98-99; Smith, Andre 1994; Smith, Leonard W. 1970; Smith, Oliver J. 1911-12; Smith, Jr., R. Calvin 1953-54-55; Smith, Roger H. 1965-66; Smith, Thomas J. 1961; Smith, Thomas S. 1969; Smith, Walter S. ; Smith, Wilber F. 1898-99; Smith, William H. 1967-68; Smithson, William B. 1913-15; Smyrl, Charles J. 1972-73; Snider, John E. 1961-62-63; Snyder, Earle D. 1910 (Mgr.); Snyder, Eric J. 1966; Snyder, George L. 1972 (Mgr.); Sobul, Jerald B. 1961; Sofsian, Walter J. 1961-62-63; Sokol, Stanley E. 1961; Southwick, David 1951 (Mgr.); Sparks, Brian 1995; Sparfield, Lawrence J. ; Spector, Andrew E. 1964-65 (Mgr.); Spencer, James 1992; Spicer, Lewis 1944; Spillett, John J. 1973; Spillett, Thomas 1960-61; Spinney, Stephen A. 1975-76-77-78; Spitz, Russell 1978-79-80; Sposato, Ross D. 1969-71-72; Sproule, William J. 1959; Stach, Kenneth J. 1973; Stafford, Albert E. 1899-1900;

Stamelman, Louis R. 1930; Stancin, Eugene 1960-61-62; Stark, Charles G. 1931; Stark, Harry ; Stark, S. Louis 1932-33-34; Stark, Peter G. 1951-52-53; Stark, William B. 1945 (Mgr.); Starobin, Mordecai 1922-23-24; Stecker, Charles R. 1965; Stecker, Herbert W. 1964-65-66; Stedman, Murray S. ; Steele, Allen D. 1892; Steele, Clifford 1916-17-18; Steen, Gregory K. 1972-73-74; Steen, James 1932-33-34; Stefanelli, Dominick 1932; Stefanski, Gary 1978 (Mgr.); Steigler, Herbert F. 1951-52-53; Stein, Arthur H. 1905-06-07-08; Steiner, Richard P. 1970-71-72; Stem, Robert P. 1959-60-61; Stephens, Thomas 1982-83-84; Stephens, Thomas G. 1956-57-58; Stephenson, Franklin 1904; Stevens, Warren 1928-29-30; Stewart, Robert J. 1936; Stimson, James P. 1904-05-06-07; Stock, George J. 1956-57; Stoeppel, Craig S. 1985-86-87-88; Stonberg, Abraham 1929-30-31; Stone, Avatus H. 1950-51; Stout, Horace E. 1889-91; Strayer, George 1936; Striba, George 1936; Strid, Charles H. 1955-56-57; Stuhlweissenburg, Claus 1987; Sudnick, Charles 1933; Sullivan, Daniel E. 1908; Sullivan, Daniel R. 1961; Sullivan, Jeremiah H. ; Sullivan, Thomas 1944-45; Sutton, Robert F. 1972-73; Svanson, Gust G. 1966; Swarr, John L. 1937-38; Sweat, Gary L. 1971-72-73; Sweeney, Charles P. 1983; Sweeney, Walter F. 1960-61-62; Swinson, Mark A. 1988; Sydnor, Willie 1981; Szombathy, Joseph 1950-51-52.

**T** Tabor, Don 1929 (Mgr.); Tait, James 1983-84-85; Tarbox, Bruce B. 1958-59-60; Tarrant, Brian K. 1994-95; Tate, David R. 1974-75; Tate, Robert P. 1977-78; Taylor, Anthony L. 1990; Taylor, John H. 1936-37-38; Taylor, John O. 1926-27; Taylor, Lee 1941 (Mgr.); Taylor, Richard L. 1956; Telinski, S. Stephen 1948-49; Ten Eyck, Gerald ; Terry, Reginald V. 1991 & 93; Thomas, Malcolm L. 1993-94-95; Thomas, Jr., Robert W. 1958; Thomas, Willard 1937-38-39; Thompson, G. Bryant 1916-17-18-19-20; Thoms, Arthur 1966-67-68; Thomson, Robert M. 1987-88-89-90; Thornburn, A.D. 1898-99; Throckmorton, L.S. 1912; Thurlow, Thomas H. 1926 (Mgr.); Thurston, George G. ; Tice, Raymond L. 1939-40-41; Tindall, Francis G. 1931-32; Tisdale, Francis 1932-33; Titmas, Herbert J. 1928-29-30; Todd, Carroll A. 1991-92-93; Todd, James 1898; Tooke, Charles W. 1889-90; Touchton, George E. 1935-36; Towne, Richard E. 1965-66; Trapasso, Timothy L. 1976-77-78; Trask, Ronald C. 1968-70; Traver, Herman D. 1890; Travis, Leslie M. 1913-14-15; Travostino, Peter 1942 (Mgr.); Trento, Angelo 1934; Trigg, Joseph E. 1914-15; Troilo, Arthur 1952-53-54; Troup, Paul A. 1937-39; Trout, Charles W. 1921-22-23; Tsarnas, John 1945-46; Tucker, David L. 1903-04-05; Turner, Jim A. 1994-95; Tuten, Jr., Melvin A. 1992-93-94; Twaddle, Harry L. 1909; Tyger, Larry J. 1995; Tyler, Ronald G. 1954-55.

**U** Urban, Edward A. 1948-49; Urban, George J. 1947-48-49; Usher, Louis C. 1918; Uyeda, Carl 1944.

**V** Valchar, Frank J. 1958; Van Arnam, John R. 1906; Van Blarcum, Clarence 1921-22; Vanca, William 1978 (Mgr.); Van Deusen, H.S. ; Van Deusen, Edward S. 1894-95; Van Duyn, Cornelius 1904; Van Duyne, Wilber ; Van Lengen, F.W. 1894-95; Van Lengen, W.H. 1923-25; Van Ness, Albert W. 1927-28-29; Varvari, William D. 1975; Vaughan, Ernest F. 1961; Vaughn, Earl 1975-76; Vavra, Joseph A. 1932-33-34; Vergara, Albert 1951-52-53; Vergara, Anthony 1950-52; Vergara, Vincent 1950-52; Vernon, Elliott E. 1893-94-96; Vesling, Timothy 1985-86-87; Vesper, Donald 1941; Vickery, Stephen A. ; Villanti, Steve 1981-82-83-84; Vincett, Reed W. 1922; Virgilio, Lawrence A. 1965; Voegler, Nicholas 1950-52; Vogt, Gerald J. 1967-68-69; vonBischoffshausen, John 1964; Voorhees, Karl B. 1897; Voyda, Jr., Thomas J. 1974-75-76-77.

**W** Wade, Eric 1982; Waite, Dean H. 1910; Waldorf, Lynn O. 1922-23-24; Waldron, Harold R. 1909-10; Walker, Anthony Jr. 1995; Walker, David L. 1989-90-91-92; Walker, Duane L. 1968-69; Walker, Gregory E. 1988-89-90-91; Walker, Jr., Matthew C. 1982-83; Walker, William H. 1993-94; Walters, Herbert 1912; Walters,

Jason A. 1994-95; Walters, Stanley P. 1970-71; Wansack, Jr., Matthew 1932-33-34; Ward, Derek 1986-87; Warholak, Ted 1955-56; Warner, David 1979-80-81; Warren, Brent T 1995; Warren, Ulysses G. 1893-94-95; Watkins, Frederick H. 1889-90-91; Watrel, Albert A. 1948-49; Watrel, Warren E. 1956; Watson, Thomas 1985-86; Watt, Joseph 1940-41-46; Watt, Joseph C. 1964; Watts, Leon 1978; Waugh, Orlo L. 1905-06-07-08; Waxman, Michael 1962; Weaver, Leo 1941-42; Weber, Mark A. 1958-59-60; Weber, Richard 1940-41-42; Webster, Parker 1935-36-37; Webster, Steven E. 1972-73; Weeks, Harry G. 1900-01-02; Weir, Dennis J. 1962; Weisenburger, Gregg M. 1988; Weiss, John 1944; Welch, Darren 1975-76-77-78; Welch, Robert B. 1950; Wells, Donald E. 1974-75-76-77; Wentworth, James M. 1988-89-90-91; Werner, Howard 1942; Werth, John 1983; Wetzel, William A. 1952-53-54; Whitaker, Spencer J. 1913; Whitcomb, Frank E. 1920; White, George H. 1891-94; White, Harold A. 1913-14-15-16; White, John 1979; White, Raymond C. 1968-69-70; Whiteman, Sean R. 1988-89; Whitesell, Richard 1941-42-46; Whiteside, Milford J. 1891; Whitfield, George F. 1890-91; Whitney, Robert 1926; Wiederkehr, Hans 1985; Wienke, Harris L. 1964-65-66; Wier, Edward J. ; Wilcox, Morgan A. 1894-96; Wilcox, Ralph E. 1894-96; Wilcox, William W. 1890; Wilhelm, Thomas D. 1962-63-64; Wilkinson, Marcus E. 1910-14-15; Williams, Boyd 1941-42; Williams, Glenn K. 1975-76-77-78; Williams, Gregory B. 1976-77-78-79; Williams, James D. 1973; Williams, Roland L. 1994-95; Williams, Timothy C. 1972-73; Willis, Roy D. 1994; Wills, Donald E. 1950; Wilson, Clifford B. 1938-39-40; Wilson, Glenn A. 1975-76-77; Wilson, James A. 1961; Wilson, Sir Mawn J. 1993-94-95; Wilson, Timothy A. 1977-78-80; Wilson, Otis 1975; Winick, Walter L. 1926-27-28; Wink, Charles J. 1957-61; Winter, Blaise 1980-81-82-83; Winters, Bernard A. 1974-75-76-77; Wisdom, Terrence B. 1989-90-91-92; Wiseman, Rebern 1950-51; Wittman, Robert 1925-27; Wohlabaugh, David V. 1992-93-94; Wolf, James B. 1907; Wolfley, Craig A. 1976-77-78-79; Womack, Douglas R. 1991-92-93; Womack, Ronald J. 1968; Wood, Olin B. 1890-91; Wood, W.W. 1895-96; Wooden, Edward L. 1990-91-92; Wooden, Terrence T. 1986-87-88-89; Woodruff, Leroy T. 1912-13-14; Woodruff, Robert B. 1970-71-72; Wooten, Alfred J. 1990-91-92-93; Wosilius, William T. 1965-66; Wright, Arthur 1927 (Mgr.); Wright, Harold E. ; Wright, James A. 1961; Wright, Joseph A. 1890-91; Wright, Nathaniel 1974-75-76; Wycoff, Lynn B. 1897-98-1900-01-02; Wycoff, Jennifer 1989 (Mgr.); Wysocki, Gregory M. 1970-71.

**Y** Yancey, Bruce 1951-52-53; Yaple, Edward 1950-51-52; Yard, Kevin M. 1976-77; Yates, Robert E. 1958-59; Yencho, George M. 1970-71-72; Yochum, Daniel L. 1970-71; Youmans, Maurice E. 1958-59; Young, Glen H. 1989-90-91-92; Young, Robert 1949-50-51; Young, Sidney W. 1958; Young, William 1945; Yost, Jr., George D. 1974-75.

**Z** Zamaitis, Edward S. 1972-73-74; Zambuto, Paul 1978-79-80-81; Zanieski, William J. 1965-66-67; Zanovitch, William J. 1973-75-76; Zaso, Gus C. 1954-55-56; Zegalia, Stephen C. 1966-67-68; Zeglen, Joseph J. 1973; Ziegler, Brent 1980-81-82-83; Ziff, David 1922; Zimdahl, Walter 1937-38-39; Zimmerman, Charles D. 1956-57-58; Zimmerman, Eric R. 1965; Zimmerman, Gifford G. 1921-22-23; Zimmerman, Robert A. 1970-71; Zunic, Michael J. 1978-79-80-81; Zur, Randolph C. 1969-70.

# BASKETBALL
# SEASON-BY-SEASON SUMMARY

| Year | Record Won | Lost | Scoring SU | Opp. | Year | Record Won | Lost | Scoring SU | Opp. |
|------|-----|------|-----|------|------|-----|------|-----|------|
| 1900-01 | 2 | 1 | 47 | 51 | 1949-50 | 18 | 9 | 1,830 | 1,590 |
| 1901-02 | 2 | 2 | 81 | 74 | 1950-51 | 19 | 9 | 1,915 | 1,662 |
| 1902-03 | 1 | 8 | 124 | 223 | 1951-52 | 14 | 6 | 1,516 | 1,384 |
| 1903-04 | 11 | 8 | 417 | 337 | 1952-53 | 7 | 11 | 1,320 | 1,377 |
| 1904-05 | 15 | 7 | 717 | 380 | 1953-54 | 10 | 9 | 1,438 | 1,450 |
| 1905-06 | 9 | 3 | 365 | 239 | 1954-55 | 10 | 11 | 1,605 | 1,665 |
| 1906-07 | 4 | 3 | 195 | 158 | 1955-56 | 14 | 8 | 1,757 | 1,639 |
| 1907-08 | 11 | 2 | 329 | 237 | 1956-57 | 18 | 7 | 1,969 | 1,767 |
| 1908-09 | 7 | 8 | 346 | 380 | 1957-58 | 11 | 10 | 1,377 | 1,316 |
| 1909-10 | 3 | 11 | 244 | 362 | 1958-59 | 14 | 9 | 1,725 | 1,625 |
| 1910-11 | 6 | 11 | 313 | 410 | 1959-60 | 13 | 8 | 1,604 | 1,535 |
| 1911-12 | 11 | 3 | 397 | 288 | 1960-61 | 4 | 19 | 1,587 | 1,854 |
| 1912-13 | 8 | 3 | 393 | 288 | 1961-62 | 2 | 22 | 1,494 | 1,899 |
| 1913-14 | 12 | 0 | 369 | 214 | 1962-63 | 8 | 13 | 1,302 | 1,431 |
| 1914-15 | 10 | 1 | 315 | 203 | 1963-64 | 17 | 8 | 2,078 | 1,869 |
| 1915-16 | 9 | 3 | 315 | 224 | 1964-65 | 13 | 10 | 1,898 | 1,762 |
| 1916-17 | 13 | 3 | 405 | 311 | 1965-66 | 22 | 6 | 2,773 | 2,311 |
| 1917-18 | 16 | 1 | 476 | 293 | 1966-67 | 20 | 6 | 2,156 | 1,949 |
| 1918-19 | 12 | 4 | 342 | 290 | 1967-68 | 11 | 14 | 1,979 | 1,991 |
| 1919-20 | 15 | 3 | 504 | 345 | 1968-69 | 9 | 16 | 1,908 | 2,050 |
| 1920-21 | 11 | 7 | 418 | 360 | 1969-70 | 12 | 12 | 2,078 | 2,074 |
| 1921-22 | 11 | 7 | 418 | 360 | 1970-71 | 19 | 7 | 2,158 | 1,971 |
| 1922-23 | 8 | 12 | 428 | 496 | 1971-72 | 22 | 6 | 2,447 | 2,267 |
| 1923-24 | 8 | 10 | 438 | 417 | 1972-73 | 24 | 5 | 2,316 | 2,106 |
| 1924-25 | 14 | 2 | 539 | 361 | 1973-74 | 19 | 7 | 2,097 | 1,837 |
| 1925-26 | 19 | 1 | 643 | 421 | 1974-75 | 23 | 9 | 2,627 | 2,370 |
| 1926-27 | 15 | 4 | 687 | 416 | 1975-76 | 20 | 9 | 2,299 | 2,155 |
| 1927-28 | 10 | 6 | 443 | 386 | 1976-77 | 26 | 4 | 2,608 | 2,107 |
| 1928-29 | 11 | 4 | 448 | 379 | 1977-78 | 22 | 6 | 2,459 | 2,004 |
| 1929-30 | 18 | 2 | 749 | 460 | 1978-79 | 26 | 4 | 2,660 | 2,145 |
| 1930-31 | 16 | 4 | 755 | 517 | 1979-80 | 26 | 4 | 2,575 | 2,113 |
| 1931-32 | 13 | 7 | 570 | 442 | 1980-81 | 22 | 12 | 2,630 | 2,440 |
| 1932-33 | 14 | 2 | 561 | 399 | 1981-82 | 16 | 13 | 2,296 | 2,197 |
| 1933-34 | 15 | 2 | 649 | 366 | 1982-83 | 21 | 10 | 2,612 | 2,311 |
| 1934-35 | 15 | 2 | 662 | 468 | 1983-84 | 23 | 9 | 2,512 | 2,311 |
| 1935-36 | 12 | 5 | 672 | 556 | 1984-85 | 22 | 9 | 2,263 | 2,104 |
| 1936-37 | 13 | 4 | 696 | 555 | 1985-86 | 26 | 6 | 2,674 | 2,184 |
| 1937-38 | 13 | 5 | 795 | 656 | 1986-87 | 31 | 7 | 3,145 | 2,766 |
| 1938-39 | 14 | 4 | 783 | 586 | 1987-88 | 26 | 9 | 2,965 | 2,466 |
| 1939-40 | 10 | 8 | 711 | 657 | 1988-89 | 30 | 8 | 3,410 | 2,891 |
| 1940-41 | 14 | 5 | 864 | 699 | 1989-90 | 26 | 7 | 2,721 | 2,349 |
| 1941-42 | 15 | 6 | 925 | 756 | 1990-91 | 26 | 6 | 2,681 | 2,380 |
| 1942-43 | 8 | 10 | 843 | 816 | 1991-92 | 22 | 10 | 2,383 | 2,259 |
| 1943-44 | Suspended | | | | 1992-93 | 20 | 9 | 2,303 | 2,139 |
| 1944-45 | 7 | 12 | 792 | 863 | 1993-94 | 23 | 7 | 2,517 | 2,248 |
| 1945-46 | 23 | 4 | 1,699 | 1,101 | 1994-95 | 20 | 10 | 2,471 | 2,202 |
| 1946-47 | 19 | 6 | 1,524 | 1,268 | 1995-96 | 29 | 9 | 2,897 | 2,607 |
| 1947-48 | 11 | 13 | 1,374 | 1,300 | **Total** | **1432** | **670** | **132,472** | **117,907** |
| 1948-49 | 18 | 7 | 1,600 | 1,348 | | | | | |

# COACHING RECORDS

| Year | Coach | W | L | Pct. |
|------|-------|---|---|------|
| 1900-03 | No Coach | 5 | 11 | .313 |
| 1903-11 | John A.R. Scott | 66 | 53 | .559 |
| 1911-24 | Edmund Dollard | 148 | 56 | .725 |
| 1924-50 | Lewis P. Andreas | 355 | 134 | .726 |
| 1950-62 | Marc Guley | 136 | 129 | .513 |
| 1962-68 | Fred Lewis | 91 | 57 | .615 |
| 1968-76 | Roy Danforth | 148 | 71 | .676 |
| 1976-pre. | James Boeheim | 483 | 159 | .752 |
| **Total** | | **1432** | **670** | **.681** |

# TEAM RECORDS

## GAME

Points scored — 144 vs. Siena, 1978-79
Points allowed — 127 vs. Pittsburgh, 1969-70
Field goals — 55 vs. Siena, 1978-79
Field goals attempted — 102 vs. Colgate, 1963-64
Field goal pct. — .733 vs. Utica (44-60), 1982-83
Free throws — 36 vs. Connecticut, 1981-82; vs. Pittsburgh, 1969-70
Free throws attempted — 48 vs. Siena, 1987-88
Free throw pct. — 1.000 vs. Montana State (12-12), 1995-96; vs. Duquesne (17-17), 1983-84
3-point FG made — 12 vs. Notre Dame, 1991-92; 12 vs. Boston College, 1994-95
3-point FG attempted — 37 vs. Notre Dame, 1991-92
3-point FG pct. (min. 5 att.) — 1.000 vs. Pittsburgh (6-6), 1986-87
3-point FG pct. (min. 10 att.) — .638 vs. So. Illinois (7-13), 1994-95
Rebounds — 84 vs. Massachusetts, 1965-66
Assists — 38 vs. Rutgers, 1972-73
Steals — 22 vs. St. Francis, PA, 1988-89
Blocked shots — 15 vs. Seton Hall, 1980-81
Turnovers — 33 at Kentucky, 1994-95
Personal fouls — 36 vs. Siena, 1978-79

## SEASON

Points scored — 3,410, 1988-89 (38 games)
Points allowed — 2,891, 1988-89 (38 games)
Scoring average — 99.0, 1965-66 (2773 points, 28 games)
Field goals — 1,334, 1988-89 (38 games)
Field goals attempted — 2,456, 1988-89 (38 games)
Field goal pct. — .543, 1988-89 (1334-2456, 38 games)
Free throws — 644, 1995-96 (38 games)
Free throw attempted — 980, 1986-87 (38 games)
Free throw pct. — .751, 1983-84 (518-690, 32 games)
3-point FG made — 209, 1991-92 (32 games)
3-point FG attempted — 624, 1991-92 (32 games)
3-point FG pct. — .403, 1986-87 (100-248, 38 games)
Rebounds — 1,524, 1986-87 (38 games)
Rebounding average — 51.4, 1969-70 (24 games)
Assists — 762, 1988-89 (38 games)
Steals — 340, 1988-89 (38 games)
Blocked shots — 207, 1988-89 (38 games)

# INDIVIDUAL RECORDS

# modern NCAA record
+ former NCAA record

## POINTS

Game: 47, Bill Smith vs. Lafayette, Jan. 14, 1971
Season: 845, John Wallace, 1995-96

## SCORING AVERAGE

Season: 28.4, Dave Bing, 1965-66
Career: 24.7, Dave Bing, 1963-66

## 1,000 POINT CLUB

*Denotes three years of varsity competition

| | Name | Pts. | Avg. | Years |
|---|---|---|---|---|
| 1. | Lawrence Moten | 2,334 | 19.3 | 1991-95 |
| 2. | Derrick Coleman | 2,143 | 15.0 | 1986-90 |
| 3. | John Wallace | 2,119 | 16.7 | 1992-96 |
| 4. | Sherman Douglas | 2,060 | 14.9 | 1985-89 |
| 5. | Stephen Thompson | 1,956 | 13.6 | 1986-90 |
| 6. | Dave Bing | 1,883 | 24.8 | 1963-66* |
| 7. | Rafael Addison | 1,876 | 14.9 | 1982-86 |
| 8. | Erich Santifer | 1,845 | 14.9 | 1979-83 |
| 9. | Billy Owens | 1,840 | 17.7 | 1988-91* |
| 10. | Rony Seikaly | 1,716 | 12.6 | 1984-88 |
| 11. | Dave Johnson | 1,614 | 12.2 | 1988-92 |
| 12. | Roosevelt Bouie | 1,560 | 13.2 | 1976-80 |
| 13. | Adrian Autry | 1,538 | 12.7 | 1990-94 |
| 14. | Dennis DuVal | 1,504 | 15.0 | 1971-74* |
| 15. | Rudy Hackett | 1,496 | 17.2 | 1972-75* |
| | Dale Shackleford | 1,496 | 12.8 | 1975-79 |
| 17. | Dwayne Washington | 1,490 | 15.7 | 1983-86* |
| 18. | Louis Orr | 1,487 | 12.8 | 1976-80 |
| 19. | Bill Smith | 1,451 | 20.7 | 1968-71* |
| 20. | Greg Kohls | 1,360 | 19.2 | 1969-72* |
| 21. | Mike Lee | 1,351 | 16.3 | 1970-73* |
| 22. | Billy Gabor | 1,344 | 14.0 | 1942-48 |
| 23. | Vinnie Cohen | 1,337 | 19.7 | 1953-56* |
| 24. | Tony Bruin | 1,294 | 11.6 | 1979-83 |
| 25. | George Hicker | 1,245 | 16.0 | 1965-68* |
| 26. | Wendell Alexis | 1,212 | 9.7 | 1982-86 |
| 27. | Jack Kiley | 1,193 | 15.1 | 1948-51* |
| 28. | Jim Lee | 1,165 | 13.4 | 1972-75* |
| 29. | Marty Byrnes | 1,159 | 11.0 | 1974-78 |
| | Marty Headd | 1,159 | 10.9 | 1977-81 |
| 31. | James Williams | 1,119 | 11.0 | 1973-77 |
| 32. | Ed Stickel | 1,096 | 16.1 | 1946-49* |
| 33. | Jon Cincebox | 1,087 | 15.8 | 1956-59* |
| 34. | Pete Chudy | 1,079 | 16.1 | 1958-61* |
| 35. | Vaughn Harper | 1,070 | 13.5 | 1965-68* |
| 36. | Leo Rautins | 1,031 | 12.1 | 1980-83* |

## FIELD GOALS MADE

Game: 19, Dave Bing vs. Colgate, Feb. 17, 1965
Season: 308, Dave Bing, 1965-66
Career: 838, Lawrence Moten, 1991-95

## FIELD GOAL ATTEMPTED

Game: 34, Greg Kohls at Colgate, March 4, 1972
Season: 636, Jack Kiley, 1949-50
Career: 1,736, Lawrence Moten, 1991-95

## FIELD GOAL PCT. (MIN 10 ATT.)

Game: 1.000, Rick Dean (13-13) vs. Colgate, Feb. 14, 1966
Season: 65.4, Roosevelt Bouie (189-289), 1979-80
Career: .596, Bill Smith (563-900), 1968-71

## CAREER FIELD GOAL PERCENTAGE LEADERS

(min. 500 attempts)

| Name | FGM/FGA | Pct. | Years |
|------|---------|------|-------|
| 1. Bill Smith | 536/900 | .596 | 1968-71 |
| 2. Roosevelt Bouie | 631/1064 | .593 | 1976-80 |
| 3. Derrick Coleman | 770/1356 | .568 | 1986-90 |
| 4. John Wallace | 491/872 | .563 | 1992- |
| 5. Stephen Thompson | 801/1431 | .560 | 1986-90 |
| Rony Seikaly | 652/1165 | .560 | 1984-88 |
| 7. Rick Dean | 352/640 | .550 | 1964-67 |
| 8. Conrad McRae | 282/515 | .548 | 1992-93 |
| 9. Andre Hawkins | 313/572 | .547 | 1981-85 |
| 10. Erich Santifer | 742/1362 | .545 | 1979-83 |

## FREE THROWS MADE

Game: 17, Greg Kohls vs. Fordham, Feb. 9, 1972
Season: 222, Greg Kohls, 1971-72; John Wallace, 1995-96
Career: 587, Derrick Coleman, 1986-90

## FREE THROW ATTEMPTED

Game: 21, Chuck Richards at Pittsburgh, Feb. 7, 1964; Greg Kohls vs. Pittsburgh, Jan. 9, 1971
Season: 291, John Wallace, 1995-96
Career: 858, Derrick Coleman, 1986-90

## FREE THROW PCT. (MIN 10 ATT.)

Game: 1.000, Greg Kohls (17-17) vs. Fordham, Feb. 9, 1972
Season: 88.6, Jimmy Lee (93-105), 1972-73
Career: .861, Rich Cornwall (217-252), 1966-68

## CONSECUTIVE FREE THROWS

Season: 34, Mike Lee, 1970-71

## CAREER FREE THROW PERCENTAGE LEADERS

(min. 150 attempts)

| Name | FTM/FTA | Pct. | Years |
|------|---------|------|-------|
| 1. Rich Cornwall | 217/252 | .861 | 1965-68 |
| 2. Jim Lee | 243/283 | .859 | 1972-75 |
| 3. Greg Kohls | 388/471 | .824 | 1969-72 |
| 4. John Suder | 146/179 | .816 | 1967-70 |
| 5. Marty Headd | 163/201 | .811 | 1977-81 |
| 6. Dan Schayes | 315/391 | .806 | 1977-81 |
| 7. Wendell Alexis | 280/354 | .791 | 1982-86 |
| 8. Mike Lee | 363/461 | .787 | 1970-73 |
| 9. Louis Orr | 301/391 | .770 | 1976-80 |
| 10. Leo Rautins | 171/223 | .767 | 1980-83 |

## THREE-POINT FIELD GOALS MADE

Game: 7, Dave Johnson vs. Florida State, Dec. 3, 1992
Season: 83, Matt Roe, 1988-89

## CAREER 3-POINT FIELD GOAL LEADERS

| Name | 3FG/3FGA | Pct. | Years |
|------|----------|------|-------|
| 1. Lawrence Moten | 197/624 | .316 | 1991-95(4) |
| 2. Matt Roe | 159/367 | .433 | 1986-89 (3) |
| 3. Adrian Autry | 139/417 | .333 | 1990- 94(4) |
| 4. Dave Johnson | 116/344 | .337 | 1988-92 (4) |
| 5. Lucious Jackson | 98/286 | .343 | 1991-95(4) |
| 6. Michael Edwards | 90/272 | .331 | 1989-93 (4) |
| 7. Greg Monroe | 79/180 | .439 | 1983-87 (1) |
| Sherman Douglas | 79/208 | .380 | 1987-90 (3) |
| 9. Billy Owens | 50/154 | .325 | 1988-91 (3) |
| 10. Scott McCorkle | 38/104 | .365 | 1990-94 (4) |

## THREE-POINT FIELD GOAL ATTEMPTS

Game: 13, Lawrence Moten vs. Connecticut, Jan. 10, 1994
Season: 199, Dave Johnson, 1991-92

## THREE-POINT FIELD GOAL PCT. (MIN. 5 ATT.)

Game: 1.000, Greg Monroe (5-5) at Pittsburgh, Mar. 7, 1987
Season: .474, Matt Roe (83-175), 1988-89

## CAREER 3-POINT FIELD GOAL PERCENTAGE LEADERS

(min. 25 made)

| Name | 3FG/3FGA | Pct. | Years |
|------|----------|------|-------|
| 1. Greg Monroe | 79/180 | .439 | 1983-87 (1) |
| 2. Matt Roe | 159/367 | .433 | 1986-89 (3) |
| 3. Earl Duncan | 26/63 | .413 | 1987-88 (1) |
| 4. Sherman Douglas | 79/208 | .380 | 1987-90 (3) |
| 5. Scott McCorkle | 38/104 | .365 | 1990-94 (4) |
| 6. Tony Scott | 26/73 | .356 | 1988-90 (2) |
| 7. Lucious Jackson | 98/286 | .343 | 1991-95(4) |
| 8. Dave Johnson | 116/344 | .337 | 1988-92 (4) |
| 9. Adrian Autry | 139/417 | .333 | 1990- 94(4) |
| 10. Michael Edwards | 90/272 | .331 | 1989-93 (4) |

Three-point field goal began in the 1986-87 season
Number of years played with three-point shot in parentheses.

## REBOUNDS

Game: 25, Dave Bing vs. Cornell, Feb. 8, 1966
Season: 422, Derrick Coleman, 1988-89
Career: 1,537, Derrick Coleman, 1986-90

## REBOUND AVERAGE

Season: 16.4, Jon Cincebox, 1957-58
Career: 14.6, Jon Cincebox, 1956-59

## CAREER REBOUNDING LEADERS

| Name | Rebs. | Avg. | Years |
|------|-------|------|-------|
| 1. Derrick Coleman | #1,537 | 10.7 | 1986-90 |
| 2. Rony Seikaly | 1,094 | 8.0 | 1984-88 |
| 3. Jon Cincebox | 1,004 | 14.6 | 1956-59 |
| 4. Rudy Hackett | 990 | 11.4 | 1972-75 |
| 5. Roosevelt Bouie | 987 | 8.4 | 1976-80 |
| 6. Billy Owens | 910 | 8.8 | 1988-91 |
| 7. Bill Smith | 903 | 12.9 | 1968-71 |
| 8. Louis Orr | 881 | 7.6 | 1976-80 |
| 9. Vaughn Harper | 866 | 11.0 | 1965-68 |
| 10. Dale Shackleford | 851 | 7.3 | 1975-79 |

## ASSISTS

Game: 22, Sherman Douglas vs. Providence, Jan. 28, 1989
Season: 326, Sherman Douglas, 1988-89
Career: 960, Sherman Douglas, 1985-89

## ASSIST AVERAGE

Season: 8.6, Sherman Douglas, 1988-89
Career: 7.0, Sherman Douglas, 1985-89

## CAREER ASSISTS LEADERS

| Name | Assists | Avg. | Years |
|------|---------|------|-------|
| 1. Sherman Douglas | +960 | 7.0 | 1985-89 |
| 2. Dwayne Washington | 637 | 6.7 | 1983-86 |
| 3. Adrian Autry | 631 | 5.2 | 1990-94 |
| 4. Eddie Moss | 539 | 4.6 | 1977-81 |
| 5. Leo Rautins | 423 | 5.0 | 1980-83 |
| 6. Gene Waldron | 410 | 3.3 | 1980-84 |
| 7. Greg Monroe | 400 | 3.1 | 1983-87 |
| Lazarus Sims | 400 | 3.1 | 1993-96 |
| 9. Billy Owens | 381 | 3.7 | 1988-91 |
| 10. Dale Shackleford | 358 | 3.1 | 1975-79 |

## STEALS

Game: 8, Matt Roe vs. St. Francis, PA, Dec. 30, 1988
Season: 85, Eddie Moss, 1980-81
Career: 235, Sherman Douglas, 1985-89

## STEAL AVERAGE

Season: 2.6, Dwayne Washington, 1985-86
Career: 2.3, Dwayne Washington, 1983-86

## CAREER STEAL LEADERS

| Name | Steals | Avg. | Years |
|------|--------|------|-------|
| 1. Sherman Douglas | 235 | 1.7 | 1985-89 |
| 2. Eddie Moss | 230 | 2.0 | 1977-81 |
| 3. Dwayne Washington | 220 | 2.3 | 1983-86 |
| 4. Adrian Autry | 217 | 1.8 | 1990-94 |
| 5. Billy Owens | 216 | 2.1 | 1988-91 |
| 6. Lawrence Moten | 215 | 1.8 | 1991-95 |
| 7. Dale Shackleford | 207 | 1.8 | 1975-79 |
| 8. Derrick Coleman | 187 | 1.3 | 1986-90 |
| 9. Erich Santifer | 185 | 1.5 | 1979-83 |
| 10. Stephen Thompson | 184 | 1.2 | 1986-90 |

## BLOCKED SHOTS

Game: 8, (By many, most recently:) LeRon Ellis vs.
  Boston College, Feb. 2, 1991
Season: 127, Derrick Coleman, 1988-89
Career: 327, Roosevelt Bouie, 1976-80

## BLOCKED SHOT AVERAGE

Season: 3.4, Derrick Coleman, 1988-89
Career: 2.8, Roosevelt Bouie, 1976-80

## CAREER BLOCKED SHOTS LEADERS

| Name | Blocks | Avg. | Years |
|------|--------|------|-------|
| 1. Roosevelt Bouie | 327 | 2.8 | 1976-80 |
| 2. Rony Seikaly | 319 | 2.3 | 1984-88 |
| Derrick Coleman | 319 | 2.2 | 1986-90 |
| 4. Conrad McRae | 203 | 2.0 | 1989-93 |
| 5. John Wallace | 146 | 1.6 | 1992-96 |
| 6. Dan Schayes | 134 | 1.1 | 1977-81 |
| 7. LeRon Ellis | 104 | 1.6 | 1989-91 |
| 8. Wendell Alexis | 103 | 0.8 | 1982-86 |
| 9. Billy Owens | 97 | 0.9 | 1988-91 |
| 10. Lawrence Moten | 85 | 0.7 | 1991-95 |

# ORANGEMEN IN THE NBA DRAFT

| Player | Position | Rnd (#) | Team |
|--------|----------|---------|------|
| **1984** | | | |
| Sean Kerins | Forward | 7th (155) | New Jersey Nets |
| **1986** | | | |
| Dwayne Washington | Guard | 1st (13) | New Jersey Nets |
| Rafael Addison | Forward | 2nd (39) | Phoenix Suns |
| Wendell Alexis | Forward | 3rd (59) | Golden State Warriors |
| **1987** | | | |
| Howard Triche | Forward | 6th (117) | New York Knicks |
| **1988** | | | |
| Rony Seikaly | Center | 1st (9) | Miami Heat |
| **1989** | | | |
| Sherman Douglas | Guard | 2nd (28) | Miami Heat |
| **1990** | | | |
| Derrick Coleman | Forward | 1st (1) | New Jersey Nets |
| **1991** | | | |
| Billy Owens | Forward | 1st (3) | Sacramento Kings |
| LeRon Ellis | Forward | 1st (22) | Los Angeles Clippers |
| **1992** | | | |
| Dave Johnson | Forward | 1st (26) | Portland Trailblazers |
| **1993** | | | |
| Conrad McRae | Forward | 2nd (38) | Washington Bullets |
| **1995** | | | |
| Lawrence Moten | Guard | 2nd (36) | Vancouver Grizzlies |
| **1996** | | | |
| John Wallace | Foward | 1st (18) | New York Knicks |

# HONORS

# BASKETBALL LETTERMEN

**A** Ableman, Richard M. 1964-65-66; Ackerson, James 1943; Ackley, Albert 1925; Ackley, Earl E., Jr. 1948-49-50; Acocella, Angelo 1945; Addison, Rafael 1983-84-85-86; Albanese, Vincent J. 1956-57; Aldrich, David G. 1967-68-69; Alexis, Wendell 1983-84-85-86; Alkoff, Louis 1933-34-35; Amster, Glenn, Jr. (mgr.) 1968-69; Andrew, David (mgr.) 1989; Ansley, Ernest C. 1910; Ardison, Robert (mgr.) 1932; Armstrong, George 1930-31-32; Arrington, Larry 1975-76; Austin, Ernest 1968-69-70; Autry, Adrian 1991-92-93-94; Axelrod, Leonard (mgr.) 1942; Axtmann, O.J. (mgr.) 1914.

**B** Balinsky, John 1935-36-37; Balukas, Raymond R. 1967-68; Banks, M.B. 1909; Barlok, Todd 1992; Barlow, Michael R. 1968-69; Barnes, Renard 1986; Barsha, John 1918-19-20; Bartholomew, Bruce 1972-73; Baylock, Victor 1936-37-38; Beagle, Kenneth 1929-30-31; Beck, John F. 1948-49-50; Bednark, Thomas R. 1966-67; Beech, George 1932-33; Begovich, Mike 1994; Beisswanger, Russell W. 1962; Bennett, Milton 1921; Berkenfeld, Stephen M. 1959-60-61; Berger, Eugene 1940-41-42; Besdin, Melvin 1952-53-54; Beverly, Lewis M. 1954; Bibbens, Ross 1921; Biener, Jerald H. (mgr.) 1953-54; Bing, David 1964-65-66; Blazey, Scott (mgr.) 1971-72; Bloom, Myer 1911-12-13-14; Blumen, Kyle (mgr.) 1993; Blumen, Todd (mgr.) 1990; Boax, James 1927; Bock, Milton 1931-32-33; Boeheim, James A. 1964-65-66; Boetcher, Maynard 1930; Bohr, F.M. 1903; Bolton, William 1940; Bouie, Roosevelt 1977-78-79-80; Boyce, Richard L. (mgr.) 1960-61; Brady, E.J. 1903; Breland, Emanuel E. 1954-55-57; Brenneman, George 1929; Brickman, H. 1918; Brodsky, Jon D. (mgr.) 1958; Brodsky, William J. (mgr.) 1964-65; Bromberg, Fred 1931; Brower, Derek A. 1985-86-87-88; Brown, James N. 1955-56; Brown, Melvin 1985-86; Brown, Michael 1985; Brown, Willis (mgr.) 1932; Brucker, Joseph 1922; Bruett, William 1941; Bruin, Tony 1980-81-82-83; Burgan, Todd 1995-96; Byrnes, Martin W. 1975-76-77-78.

**C** Carello, Sam (mgr.) 1987; Carr, Harlan 1925; Case, William R. 1968-69-70; Casey, James 1916-17; Castellini, August 1954-55; Castle, Lewis S. 1912-13-14; Catchpole, Park (mgr.) 1940; Cegala, Louis 1954-55-56; Cheney, Guy W. 1908; Chudy, Peter K. 1959-60-61; Church, Lewis W. (mgr.) 1924; Cincebox, W. Jon 1957-58-59; Cipolla, Jason 1996; Clark, David L. 1973; Clark, Gary L. 1955-56-57; Clark, Robert (mgr.) 1927; Clary, Robert 1968-69-70; Coffee, Jack (mgr.) 1933; Coffman, David (mgr.)

1938; Cohen, Ronald P. (mgr.) 1965; Cohen, Hal 1977-78-79-80; Cohen, Vincent 1955-56-57; Cohen, Jr., Vincent 1992; Coleman, Derrick D. 1987-88-89-90; Coman, A.P. (mgr.) 1916; Conderman, Joseph (mgr.) 1920; Conlin, Frank 1919-20-21; Connors, William J. 1961; Conover, Richard 1958-59-60; Cornwall, Richard T. 1966-67-68; Cosentino, Rudolph 1945; Cotton, Lewis D. 1973; Cracker, William (mgr.) 1926; Crandall, Lawrence 1946-47-48; Crisp, Wilbur 1914-15-16-17; Crofoot, George 1958; Cronauer, Ed 1918; Cronauer, John 1918; Cubit, Mark 1978-79; Cummings, Charles F. (mgr.) 1911; Curran, Jack 1936.

**D** Danforth, Michael R. 1976; Darby, Walter A. 1909; Davey, Walter V. 1911-12; Davis, Ernest R. 1961; Davis, Ken 1979-80-81; Dean, Herbert 1939; Dean, Richard I. 1965-66-67; Deer, A. Carmine 1948-49-50; DeFillippo, Tony 1929; Degner, Donald L. 1973-74-75; Delp, M.Z. (mgr.) 1909; DeMarle, William 1974-75; DeYoung, John 1933-34-35; Dickie, William 1945; DiPace, Daniel 1941-42-43; Dodge, Stephen B. 1962; Dollard, E.A. 1905-06-07-08; Dollard, Edmund (mgr.) 1939; Dolley, Charles 1917-18-19; Dooms, Robert A. 1972-73-74; Douglas, Sherman 1986-87-88-89; Dressler, Frederic (mgr.) 1962-63; Drew, William 1977-78; Duffy, Richard M. 1963-64-65; Duncan, James Earl 1988; Duncan, G.O.L. 1909; DuVal, Dennis 1972-73-74.

**E** Edwards, Michael E. 1990-91-92-93; Egan, Patrick 1932; Eisemann, William 1926-27; Elliott, Alton 1930-31-32; Ellis, LeRon P. 1990-91; Evans, Gary 1957.

**F** Face, Charles F. 1923; Farnsworth, Alton 1935; Farrell, S.A. 1907; Fash, William, D. 1948-49-50; Feldman, Dan 1931; Ferris, Paul 1943; Ferris, William 1934; Fine, Bernard A. (mgr.) 1966-67; Finley, Robert C. 1962-63; Finney, William 1969-70-72; Fisher, George 1921-22-23; Fisher, W. Claude 1909; Fitzpatrick, Richard 1933; Flynn, Raymond 1946; Fogarty, Daniel 1929-30-31; Foster, Herbert 1962-63; Frank, Mike (mgr.) 1995; Fredericks, Paul 1907.

**G** Gabor, William 1943-46-47-48; Gallivan, John F. 1923; Gelatt, Charles 1994; Getzfeld, Robert (mgr.) 1946-47; Giles, Clarence W. 1911; Gillespie, Ronald C. 1954-55-56; Gipson, Bernard F. 1968-69; Glacken, Edward 1947; Glacken, Joseph 1942-43-47; Gluck, Jason 1994; Gluckman, Harold (mgr.) 1939-40; Gobobe, Zangwill 1930; Goercki, John 1936-37-38; Goldberg, Edward D. 1958-59-60; Goldman, Scott (mgr.) 1990; Goldsmith, Norman B. 1964-65-66;

Gordon, Sidney (mgr.) 1931; Green, John (mgr.) 1979; Green, Martin A. (mgr.) 1975; Green, Thomas M. 1969-70-71; Greenman, Lloyd 1919; Greve, Henry 1923-24-25; Guerrero, Gilbert 1970; Guley, Marcel 1935-36.

**H** Hackett, Rudolph 1973-74-75; Haley, Robert (mgr.) 1933; Haller, Mark 1938-39; Hamblen, Frank A. II 1967-68-69; Hanson, Victor A. 1925-26-27; Harmon, David 1969-70; Harper, Vaughn 1966-67-68; Harried, Herman 1985-87-88-89; Harris, Anthony E. 1992; Harris, Kenneth 1916; Harwood, John 1928-29-30; Hauck, Walter (mgr.) 1976; Hawkins, Andre 1982-83-84-85; Hayman, Louis 1929-30-31; Hayes, Jim 1994-95-96; Headd, Martin 1978-79-80-81; Healy, Willard (mgr.) 1941; Henderson, Jack (mgr.) 1936; Hennemuth, William 1945; Hicker, George P. 1966-67-68; Hill, Otis 1994-95-96; Hladik, Anthony, Jr. 1949-50-51; Holbrook, Bernard 1930; Hollenbeck, David A. 1958; Hopkins, Michael G. 1990-91-92-93; Horn, Harry 1938-39; Horowitz, Paul 1928; Houseknecht, C.J. 1903; Hudson, Joseph (mgr.) 1935; Huggins, Eric H. 1950-51-52; Hughes, Keith 1987; Hutt, Less (mgr.) 1928.

**J** Jackson III, Lucious B. 1992-93-94-95; Jaffe, Myron T. 1950; James, Kevin O. 1976-77-78; James, Loren O. 1961; Janulis, Marius 1995-96; Jarvis, George 1947-48-49; Jaskot, Richard C. 1954; Jensen, Richard 1939-40; Jerebko, Christopher 1978-79-80-81; Jockle, Thomas 1950-51; Johnson, Dave M. 1989-90-91-92; Johnson, Derrick 1995; Jones, Stuart (mgr.) 1959; Jordan, John 1972.

**K** Karpis, John 1983-84; Kartluke, Paul 1939-40-41; Kasbar, Brenda (mgr.) 1990; Kates, Bernard 1923; Katz, Everett 1929-30-31; Katz, Joel 1985-86-87; Katz, Lawrence D. 1967; Katz, Milton 1931; Keating, D.J. 1910; Keating, Steven 1992; Keefer, Ralph 1917; Keib, J.E. 1914-15; Kelley, Lawrence 1975-76-77; Kellogg, William 1922; Kerins, Sean 1981-82-83-84; Kernan, James 1919; Keys, William 1976-77; Kiley, John F. 1949-50-51; Kilpatrick, John 1909-10; Kilpatrick, Ronald N. 1953; Kindel, Ross 1975-76-77-78; King, Donald A. 1961; King, Kevin 1974-75-76; Kingsley, J.E. 1912; Kinne, Charles C. (mgr.) 1905-06; Kirchgasser, George 1904-05-06; Kline, David 1953-54; Klutchkowski, Manfred 1962-63; Kohls, Gregory 1970-71-72; Kohm, Joseph 1986-87; Kollath, D. Bruce 1959-60; Konstanty, Casimer J. 1939; Kouray, Christian 1940-41; Kouwe, Robert L. 1967-69; Kruse, Stanley 1940-41.

**L** Label, William (mgr.) 1950; Lambert, David (mgr.) 1988; Lambert, Robert 1928; Larned, John E. 1953-54-55; Lavin, Kenneth 1922; Lazor, Bobby 1995-96; Leavitt, Norman 1936-37-38; Lee, Charles 1925-26-27; Lee, David F. (mgr.) 1907; Lee, James P. 1973-74-75; Lee, Matthew T. 1908-09-10; Lee, Michael 1971-72-73; Leonard, John 1919; Lewis, Chris 1982-83; Lighton, Lewis (mgr.) 1925; Lloyd, Michael 1995; Lockwood, Charles 1994; Loll, Scott B. 1965; Lotano, Ernest 1961; Loudis, Laurence G. 1956-57-58; Lowe, H.B. (mgr.) 1919; Lowe, W.R. 1922; Ludd, Steven O. 1966-67; Ludka, John 1945-46-47; Lynch, Paul 1908; Lyon, F. Murray 1910.

**M** Machemer, Fred E. 1960-61-62; Mackey, John 1961; MacNaughton, Donald 1937-38-39; MacRae, Evander G. 1922-23-24; Maister, Elmer 1932-33-34; Manikas, William 1951-52-53; Manning, Richard A. 1989-90; Mantho, Timothy A. 1967; Marcus, Abraham 1939; Marcus, Leon 1918-19; Markowitz, Harry (mgr.) 1926; Martin, Daniel 1919; Maxon, H.F. (mgr.) 1913; May, James 1994-95-96; Mayley, Gordon 1926; McCarthy, C.H. 1922; McCarthy, Charles 1924; McCorkle, Scott 1991-92-93-94; McDaniel, Robert 1970; McFadden, Gerald 1969-70; McGough, Michael (mgr.) 1985; McMillian, J. Paul 1939-40; McRae, Conrad B. 1990-91-92-93; McTiernan, Thomas 1943; Meadors, Mark 1974-75; Mendell, Irving 1925; Mendelson, Sidney 1924-25; Miller, Edwin B. 1950-51-52; Miller, Francis J. 1945-48-49-50; Mogish, Andrew 1943-46-47; Monroe, Greg 1984-85-86-87; Moss, Eddie 1978-79-80-81; Mossey, Thomas E. 1958-59-60; Moten III, Lawrence E. 1992-93-94-95; Munro, James (mgr.) 1935; Murray, Robert S. 1962-63-64; Mustion, John M. 1960.

**N** Nelson, Elimu 1994-95-96; Nelson, William 1954; Newell, Royce 1946-47-48-49; Newton, Lewis 1932; Nicoletti, Frank G. 1964-65-66; Niles, Earl B. 1904; Notman, W.J. 1912-13-14; Noyes, Harold A. 1958-59.

**O** O'Byrne, John C. (mgr.) 1914; O'Connor, Donald (mgr.) 1982-83; O'Neill, Larry 1981-83; Orr, Louis 1977-78-79-80; Osman, A.J. 1915; Osborne, Josh (mgr.) 1992; Ovcina, Elvir 1996; Owens, William C. 1989-90-91.

**P** Papadakos, George 1984; Parker, Robert M. 1975-76-77; Parker, Wallace 1920-21; Patrick, David 1996; Patton, Howard (mgr.) 1936; Payton, Ron 1979-80-81-82; Penceal, Sam 1964-65-66; Perry, Calvin 1980-81-82-83; Peters, Roy 1946-47; Peters, W.L. 1918; Phillips, Ronald 1932-33-34; Pickard, Donald 1933-35; Piotrowski, Paul 1970-71-72; Post, Richard (mgr.) 1951; Potter, A.D. 1915; Powell, Arthur L. 1904-05-06-07; Powell, Reginald 1976-77; Price, Delbert (mgr.) 1942; Propst, Rudolph W. 1911; Quigley, Terrence J. 1961.

**R** Raff, E. (mgr.) 1917; Rafter, William J. 1915-16-17; Rakov, Phillip 1925-26; Rautins, Leo 1981-82-83; Reafsnyder, J.B. 1993-94-95-96; Reddout, Franklin P. 1951-52-53; Redlein, George L. 1905-06; Reid, Valentine 1965-66; Renzi, Oliver 1945-46-47-48; Rice, E.G. 1903; Richards, Charles S. 1964-65; Richtmeyer, Stanley 1926-27-28; Riehl, A.H. 1912-13; Riehl, Frank H. 1905-06-07-08; Ringelmann, Thomas C. 1966-67; Roche, Robert P. 1951-52; Rochester, Stephen S. (mgr.) 1966-67; Roe, Matthew R. 1987-88-89; Rogers, Erik C. 1987-88-89-90; Rose, Stanley H. (mgr.) 1952; Rosen, Edward L. 1949-50; Rosen, Emanuel 1927-28; Rosser, M. 1927; Ruby, David (mgr.) 1970; Ruffin, H.E. 1917; Rugg, W.D. 1911-12; Ryan, L.C. 1911-12.

**S** Salz, Sanford 1960-61; Sanford, Lloyd 1933-34-35; Santifer, Erich 1980-81-82-83; Saperstein, Gerald 1929; Sarvay, Merton (mgr.) 1951; Savage, Robert P. 1948-49-50; Sayle, Donald 1940-41-42; Schank, George (mgr.) 1917; Schayes, Dan 1978-79-80-81; Schmeizer, R. Bruce 1958-59; Schoff, Phillip H. 1963-64-65; Schroeder, John 1937-38-39; Schubert, William 1946; Schulz, Henry 1947-48-49; Schwarzer, Joseph 1916-17-18; Scott, Oliver 1935-36; Scott, Anthony A. 1989-90; Scott, Walter H. 1954; Scully, John R. 1910; Seaman, James H. 1962-63; Sease, Christopher 1974-75-76; Seibert, Ernest R. 1975-76; Seikaly, Rony F. 1985-86-87-88; Sekunda, Glenn E. 1992-93; Semple, Robert (mgr.) 1924-25; Seymour, R.D. 1913-14-15; Shackleford, Dale P. 1976-77-78-79; Shaddock, Robert 1942-43; Shaw, Bart 1928-29; Shaw, Steven 1973-74-75; Sheehey, Michael 1980-81; Sherk, Douglas (mgr.) 1977-78; Sidat-Singh, Wilmeth 1937-38-39; Silverstein, Carl (mgr.) 1950; Simonaitis, John 1935-36-37; Sims, Lazarus 1993-94-95-96; Siock, David A. 1989-91-92-93; Siroty, David (mgr.) 1985; Smith, John T. (mgr.) 1923; Smith, William A. 1969-70-71; Snyder, James J. 1955-56-57; Solomon, Ira R. (mgr.) 1937; Sonderman, Edgar 1935-37; Spector, Joseph (mgr.) 1938; Spencer, Robert S. (mgr.) 1910; Spera,

Sonny 1982-83-84-85; Spicer, Lewis 1945-46; Stanton, Charles 1941-42-43; Stapleton, S. Scott 1972-73-74; Stark, J.J. 1905; Stark, Lewis G. 1956; Stark, Michael 1948-49-50; Stark, Peter G. 1952-53; Stearns, Chester 1931; Stearns, Robert (mgr.) 1934; Steere, Robert (mgr.) 1943; Stevesky, Charles 1950-51; Stewart, Robert 1937-38-39; Stickel, Edward 1946-47-48-49; Stickney, Russell 1942; Stundis, Thomas J. 1972-73-74; Suder, John M. 1968-69-70; Sugarman, Louis 1908; Suprunowicz, Richard 1949-50-51; Suprunowicz, William R. 1973-74; Swanson, Stanley R. 1951-52; Sylvester, Joseph 1942-43.

**T** Taggart, Charles 1933-34; Taub, Lawrence S. (mgr.) 1968; Taylor, Richard W. 1962-63; Taylor, William 1923; Thaw, Charles 1953; Thomas, Jay 1943; Thompson, Robert (mgr.) 1928; Thompson, Stephen M. 1987-88-89-90; Thompson, William 1937-38-39; Thorne, Dudley 1940; Tichnor, B.C. 1910-11; Ticktin, Richard (mgr.) 1948-49; Timberlake, Chris 1982; Triche, Howard 1984-85-86-

87; Trobridge, Rex C. 1964-65-66; Trout, Charles 1924; Twiford, Robert 1939; Twombley, E.D. 1903; Tydeman, William E. 1962.

**V** Vernick, Carl 1962-63-64.

**W** Wadach, Mark 1971-72-73; Waldron, Eugene T. 1981-82-83-84; Walker, Rodney 1986; Walkov, William 1928-29-30; Wallace, John 1993-94-95-96; Wallach, Robert C. 1948-49-50; Walters, Herbert H. (mgr.) 1915; Ward, Wayne H. 1968; Warwell, Cliff 1977; Washington, Dwayne 1984-85-86; Watson, Greg 1982; Weltman, Abraham 1921-22; Werner, Donald 1940; Wichman, Charles 1971-72-73; Wiles, Benjamin J. (mgr.) 1937; Wilmott, Raymond 1940-41-42; Williams, James L. 1974-75-76-77; Wills, Edward 1934; Wills, Howard 1933; Wynne, Peter 1982-83.

**Y** Yarnall, Charles D. 1960; Yoo, Henry 1994.

**Z** Zimmerman, Gifford 1922; Zimmick, Conrad C. 1954; Ziolko, Mark 1971-72.

# LACROSSE
## SEASON-BY-SEASON SUMMARY

| Year | W | L | T | Year | W | L | T | Year | W | L | T | Year | W | L | T |
|---|---|---|---|---|---|---|---|---|---|---|---|---|---|---|---|
| 1916 | 2 | 4 | 1 | 1937 | 6 | 4 | 0 | 1958 | 6 | 3 | 0 | 1979 | 10 | 5 | 0 |
| 1917 | No Games | | | 1938 | 5 | 5 | 0 | 1959 | 3 | 6 | 0 | 1980 | 12 | 2 | 0 |
| 1918 | 3 | 4 | 0 | 1939 | 4 | 2 | 0 | 1960 | 6 | 4 | 0 | 1981 | 7 | 4 | 0 |
| 1919 | 5 | 4 | 1 | 1940 | 5 | 4 | 0 | 1961 | 4 | 4 | 0 | 1982 | 6 | 4 | 0 |
| #1920 | 5 | 3 | 4 | 1941 | 6 | 3 | 0 | 1962 | 7 | 2 | 0 | *1983 | 14 | 1 | 0 |
| 1921 | 11 | 3 | 1 | 1942 | 2 | 4 | 0 | 1963 | 6 | 4 | 0 | 1984 | 15 | 1 | 0 |
| #1922 | 17 | 0 | 0 | 1943 | Suspended | | | 1964 | 6 | 4 | 0 | 1985 | 14 | 2 | 0 |
| 1923 | 11 | 2 | 2 | 1944 | Suspended | | | 1965 | 6 | 5 | 0 | 1986 | 14 | 3 | 0 |
| #1924 | 13 | 0 | 1 | 1945 | Suspended | | | 1966 | 3 | 7 | 0 | 1987 | 9 | 4 | 0 |
| #1925 | 14 | 1 | 0 | 1946 | 7 | 5 | 0 | 1967 | 5 | 7 | 0 | *1988 | 15 | 0 | 0 |
| 1926 | 12 | 1 | 0 | 1947 | 10 | 6 | 0 | 1968 | 9 | 4 | 0 | *1989 | 14 | 1 | 0 |
| 1927 | 11 | 3 | 2 | 1948 | 11 | 3 | 0 | 1969 | 11 | 3 | 0 | *1990 | 13 | 0 | 0 |
| 1928 | 8 | 2 | 1 | 1949 | 14 | 1 | 0 | 1970 | 7 | 2 | 0 | 1991 | 12 | 3 | 0 |
| 1929 | 5 | 3 | 1 | 1950 | 11 | 2 | 0 | 1971 | 9 | 4 | 0 | 1992 | 13 | 2 | 0 |
| 1930 | 3 | 8 | 0 | 1951 | 6 | 4 | 0 | 1972 | 8 | 8 | 0 | *1993 | 12 | 2 | 0 |
| 1931 | 7 | 4 | 0 | 1952 | 6 | 2 | 0 | 1973 | 4 | 6 | 0 | 1994 | 13 | 2 | 0 |
| 1932 | 6 | 1 | 1 | 1953 | 6 | 3 | 0 | 1974 | 2 | 9 | 0 | *1995 | 13 | 2 | 0 |
| 1933 | 7 | 2 | 0 | 1954 | 8 | 2 | 0 | 1975 | 3 | 8 | 0 | **Tot.** | **629** | **254** | **15** |
| 1934 | 10 | 2 | 0 | 1955 | 6 | 4 | 0 | 1976 | 7 | 4 | 0 | * NCAA Champions | | | |
| 1935 | 5 | 5 | 0 | 1956 | 8 | 5 | 0 | 1977 | 8 | 6 | 0 | # USILA Champions | | | |
| 1936 | 7 | 2 | 0 | 1957 | 10 | 0 | 0 | 1978 | 10 | 3 | 0 | | | | |

## COACHING RECORDS

| | Years | Record | Pct. |
|---|---|---|---|
| Laurie Cox | 1916-30 | 120-38-14 | .738 |
| Roy Simmons Sr. | 1931-70 | 252-130-1 | .659 |
| Roy Simmons Jr. | 1971-present | 257-86-0 | .749 |
| **All-time SU Record** | | **629-254-15** | **.709** |

## SYRACUSE IN THE NCAAs

| Year | Seed | Round | Opponent | W-L | Score | Site |
|---|---|---|---|---|---|---|
| 1979 | 7th | First | Maryland | L | 16-13 | Maryland |
| 1980 | 3rd | First | Washington & Lee | W | 12-4 | Coyne Field |
| | | Semis | Johns Hopkins | L | 18-11 | Johns Hopkins |
| 1981 | 7th | First | North Carolina | L | 13-6 | North Carolina |
| 1983 | 2nd | First | Pennsylvania | W | 11-8 | Coyne Field |

|      |      | Semis    | Maryland       | W | 12-5       | Carrier Dome  |
|------|------|----------|----------------|---|------------|---------------|
|      |      | Finals   | Johns Hopkins  | W | 17-16      | Rutgers       |
| 1984 | 2nd  | First    | Rutgers        | W | 8-7 (ot)   | Carrier Dome  |
|      |      | Semis    | Army           | W | 11-9       | Carrier Dome  |
|      |      | Finals   | Johns Hopkins  | L | 13-10      | Delaware      |
| 1985 | 2nd  | First    | Pennsylvania   | W | 14-7       | Carrier Dome  |
|      |      | Semis    | North Carolina | W | 14-13 (ot) | Carrier Dome  |
|      |      | Finals   | Johns Hopkins  | L | 11-4       | Brown         |
| 1986 | 2nd  | Quarters | Rutgers        | W | 17-5       | Carrier Dome  |
|      |      | Semis    | Virginia       | L | 12-10      | Delaware      |
| 1987 | 3rd  | Quarters | Navy           | W | 19-5       | Carrier Dome  |
|      |      | Semis    | Cornell        | L | 18-15      | Rutgers       |
| 1988 | 1st  | Quarters | Navy           | W | 23-5       | Carrier Dome  |
|      |      | Semis    | Pennsylvania   | W | 11-10      | Carrier Dome  |
|      |      | Finals   | Cornell        | W | 13-8       | Carrier Dome  |
| 1989 | 1st  | Quarters | Navy           | W | 18-11      | Carrier Dome  |
|      |      | Semis    | Maryland       | W | 18-8       | Maryland      |
|      |      | Finals   | Johns Hopkins  | W | 13-12      | Maryland      |
| 1990 | 1st  | Quarters | Brown          | W | 20-12      | Carrier Dome  |
|      |      | Semis    | North Carolina | W | 21-10      | Rutgers       |
|      |      | Finals   | Loyola         | W | 21-9       | Rutgers       |
|      |      | 1990 Championship vacated by NCAA |||||
| 1991 | 5th  | First    | Michigan State | W | 28-7       | Carrier Dome  |
|      |      | Quarters | Johns Hopkins  | W | 11-8       | Johns Hopkins |
|      |      | Semis    | North Carolina | L | 19-13      | Carrier Dome  |
| 1992 | 1st  | Quarters | Yale           | W | 17-8       | Carrier Dome  |
|      |      | Semis    | Johns Hopkins  | W | 21-16      | Pennsylvania  |
|      |      | Finals   | Princeton      | L | 10-9 (2ot) | Pennsylvania  |
| 1993 | 3rd  | Quarters | Hofstra        | W | 20-8       | Carrier Dome  |
|      |      | Semis    | Princeton      | W | 15-9       | Maryland      |
|      |      | Finals   | North Carolina | W | 13-12      | Maryland      |
| 1994 | 1st  | Quarters | Duke           | W | 12-11      | Carrier Dome  |
|      |      | Semis    | Virginia       | L | 15-14 (ot) | Maryland      |
| 1995 | 3rd  | Quarters | Princeton      | W | 15-11      | Carrier Dome  |
|      |      | Semis    | Virginia       | W | 20-13      | Maryland      |
|      |      | Finals   | Maryland       | W | 13-9       | Maryland      |

# TEAM RECORDS

\* USILA record

## GAME

Most Goals Scored — 30, Colgate, 1977; Hofstra, 1991
Most Goals Allowed — 27, Cornell, 1974
Fewest Goals Scored — 0, six times (most recent - 1931, Johns Hopkins 0-20)
Fewest Goals Allowed — 0, 43 times (most recent - 1973, Colgate 14-0)
Most Goals, both teams — 42, Rutgers (19-23), 1955
Fewest Goals, both teams — 0, New York Lacrosse Club (0-0), 1920; 1, Stevens (0-1), 1919 (collegiate record)
Largest Margin of Victory — 28, Colgate (30-2), 1977
Largest Margin of Defeat — 23, Cornell (4-27), 1974

## SEASON

Most Wins — 17\*, 1922 (17 games)
Highest Winning Percentage — 1.000, 1922 (17-0\*), 1957 (10-0), 1988 (15-0), 1990 (13-0)
Fewest Wins — 2, 1916 (7 games), 1942 (6 games), 1974 (11 games)
Lowest Winning Percentage — .182, 1974 (2-9)
Most Losses — 9, 1974 (11 games)
Fewest Losses — 0, 1922 (17 games), 1924 (14 games), 1957 (10 games), 1988 (15 games), 1990 (13 games)
Most Goals Scored — 274, 1991 (15 games)
Highest Scoring Average — 20.8, 1990 (13 games)
Highest Average Margin of Victory — 11.3, 1990 (13 games)
Most Goals Allowed — 194, 1972 (16 games)
Highest Scoring Average Against — 15.9, 1974 (11 games)
Fewest Goals Scored — 14, 1918 (7 games)
Lowest Scoring Average — 2.0, 1918 (7 games)
Fewest Goals Allowed — 19, 1922 (17 games)
Lowest Scoring Average Against — 1.1, 1922 (17 games)

# INDIVIDUAL RECORDS

(Since 1967)* - NCAA game    % - at Manhasset, NY

## GOALS, GAME

| | | | |
|---|---|---|---|
| 1. | 9 | Greg Tarbell | Bucknell | 1982 |
| | | Gary Gait | Navy * | 1988 |
| 3. | 8 | Tom Korrie | Cortland | 1984 |
| | | Ralph Spinola | Union | 1981 |
| | | Larry Storrier | Colgate | 1977 |
| | | Gary Gait | Army | 1988 |
| 7. | 7 | Tim O'Hara | Bucknell | 1980 |
| | | Tom Abbott | Union | 1978 |
| | | Larry Storrier | Princeton | 1976 |
| | | Larry Storrier | RPI | 1976 |
| | | Larry Storrier | Cortland | 1976 |
| | | John Engelken | Wm. & Mary | 1975 |
| | | Ron Hill | Clarkson | 1972 |
| | | Oliver Hill | Union | 1972 |
| | | Ron Hill | Colgate | 1971 |
| | | Gary Gait | Cortland | 1988 |
| | | Gary Gait | Hobart | 1988 |
| | | Paul Gait | Navy * | 1988 |
| | | Gary Gait | Cortland | 1989 |
| | | Matt Riter | C.W. Post | 1992 |
| | | Matt Riter | Hofstra * | 1993 |
| | | Roy Colsey | at Loyola | 1995 |

## POINTS, GAME

| | | | | |
|---|---|---|---|---|
| 1. | 12 | (4-8) | Tim Nelson | Cortland | 1984 |
| | | (9-3) | Gary Gait | Navy (NCAA) | 1988 |
| 3. | 11 | (6-5) | Tim Nelson | Adelphi | 1983 |
| | | (9-2) | Greg Tarbell | Bucknell | 1982 |
| | | (6-5) | Tim O'Hara | Hobart | 1980 |
| | | (4-7) | Tim O'Hara | N. C. St. | 1979 |
| | | (8-3) | Larry Storrier | Colgate | 1977 |
| | | (4-7) | Mike Cornelius | Colgate | 1974 |
| | | (7-4) | Paul Gait | Navy * | 1988 |
| 10. | 10 | (3-7) | Tim Nelson | Hobart % | 1984 |
| | | (1-9) | Tim Nelson | at Hobart | 1984 |
| | | (7-3) | Tim O'Hara | Bucknell | 1980 |
| | | (7-3) | Tom Abbott | Union | 1978 |
| | | (6-4) | Tom Abbott | Cortland | 1976 |
| | | (7-3) | Larry Storrier | Cortland | 1976 |
| | | (7-3) | Larry Storrier | RPI | 1976 |
| | | (3-7) | John Zulberti | Rutgers | 1989 |
| | | (4-6) | Gary Gait | Adelphi % | 1990 |
| | | (4-6) | Paul Gait | at Cornell | 1990 |

## SAVES, GAME

| | | | | |
|---|---|---|---|---|
| 1. | 34 | Paul Bishop | Army | 1973 |
| 2. | 33 | Paul Bishop | Towson St. | 1973 |
| 3. | 32 | Alan Brown | Navy | 1968 |
| 4. | 29 | Jamie Molloy | Cornell | 1980 |
| | | Thompson Gregg | Cortland St. | 1970 |
| 6. | 28 | Tom Nims | UNC | 1985 |
| | | Tom Nims | Delaware | 1985 |
| | | Jamie Molloy | Adelphi | 1977 |
| | | Jason Gebhardt | Johns Hopkins | 1996 |
| 10. | 27 | Jamie Molloy | Mass. | 1977 |
| | | Alex Rosier | Loyola | 1994 |
| | | Jason Gebhardt | Virginia | 1996 |

## ASSISTS, GAME

| | | | | |
|---|---|---|---|---|
| 1. | 9 | Tim Nelson | Penn | 1985 |
| | | Tim Nelson | at Hobart | 1984 |
| | | Tim Nelson | Loyola | 1983 |
| 4. | 8 | Tim Nelson | Cortland | 1984 |
| 5. | 7 | Tim Nelson | at Adelphi | 1985 |
| | | Tim Nelson | Hobart % | 1984 |
| | | Tim Nelson | at Rutgers | 1984 |
| | | John Zulberti | at J. Hopkins | 1988 |
| | | John Zulberti | Rutgers | 1989 |
| | | Rob Kavovit | Yale | 1995 |
| | | Casey Powell | Pennsylvania | 1996 |

## GOALS, SEASON

| | | | |
|---|---|---|---|
| 1. | 70 | Gary Gait | 1988 |
| 2. | 56 | Tom Korrie | 1986 |
| 3. | 55 | Tom Abbott | 1977 |
| 4. | 53 | Tom Marechek | 1991 |
| 5. | 51 | Tom Korrie | 1984 |
| | | Gary Gait | 1989 |
| 7. | 49 | Matt Riter | 1993 |
| 8. | 47 | Paul Gait | 1988 |
| | 47 | Tom Marechek | 1992 |
| 10. | 46 | Tom Abbott | 1978 |
| | | Tom Marechek | 1989 |
| | | Gary Gait | 1990 |
| | | Matt Riter | 1992 |

## POINTS, SEASON

| | | | | |
|---|---|---|---|---|
| 1. | 103 | (36-67) | Tim Nelson | 1984 |
| 2. | 96 | (56-40) | Tom Korrie | 1986 |
| 3. | 89 | (37-52) | Tim O'Hara | 1979 |
| 4. | 87 | (70-17) | Gary Gait | 1988 |
| 5. | 85 | (21-64) | Tim Nelson | 1985 |
| 6. | 83 | (27-56) | Tim Nelson | 1983 |
| 7. | 78 | (30-48) | John Zulberti | 1989 |
| 8. | 77 | (38-39) | Tim O'Hara | 1980 |
| 9. | 76 | (55-21) | Tom Abbott | 1977 |
| | 76 | (53-23) | Tom Marechek | 1991 |

## SAVES, SEASON

| | | | |
|---|---|---|---|
| 1. | 307 | Paul Bishop | 1972 |
| 2. | 267 | Tom Nims | 1985 |
| 3. | 265 | Jason Gebhardt | 1996 |
| 4. | 260 | Tom Nims | 1984 |
| 5. | 259 | Travis Solomon | 1983 |
| 6. | 245 | Alex Rosier | 1994 |
| 7. | 235 | Chris Surran | 1993 |
| 8. | 229 | Alan Brown | 1968 |
| | 229 | Chris Surran | 1992 |
| 10. | 221 | Jamie Molloy | 1980 |
| | 221 | Alex Rosier | 1995 |

## ASSISTS, SEASON

| | | | |
|---|---|---|---|
| 1. | 67 | Tim Nelson | 1984 |
| 2. | 64 | Tim Nelson | 1985 |
| 3. | 56 | Tim Nelson | 1983 |
| 4. | 52 | Tim O'Hara | 1979 |
| 5. | 48 | John Zulberti | 1989 |
| 6. | 47 | John Zulberti | 1988 |
| 7. | 41 | Tim O'Hara | 1978 |
| | | John Zulberti | 1986 |
| 9. | 40 | Tom Korrie | 1986 |
| 10. | 39 | Tim O'Hara | 1980 |

## GOALS, CAREER

| 1. | 192 | Gary Gait | 1987-90 |
|---|---|---|---|
| 2. | 182 | Tom Marechek | 1989-92 |
| 3. | 155 | Tom Korrie | 1983-86 |
| 4. | 142 | Tom Abbott | 1975-78 |
| 5. | 129 | Brad Kotz | 1982-85 |
| 6. | 128 | Matt Riter | 1990-93 |
| 7. | 127 | Paul Gait | 1987-90 |
| 8. | 124 | Tim O'Hara | 1977-80 |
| | 124 | Roy Colsey | 1992-95 |
| 10. | 109 | John Zulberti | 1986-89 |

## POINTS, CAREER

| 1. | 282 | (124-158) | Tim O'Hara | 1977-80 |
|---|---|---|---|---|
| 2. | 271 | (84-187) | Tim Nelson | 1983-85 |
| 3. | 267 | (109-168) | John Zulberti | 1986-89 |
| 4. | 258 | (182-76) | Tom Marechek | 1989-92 |
| 5. | 253 | (192-61) | Gary Gait | 1987-90 |
| 6. | 228 | (155-73) | Tom Korrie | 1983-86 |
| 7. | 212 | (127-85) | Paul Gait | 1987-90 |
| 8. | 205 | (129-76) | Brad Kotz | 1982-85 |
| 9. | 204 | (142-62) | Tom Abbott | 1975-78 |
| 10. | 192 | (84-108) | Jamie Archer | 1990-93 |

## SAVES, CAREER

| 1. | 766 | Jamie Molloy | 1977-80 |
|---|---|---|---|
| 2. | 692 | Tom Nims | 1981-85 |
| 3. | 612 | Paul Bishop | 1971-73 |
| 4. | 537 | Matt Palumb | 1987-90 |
| 5. | 476 | Chris Surran | 1991-93 |

## ASSISTS, CAREER

| 1. | 187 | Tim Nelson | 1983-85 |
|---|---|---|---|
| 2. | 158 | Tim O'Hara | 1977-80 |
| | | John Zulberti | 1986-89 |
| 4. | 108 | Jamie Archer | 1990-93 |
| 5. | 85 | Tom Nelson | 1984-87 |
| | | Paul Gait | 1987-90 |
| 7 | 84 | Rob Kavovit | 1994- |
| 8. | 81 | Jeff Davis | 1967-70 |
| 9. | 76 | Brad Kotz | 1982-85 |
| | 76 | Tom Marechek | 1989-92 |

# HONORS

## LACROSSE HALL OF FAME

| Player | Year Inducted |
|---|---|
| James N. Brown | 1984 |
| Laurie D. Cox | 1957 |
| Frederick A. Fitch | 1961 |
| Ron Fraser | 1987 |
| William L. Fuller | 1982 |
| Victor J. Jenkins | 1967 |
| Steward Lindsay Jr. | 1977 |
| Irving Lydecker | 1960 |
| Oren R. Lyons | 1992 |
| William N. Ritch | 1972 |
| Louis Robbins | 1975 |
| Victor Ross | 1962 |
| Roy Simmons Sr. | 1964 |
| Roy Simmons Jr. | 1991 |
| Glenn N. Thiel | 1965 |

## ALL-AMERICANS

(First-team selections only)
1922 Paul Lowry, Defense; George Dickson, Defense; Victor Ross, In Home
1923 Harvey MacAloney, Goal; George Fisher, Cover Point; Victor Ross, In Home
1924 Frederick Fitch, Defense; Clifford Failing, Defense; Walter Townsend, Attack
1925 Lynn Wood, Goal; Walter Townsend, Attack
1926 Fred Stoddard, Attack
1927 Willis Clark, Defense; Borden Painter, Attack
1928 Donald Harrington, Point; Borden Painter, Attack
1929 Henry Brophy, Cover Point
1930 Henry Brophy, Defense
1932 William Welch, Out Home
1934 Louis Robbins, Out Home; Thomas Delaney, Attack
1935 Walter Jensen, Center; Louis Robbins, Out Home
1936 Edward Jontos, Cover Point
1937 Arthur Morrison, Center
1949 William Fuller, Midfield
1950 William Fuller, Midfield
1954 Bruce Yancey, Midfield
1956 Stew Lindsay, Attack
1957 Jim Brown, Midfield
1962 Richard Finley, Midfield
1979 Kevin Donahue, Midfield
1980 Tim O'Hara, Attack
1981 Tom Donahue, Midfield; Jeff McKee, Defense
1983 Brad Kotz, Midfield; Jeff McCormick, Defense; Tim Nelson, Attack
1984 Brad Kotz, Midfield; Tim Nelson, Attack
1985 Jeff Desko, Defense; Brad Kotz, Midfield; Tim Nelson, Attack; Kevin Sheehan, Defense
1986 Todd Curry, Midfield; Kevin Sheehan, Defense
1987 Todd Curry, Midfield
1988 Gary Gait, Midfield; Paul Gait, Midfield; John Zulberti, Attack
1989 Gary Gait, Midfield; Paul Gait, Midfield; Pat McCabe, Defense; John Zulberti, Attack
1990 Greg Burns, Attack; Gary Gait, Midfield; Paul Gait, Midfield; Tom Marechek, Attack; Pat McCabe, Defense
1991 Tom Marechek, Attack; Pat McCabe, Defense
1992 Dom Fin, Midfield; Charlie Lockwood, Midfield; Tom Marechek, Attack
1993 Matt Riter, Attack; Dom Fin, Midfield; Roy Colsey, Midfield
1994 Dom Fin, Midfield; Roy Colsey, Midfield; Ric Beardsley, Defense
1995 Roy Colsey, Midfield; Ric Beardsley, Defense

* A list of lettermen was not available.

# TRIVIA ANSWERS

1. Shawn Halloran of Boston College, the only foe to pass for more than 425 yards vs. SU, threw for 453 yards in 1985.

2. Pittsburgh's Tony Dorsett is the only opposing back to twice rush for more than 200 yards vs. the Orange: 211 yards as a freshman in 1973, 241 as a senior in '76.

3. Linemen Joe Alexander and Lou Usher were unique for nearly 70 years as SU's only pair of consensus All-Americans (1918) until quarterback Don McPherson and nose guard Ted Gregory in 1987.

4. Johnny Michelosen coached the 1960 Pitt team that came into Archbold Stadium and ended SU's 16-game winning streak, longest in the nation at that time.

5. Placekicker John Biskup (1989-92) is SU's career bowl-game scoring leader with 25 points — five field goals, 10 of 10 points-after in four victories.

6. Among those with at least five years as SU head coach, only Chick Meehan's .787 winning percentage from 1920-24 exceeds Paul Pasqualoni's .733 entering the 1996 campaign.

7. Tight end Pat Kelly's 17-yard touchdown grab of Don McPherson's pass set the table for Michael Owens' two-point conversion dash into the left corner to beat West Virginia and complete a perfect regular season in 1987.

8. Scott Schwedes' eight catches vs. Boston College in 1985 covered 249 yards, the single-game mark for pass reception yardage.

9. Only Don McPherson's NCAA-leading 164.3 passing efficiency rating in 1987 exceeds Donovan McNabb's 162.3 PER in 1995 among Orange QBs who threw at least 100 passes in a season (Dave Sarette had a PER of 164.0 in 1959, but attempted only 83 passes).

10. Ex-Hobart College coach George Davis' 95-yard run vs. Fordham in 1949 is the longest-standing individual Orange record.

11. In the 1984 national shocker that was SU 17, No. 1 Nebraska 9, Mike Siano's leaping end zone grab came on a pass thrown by QB Todd Norley.

12. Although Dave Sarette was outstanding as the 1959 national champs' signal-caller, the starting QB for the season-opener vs. Kansas in Archbold was Gerhard Schwedes, who moved to halfback and averaged 6.3 yards-per-carry.

13. Robert B. Adams is the only player to captain the Orange three seasons (1894-96).

14. Halfback Ger Schwedes (1959), linebacker Tony Romano ('83) and defensive tackle Tim Green ('85) have been SU honorees as National Football Foundation and College Hall of Fame Scholar-Athletes.

15. On an end-around, Phil Allen was never touched darting around the Red Raiders' left side 14 yards to the Archbold end zone in 1938 as the Orange broke the Colgate jinx — or 'hoodoo,' as it was called — 7-0.

16. Among great receivers of the 1980s and '90s, Shelby Hill's No. 1 in receptions (139), Rob Moore tops in touchdowns (22), Marvin Harrison the leader in yardage (2,728), but the yards-per-catch leader is Tommy Kane (20.1 career average).

17. The 1959 national champs possessed a stifling defense and awesome offense, whose hallmark weapon in its arsenal was a misdirection running play called the 'Scissors.'

18. Oakland Raiders' General Partner Al Davis is the only SU alum in the Pro Football Hall of Fame (inducted in 1992) not to letter for the Orange.

19. Rob Moore was the player quoted as saying he was told during warmups to be ready for a trick play; Moore was on the receiving end of an 80-yard touchdown pass from Don McPherson on the first play from scrimmage in what quickly became a rout of Penn State in 1987, SU's first win over the Nittany Lions since the Schwartzwalder era.

20. Penn State is the opponent that has faced SU the most (68 meetings) and holds the most wins over the Orange (40).

21. Only Don McPherson (22 in 1987) has thrown more touchdown passes in a season than Donovan McNabb tossed last season (16).

22. Prior to this season, 11 school recorded 600 or more victories. They are: Michigan, Notre Dame, Texas, Alabama, Nebraska, Penn State, Ohio State, Oklahoma, Tennessee, Southern Cal and Georgia. SU began the season with 599, Army 597.

23. Always tough in short yardage down around the goal-line, fullback Al Wooten ranks fifth all-time in rushing touchdowns with 20, behind a quartet of great running backs named Little, Davis, Morris and Brown.

24. Ben Schwartzwalder's 22 consecutive non-losing seasons is, of course, an SU coaching standard, but the school record for successive non-losers is 23, set from 1913-35 under six coaches (Buck O'Neill, Bill Hollenback, Chick Meehan, Pete Reynolds, Lew Andreas and Vic Hanson).

25. Mark McDonald came off the bench to spell Billy Scharr and completed an SU bowl-record 76.9 percent of his passes (10 of 13) in leading the Orange to a 19-18 win over Georgia in the 1989 Peach Bowl.

26. Louisiana State is the only school to play Syracuse in more than one bowl (1965 Sugar, 1989 Hall of Fame); they split.

27. Paul Pasqualoni concedes: "I never thought, never predicted, that David Bavaro could play in the NFL. He was short, didn't run extremely well (but was an NFLer from 1990-94)." He also was the last player to lead the Orange in tackles three years running (1987-89).

28. Bob Woodruff threw the fewest interceptions-per-attempt in a season, just three out of 142 passes in 1971 (one out of every 44 attempts).

29. Career sack leader Tim Green (45 ½) also ranks 1-2-3 in season sacks with 15 in 1984, 14 ½ in '83 and 13 ½ in '85.

30. Safety Markus Paul is the only Orangemen to lead the team in interceptions four years; the two-time Jim Thorpe Award finalist was the top "thief" in 1985-86-87, sharing honors in '88 with Terry Wooden.

31. Between 1961 and '85, the only Orange QB to throw more touchdown passes than interceptions in a season was Bill Hurley, who did it in both 1976 and '77.

32. Having endured one Orange crush after another,

25 times in as many encounters by an average score of 31.9 to 1.6 (there were 18 shutouts), Hobart stopped playing SU after 1931.

33. Current running backs coach David Walker was Mr. Consistency, the highest-ranking all-time rusher never to gain 1,000 in a season (No. 4 with 2,643 yards, topped by 969 in '91).

34. The Syracuse record of 49,325 per-game attendance was set in 1992.

35. The 1913-14 team is the only unbeaten squad (12-0) in Syracuse history.

36. Host Penn State handed the 1925-26 Orangemen, declared National Champions by the Helms Foundation, their lone defeat in the 16th game of a 19-1 season, 37-31. Three games later, SU avenged the loss at home, 29-12.

37. Jim Brown did not score in the 1957 NCAA East Regional final against North Carolina because he was not a member of that team. Big Jim had been a double-figure scorer the two previous seasons, but did not play basketball as a senior.

38. Of Syracuse's five tournament games in the 1975 NCAAs, three were decided in overtime — wins over LaSalle by four and Kansas State by eight, and an 8-point loss to Louisville in the Final Four consolation game.

39. Billy Gabor, called "Bullet," was the first SU player to score 1,000 points in his career. Gabor scored 1,344 points, playing four seasons in the 1940s, interrupted by two years in the military.

40. Bill Sanford's athletic prowess was in rowing, Dave Giusti's in baseball. But the longtime SU crew coach/politico and the former pitching star of the Pittsburgh Pirates did suit up with the SU basketball team, although neither lettered.

41. The 4-19 team in the 1960-61 season that dropped its last five contests — the start of a 27-game losing streak over two campaigns — was led in scoring by southpaw Pete Chudy, who averaged 20.8 ppg. Fortunately for Chudy, he did not have to endure the agony of the 1961-62 season, that was far worse.

42. Steve Ludd had come off the bench and had been a backcourt starter in the 1960s, but he gave up the game to devote more time to academics.

43. Dave Bing — and Jim Boeheim, for that matter — was coached as a freshman by Morris Osburn, who came to Syracuse as coach of the Tangerines with Fred Lewis from Mississippi Southern.

44. Frank Hamblen sort of clicked his heels on his jump shot, which lacked elevation. But he was a good outside shooter and has proven to be a good judge of NBA talent over the years.

45. Syracuse's only national tournament title came in the 1951 National Campus Tournament in Peoria, Ill., where SU defeated Toledo and Utah, each by 17, then nipped host Bradley in the championship game, 76-75.

46. Having broken his hand, forcing him to miss the 1981 Big East Tournament and NCAAs, Marty Headd had a lot of time on his hands. Headd, a member of the 1,000-point club, admitted to me in a Herald article that classrooms were not his favorite place. Others among us may have shared that feeling.

47. False; John Wallace was not the only Orangeman named to the 1996 Final Four All-Tournament team.

Todd Burgan scored 19 points in each game and was also selected.

48. John Thompson pulled his Georgetown Hoyas off the court when an idiotic patron in the Dome threw an orange, which splattered against the backboard as Patrick Ewing was preparing to attempt a foul shot. The game was later continued.

49. Said an irate and emotional Jim Boeheim in the press room, following the 1984 Big East Tournament: "19,000 people saw (Georgetown's) Michael Graham punch my player (Andre Hawkins)." Boeheim heaved a chair in disgust … and the press, having seen what took place on the court, was not critical of his outburst.

50. Forward Wendell Alexis was not a fixture in the starting lineup until his senior year (1985-86). He's the only member of the 1,000-point club to be a one-year starter, and his 9.7 ppg career average is the only one among the 1,000-point fraternity not in double figures.

51. Freedom; that's what Bernie Fine said he's had as Jim Boeheim's right-hand man. Fine has been an SU assistant on Boeheim's staff ever since Coach Jim was named head coach in 1976.

52. Derrick Coleman (No. 2 on the all-time scoring list) and Stevie Thompson (No. 5) are the two players among SU's top dozen career scorers who never were single-season scoring leaders.

53. During the first half of the SU-Georgetown game in 1982, the Orange cheerleaders were performing a "human pyramid." Michelle Munn fell to the floor; the noise and her cries of pain were agonizing. Silence that gripped the Dome crowd was deafening, in an eerie way. Michelle was very seriously injured, but not permanently.

54. False; Jason Cipolla and Marius Janulis shared starting at the off-guard spot, but each missed a game during the 1995-96 season. Top frontline reserve J.B. Reafsnyder did play in all 38 games, along with starters John Wallace, Lazarus Sims, Todd Burgan and Otis Hill.

55. Among 1996-97 returnees, Jason Cipolla scored the most points in one game during his career — 25 at Seton Hall last season.

56. True; this coaching staff of Jim Boeheim, Bernie Fine, Louis Orr and Mike Hopkins is the first since Manley was built that is comprised totally of SU alums.

57. Syracuse (.750, 33-11).

58. 1922, when SU went 17-0.

59. Four; 1922 (17-0), 1957 (10-0), 1988 (15-0), 1990 (13-0).

60. Roy Simmons Sr.; North beat South, 13-11, in Freeport, Long Island.

61. Oren Lyons stopped 20 shots (North goalies had 31 saves) in a 26-6 loss to the South, who fired 87 shots in the 1958 North-South game.

62. Defenseman Jack Salerno played for the American team, who beat the Nationals, 12-0, in Greenvale, N.Y.; the next year, the North-South game was resumed, and played in Syracuse.

63. Greg Tarbell peppered Bucknell for nine goals in 1982; Gary Gait's nine vs. Navy came in the 1988 NCAAs.